Familienunternehmen und KMU

Reihe herausgegeben von

Andreas Hack, Institut für Organisation & Personal, Universität Bern, Bern, Switzerland

Andrea Calabrò, WIFU-Stiftungslehrstuhl, Universität Witten, Herdecke WIFU-Stiftungslehrstuhl, Witten, Germany

Thomas Zellweger, Chair of Family Business, Universtitat St. Gallen, St. Gallen, Switzerland

Franz W Kellermanns, Belk College of Business, Univ North Carolina Charlotte Belk College of Business, Charlotte, USA

Hermann Frank, Institut für KMU-Management, Universität Wien Institut für KMU-Management, Wien, Austria

Marcel Hülsbeck, Private Universität Witten/Herdecke, Fakultät für Wirtschaftswissenschaft, Witten, Germany

Sowohl Familienunternehmen als auch kleine und mittlere Unternehmen (KMU) zeichnen sich durch eine Reihe spezifischer Besonderheiten aus, die ihnen im Marktumfeld einen klaren Wettbewerbsvorteil bieten aber auch zu besonderen Risiken führen können. Die vorliegende Schriftenreihe präsentiert wissenschaftliche Arbeiten, die einen empirischen und theoretischen Beitrag zur Erkundung dieser Besonderheiten und deren Auswirkungen auf die betriebswirtschaftliche Praxis leisten. Übergeordnetes Ziel ist es, die Theorieentwicklung des Managements von Familienunternehmen und KMU voranzutreiben. Both Family Firms and Small and Medium Sized Enterprises (SME) feature a number of distinct behaviors and characteristics which could provide them with a competitive advantage in the market but could also lead to certain risks. The scientific series at hand presents research which provides an empirical and theoretical contribution to the investigation on these specific characteristics and their impact on business practice. The overall aim of this series is to advance the development of theory in the areas of family firm and SME management.

Gunther Friedl
Editor

Decarbonizing German Family Firms

Springer Gabler

Editor
Gunther Friedl
Chair of Management Accounting
Technical University Munich
Munich, Germany

ISSN 2520-1174 ISSN 2520-1182 (electronic)
Familienunternehmen und KMU
ISBN 978-3-658-47800-1 ISBN 978-3-658-47801-8 (eBook)
https://doi.org/10.1007/978-3-658-47801-8

This work was supported by Dr. Hans Riegel Foundation.

This Springer Gabler imprint is published by the registered company Springer Fachmedien Wiesbaden GmbH, part of Springer Nature.
The registered company address is: Abraham-Lincoln-Str. 46, 65189 Wiesbaden, Germany

Abstract

The European Commission (EC) published the European Green Deal to implement the sustainability goals of the United Nations 2030 Agenda and the Paris Agreement. Driven by climate change, these regulations mainly aim to limit greenhouse gas (GHG) emissions and thus keep the future temperature increase well below 2 degrees Celsius. As the third largest exporting country worldwide, Germany emits the highest amount of GHG emissions within the EU. To ensure the achievement of the EU's binding climate targets, it is necessary to focus specifically on family firms in Germany, as they cover 90% of all businesses. Thus, the dual mission of meeting regulatory requirements while maintaining global competitiveness increasingly stresses the need to support family firms on their (mandatory) decarbonization journey. Therefore, this research consortium entails four chapters providing a holistic view of the critical steps within a family firm's decarbonization. Based on qualitative and quantitative data from German family firms of different industries, we explore the measurement and accounting mechanisms of GHG emissions (Chap. 2). To create value from that emission data, we further investigate the management of goal tensions between environmental and economic goals (Chap. 3). In the course of the forthcoming Corporate Sustainability Reporting Directive (CSRD) and communicating a company's decarbonization efforts to stakeholders, we analyze the consequences of this reporting mandate for a family firm (Chap. 4). Given the high investment demand of any decarbonization measure, it is crucial for any company to remain profitable, which is especially true for family firms as they want to transfer their business to future generations. Therefore, we also focus on the link between corporate environmental performance (CEP) and corporate financial performance (CFP) (Chap. 5).

Acknowledgement

The entire research team would like to thank the Dr. Hans Riegel Foundation for their generous funding. The constructive dialogue and the workshops have significantly contributed to gaining valuable insights for research and practice within the field of family firms and sustainability including decarbonization. We would therefore also like to thank the network of the Dr. Hans Riegel Foundation and for proactively initiating a publication in ZEIT WISSEN. Finally, we thank our readers. Your interest in decarbonization in family firms shows the increasing motivation for the transition to net zero emissions, which is an essential step in the prevention of climate change and its severe consequences.

Contents

Abbreviations

B2B	Business-To-Business
B2C	Business-To-Consumer
CapEx	Capital Expenditures
CDP	Carbon Disclosure Project
CEO	Chief Executive Officer
CEP	Corporate Environmental Performance
CFP	Corporate Financial Performance
CO_2	Carbon Dioxide
CO_{2e}	Carbon Dioxide Equivalent
COP	Conference of Parties
COP 27	27th Conference Of The Parties To The United Nations Framework Convention On Climate Change
CSR	Corporate Social Responsibility
CSRD	Corporate Sustainability Reporting Directive
CSR-RUG	Corporate Social Responsibility Directive Implementation Act
DAX	Deutscher Aktienindex (Mid-Cap German Stock Index)
DNK	German Sustainability Code
EC	European Commission
ESG	Environmental, Social, Governance
ESRS	European Sustainability Reporting Standards
EU	European Union
FOC	First-Order Consequences
GHG	Greenhouse Gas
GRI	Global Reporting Initiative

ISO	International Organization for Standardization
KPI	Key Performance Indicator
MS	Member State
NFRD	Non-Financial Reporting Directive
NGO	Non-Profit Organization
NRBV	Natural Resource-Based View
PEF	Product Environmental Footprint
PFF	Private Family Firm
PIE	Public-Interest Entities
RBV	Resource-Based View
ROA	Return On Assets
ROE	Return On Equity
RV	Relational View
SBTi	Science-Based Targets Initiative
Scope 3	Scope 3 CO_2 Emission
SD	Standard Deviation
SEW	Socioemotional Wealth
SME	Small and Medium-Sized Enterprise
SOC	Second-Order Consequences
TCFD	Task Force On Climate-Related Financial Disclosures
TLGT	Too-Little-Of-A-Good-Thing
TMGT	Too-Much-Of-A-Good-Thing
TSR	Total Shareholder Return
UN	United Nations
UNFCCC	UN Framework Convention on Climate Change
WWF	World Wide Fund For Nature

List of Figures

List of Tables

Introduction

1

Gunther Friedl

> "Greenhouse gas emissions keep growing. Global temperatures keep rising. And our planet is fast approaching tipping points that will make climate chaos irreversible."

This statement was made by António Guterres, the Secretary-General of the United Nations (UN), in November 2022 at the 27th Conference of Parties (COP) in Egypt (World Economic Forum, 2022).

The United Nations (UN) is the largest association of countries worldwide that tries to secure global peace and equality on a healthy planet. Hence, ongoing climate change is defined as one of the most serious global issues that affect the alliance's goals (United Nations, 2022b). It is proven that climate change is mainly caused by anthropogenic greenhouse gases (GHG), with carbon dioxide (CO2) being the main contributor, accounting for approximately 66% (Umweltbundesamt, 2023a). To limit and reduce GHG emissions on an international level, in 1994, the UN Framework Convention on Climate Change (UNFCCC) set the course for reducing GHG by committing all involved parties, according to article 2 "to achieve […] stabilization of greenhouse gas concentrations in the atmosphere at a level that would prevent dangerous anthropogenic interference with the climate system" (UN Convention, 1992, p. 4). This framework formed the basis for the annual COP, which is the supreme decision-making body of the convention that reviews its effective implementation and regulatory instruments

G. Friedl (✉)
Chair of Management Accounting, TUM School of Management, Technical University of Munich, Munich, Germany
e-mail: gunther.friedl@tum.de

G. Friedl (ed.), *Decarbonizing German Family Firms*, Familienunternehmen und KMU, https://doi.org/10.1007/978-3-658-47801-8_1

(Kuyper et al., 2018; United Nations, 2022a). At the third COP in Japan, the objective of the UNFCCC was specified by the adoption of the Kyoto Protocol in 1997. Hence, all participating industrialized countries were obliged to reduce their GHG emissions between 2008 and 2012 by an overall 5.2% compared to 1990 (Bernard-Rau & Schnerring, 2022; Gründinger, 2012). In contrast, the Paris Agreement, as the successor to the Kyoto Protocol agreed at COP 21 in 2015, focuses mainly on a collective long-term objective instead of individual country-specific climate targets in developed markets (Leggett, 2020; van der Gaast, 2016). The overall goal of the agreement is to limit a GHG-related increase in temperature well below 2 degrees Celsius (Leggett, 2020). Despite the ambitious targets, there is still a need to accelerate the implementation of GHG emission reduction measures. The most recent COP hosted in Egypt announced that the world is currently heading for a temperature rise of approximately 2.6 degrees Celsius with severe consequences (Kerstin, 2022).

1.1 Global Political Sustainability Goals and Regulations

Regulatory instruments set by the COP should promote the effective implementation, flexibility, and reduction of costs for environmental measures to combat climate change (Bernard-Rau & Schnerring, 2022; Gründinger, 2012; United Nations, 2022a). One exemplary instrument is market-based mechanisms like the international emission trading concept initiated by the Kyoto Protocol (Gründinger, 2012). The implementation of carbon trading concepts and the main contribution of carbon to the greenhouse effect emphasized using CO_2 equivalents (CO_2e) (Lipper et al., 2018). Since the environmental impact of the main GHGs differs, CO_2e is used as a standardized metric to quantify and compare the emissions based on the Global Warming Potential (GWP) (Bernard-Rau & Schnerring, 2022). Evolved from the trading and the underlying CO_2 market, each country is allocated a certain amount of emission rights, which depend on the individual reduction commitment. If a country reduces more than its target, it can sell surplus emission rights to countries that have not managed to meet its targets (Bernard-Rau & Schnerring, 2022; Umweltbundesamt, 2023b). In 2005, the European Union (EU) extended the trading instrument through the Emission Trading Scheme (EU-ETS). Compared to international emission trading, the EU market participants are not governmental institutions but rather companies from carbon-intensive industries, particularly operators of the plans (Gründinger, 2012). Those industries include, for example, the steel, aluminum, cement, or chemical industry, which account for 40% of the European GHG emissions, of which 25% are emitted by German plants (Umweltbundestamt & Deutsche Emissionshandelsstelle, 2023).

1.2 German Sustainability Goals and Affiliated Strategy

In absolute numbers, Germany is the largest emitter of CO_2e within the EU (Umweltbundesamt, 2023a). However, a different view emerges if the CO_2e are related to the gross domestic product (GDP). Having the largest GDP within the EU, Germany is in the top third of countries with the lowest emissions (Umweltbundesamt, 2023a). Since the economic performance and the way industries operate influence the level and limitations of CO_2 emissions, a specific perspective on the German market, inclusive its plants and industries, has to be developed. With the announcement of the European Green Deal in 2019 and its goal to achieve a reduction of GHG emissions by 55% by 2030 respectively GHG neutrality by 2050, Germany has a progressive need to reduce its emissions (Perino et al., 2022; Schlacke et al., 2022). The strategic plan "Fit for 55" associated with the climate target in 2030 stipulates that the given emission reduction targets of the individual countries depend on their economic strength (Schlacke et al., 2022). Since Germany is the largest economy in the EU, it has to reduce its emissions by 50% until 2030, whereas smaller European countries have targets of around 10% (Handelsblatt, 2022).

1.3 Importance of German Family Firms

To meet the German targets, it is inevitable to focus on family firms and their sustainability approach, as they account for 90% of all active businesses and cover 60% of all workplaces within the German economy (Langenscheidt, 2020). The former federal minister for economic affairs and energy, Peter Altmaier, stated, "*Our economic model is based on medium-sized, family-owned firms. Quite appropriately, they are described as the "engine" of our national economy*" (Handelsblatt, 2019). For instance, the continued high turnover growth of family businesses justifies this statement. Between 2006 and 2016, German family businesses achieved 70 basis points higher turnover growth than the companies in the German stock market index (DAX) (Handelsblatt, 2019). Another evidence in favor of addressing the environmental behavior of family businesses is their recent involvement in mandatory non-financial reporting under the Corporate Sustainability Reporting Directive (CSRD). The CSRD, which was adopted by the European Commission (EC) in 2021, is the successor to the Non-Financial Reporting Directive (NFRD) and extends the scope from large, listed companies to large companies that meet specific criteria and therefore include family firms as well (European Commission, 2022a). These guidelines require mainly the consideration of environmental and social aspects like respect for human rights, and diversity on company boards (European Commission, 2022a). The CSRD focuses specifically on standards, including financial ratios, in line with the EU taxonomy to enable comparability between companies (Schwager, 2022). Those European directives were translated into German law by the Corporate Sustainability Reporting Directive Implementation Act (CSR-RUG) (Schwager, 2022). However, regulations differ in terms of scope and content within Europe. While in Germany, GHG non-financial reporting under the CSR-RUG refers to this date to some listed companies that meet certain size criteria which have to disclose a relatively generic set of non-financial information (§289c HGB), the UK obligates all listed companies to disclose particular GHG emission information and indicators (Hummel & Rötzel, 2019).

The short timeframe to comply with the CSRD poses challenges for companies, especially for German family firms, due to their presence and the scope expansion of the new Directive. Those challenges include particularly the transparent disclosure of CO_2 emissions, responsible corporate governance, or sustainable supply chain management (Schwager, 2022). Regarding the climate targets and the recent mandatory sustainability reports, German family firms would need guidance on how to integrate environmental, social, and governance (ESG) related topics into their business strategy, including accounting for GHG emissions.

1.4 The Definitional Dilemma of German Family Firms

This topic has currently gained strong momentum, but the ambiguity of the term "family firm" confronts researchers with a definitional dilemma (Brockhaus, 2004; Chrisman, Chua & Sharma, 2005). Although it might be clear that the family's involvement in the business is the main difference from non-family firms, the variety of involvement types, such as ownership, leadership, management, or transgenerational succession, do not lead to a trivial differentiation (Chrisman, Chua & Sharma, 2005). Therefore, Chrisman et al. (2005) recommend defining particular types of family firms before proceeding with research, which is also considered in the following chapters. Nonetheless, concepts like the agency theory, the stewardship theory, or the socioemotional wealth model (SEW) help to differentiate family-controlled firms from a behavioral perspective and to derive some common characteristics (Berrone et al., 2012). Those behavioral analyses show, for instance, that family firms pursue goals that are also not economic in nature, such as a focus on environmental performance, the family reputation, or the enduring ties to stakeholders (Berrone et al., 2012; Carney, 2005). A further characteristic shared by family firms includes a long-term-oriented decision-making approach to pave the way for a successful future for their descendants (Habibur Rahman et al., 2017). This long-term perspective is a beneficial attribute, as it could facilitate success towards a future transition to GHG neutrality while creating synergies with the goals of the Paris Agreement and its long-term focus. A clear coherence that justifies the relevance and the focus of scientific research on efficient carbon management in German family firms. Some further characteristics can also be derived from the capital structure, like a low leverage ratio due to a high-risk aversion (Gomez-Mejia et al., 2007).

1.5 Research Gap and Structure

The ambitious climate targets set by politics and the associated need for decarbonization, particularly within family firms due to their high economic impact, justify the need for research in the field of carbon emission management and their reduction within German family firms. It is decisive that companies incorporate sustainability-related topics into their strategy and holistically manage sustainability practices rather than using a "silo thinking" approach where only specific departments deal with those topics (Lai & Stacchezzini, 2021). Therefore, the following research consortium, which encompasses four chapters, takes a holistic approach by considering the issue of carbon emission management in family firms from a process-oriented perspective. First, as a prerequisite for emissions management, it is inevitable to quantify GHG emissions because "only what gets measured gets managed" (Drucker, 1954). Second, in order to also steer the company from a sustainable perspective, it is crucial to create value from the collected emission and sustainability information. For example, it can be used in strategic decision-making as performance indicators for sustainable investments. Third, to inform stakeholders about a company's sustainability efforts, companies must disclose a sustainability report, which will become mandatory due to the upcoming CSRD. Finally, it is also important to assess how these sustainability decisions may impact the financial performance of the family firm. Especially for smaller

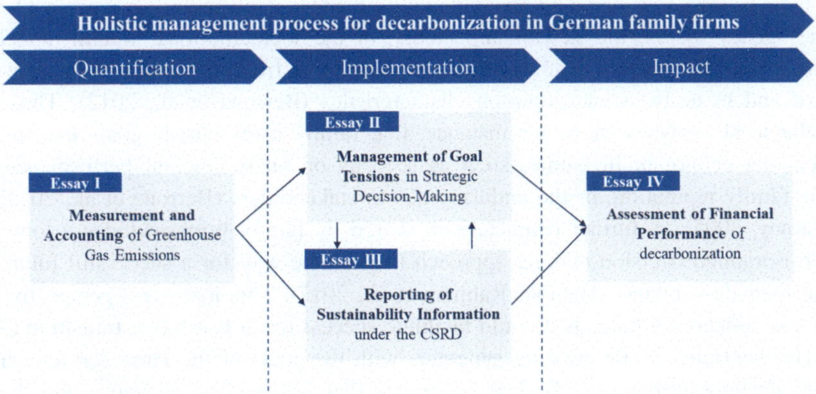

Fig. 1.1 Research consortium's structure. *Source* Own figure

family firms with limited financial resources, it is crucial to benefit from this costly process. Thus, we start with the **measurement** and accounting of greenhouse gas emissions (Chap. 2), followed by the **management** of goal tensions in strategic decision-making in the context of decarbonization (Chap. 3), then the **reporting** of mandatory sustainability reporting, including its challenges and opportunities (Chap. 4), and lastly also the **assessment** of financial performance regarding their decarbonization (Chap. 5) within German family firms. Our fours are based on this holistic carbon emission management process, as illustrated in Fig. 1.1.

Chapter 2 deals with the management and accounting of GHG emissions within family-owned companies. The focus lies on the accounting procedure of GHG emissions along their value chain. Already existing accounting standards and conceptual fallacies are discussed. Since emission data is mostly not publicly available for this company type, a qualitative research approach via interviews is most suitable.

Chapter 3 investigates the tensions between economic and environmental goals. This research topic is specifically relevant in family business research due to the overlap between the business and the family. The developed framework for balancing goals tensions is based on interview data from eleven family firms, ten expert interviews, and archival data.

Chapter 4 focuses on the reporting process of the collected sustainability information and examines the challenges and opportunities family firms face due to their socio-emotional behavior. We do not refer to voluntary reporting but examine the specific consequences based on the forthcoming European reporting obligation, the CSRD, by interviewing ten family firms.

Chapter 5 reflects the management process of decarbonization by assessing the relationship between environmental performance (CEP) and corporate financial performance (CFP) in family firms. Thus, the focus is on the question, "When does it pay to be green?" using econometric research methods in a family firm context.

The overall relevance of this research consortium is twofold. First, from a theoretical perspective, the following chapters aim to fill the research gap on GHG quantification, implementing sustainable investment decisions or business opportunities, and its impact analysis in German family firms. The results of this research go far beyond the analysis of current regulations on carbon accounting (He et al., 2022). In addition, existing research only refers to listed or non-family firms (Porter & van der Linde, 1995; Waddock & Graves, 1997). For instance, the relationship between CEP and CFP has already been analyzed by researchers. Given its special propositions, family firms are different due to ownership by one or a small number of families. Thus, findings from the non-family firms cannot necessarily be applied and the question remains open whether it pays off to be green for family firms.

Second, from a practical perspective, the results and recommendations in the chapters give clear managerial advice for decision-makers and owners of family firms concerning carbon management and accounting. Besides, there is particular room for guiding non-financial reporting. Sustainability reporting standards are formulated in a relatively descriptive manner and lack standardized KPIs. The implementation of the new CSRD regulation and the associated extension of its scope will pose further challenges for many family firms that have never published such a report before. To this purpose, we reveal several opportunities due to the integration of ESG-related topics into a family firm's strategy, and hereby incentivize firms to act sustainably and therefore aim to the European and German governments to achieve their ambitious climate goals. In summary, a decarbonization strategy is important for companies and especially for family firms in Germany, to contribute to the avoidance of climate chaos and its consequences feared by Antonio Guterres at COP 27.

Measurement and Accounting of Greenhouse Gas Emissions

2

Measurement and Accounting of Greenhouse Gas Emissions in German Family-Owned Companies

Julius C. Baumgart

This chapter explores the unique intersection of family-owned companies and their approach to environmental management in times of a growing need to fight climate change. Among various initiatives to reduce GHG emissions, the EU has been exceptionally proactive, mandating large companies to report on environmental and non-financial matters. Within Europe, this study focuses on Germany, where family-owned companies play a dominant role, comprising a significant portion of the private sector and emissions. Recognizing the distinct characteristics of these companies, such as a long-term mindset and sustainable management combined with their tendencies towards secrecy, this research aims to 1) examine whether existing conceptual frameworks on environmental management methodologies apply to family-owned firms and 2) delve into why these companies report on environmental activities beyond regulatory requirements and the challenges they face in this journey. Utilizing a qualitative approach, including semi-structured interviews and case studies, the study confirms the relevance of certain archetypes to family-owned companies while extending existing

This chapter was presented at the 3rd European Institute for Advanced Studies in Management (EIASM) Conference on Management Accounting and Control in SMEs in Assisi, Italy, in April 2023 and accepted at the 23rd European Academy of Management (EURAM) Annual Conference in Dublin, Ireland, in June 2023.

J. C. Baumgart (✉)
Chair of Management Accounting, TUM School of Management, Technical University of Munich, Munich, Germany
e-mail: baumgart.julius@bcg.com

G. Friedl (ed.), *Decarbonizing German Family Firms*, Familienunternehmen und KMU, https://doi.org/10.1007/978-3-658-47801-8_2

frameworks to include motivations, methodologies, and challenges specific to this company type. The findings highlight the importance of customer demand, generational thinking, and an intrinsic desire to mitigate GHG emissions as motivators, with the GHG Protocol emerging as the prevalent standard. Challenges such as a lack of urgency and standardized data complicate environmental reporting. This chapter contributes to the literature by offering insights into the environmental management practices of a sector known for its privacy and suggesting tailored approaches for future GHG reduction efforts.

2.1 Introduction

The world in the 2020s faces global challenges such as the COVID-19 pandemic or the Russo-Ukrainian war, which pose significant threats to today's society. However, climate change is "*the biggest threat to security that modern humans have ever faced*" (United Nations, 2021), as David Attenborough stated at the 2021 UN Security Council. Over the last four decades, global temperatures have been rising constantly, with each decade warmer than the previous decade. For instance, in the second decade of the twenty-first century, temperatures have been ~ 1.1° Celsius higher than pre-industrial temperatures (IPCC, 2021), driven to the most considerable extent by GHG emissions.[1] Now, more than ever, it is essential to reduce GHG emissions as much as possible and as soon as possible to reduce climate change risks (UNFCCC, 2015). Many initiatives have been started over the last three decades, such as, for instance, the Kyoto Protocol (signed in 1997), the Paris Agreement to limit the temperature increase to a maximum of two degrees Celsius (signed in 2016), the European Green Deal to become carbon neutral by 2050 (approved in 2020) or the European "*Fit for 55*" initiative to reduce GHG emissions by 55% until 2030. Globally, the industry is responsible for 30–40% of GHG emissions (Ritchie et al., 2023), making it evident that this constitutes one of the main levers for managing and optimizing the world's GHG emission household.

The EU is mainly active in enforcing these initiatives with the design and implementation of regulatory guidelines, thus urging companies to report on and manage their environmental emissions. In 2014, the EU approved the NFRD

[1] As defined by the Kyoto Protocol, GHG emissions include the following six gases in particular: carbon dioxide (CO_2), methane (CH_4), nitrous oxide (N_2O), hydrofluorocarbons (HCFs), perfluorocarbons (PFCs) and sulphur hexafluoride (SF_6) (UNFCCC, 2008).

(European Parliament & European Council, 2014). Later on, the CSRD (European Parliament & European Council, 2022) required companies to report on environmental performance, social and employee matters, human rights performance, corruption and anti-bribery matters (CSR Europe & GRI, 2017; European Parliament & European Council, 2022). Within the EU, Germany constitutes the largest emitter of GHG, with a share of 25% of European GHG emissions (European Environment Agency, 2023). Different to other European countries, family-owned companies constitute the predominant company type, with more than 90% of private companies being family-controlled, comprising ~ 57% of employees within the private sector and ~ 55% of total German company revenue (Stiftung Familienunternehmen, 2023b). Family-owned companies differ substantially from public corporations given their long-term mindset, their sustainable management, the will to assure the persistence of the company and a desire to hand over the company to the next generation, yet also their tendency towards privacy and secrecy (so-called hidden champions) (Stiftung Familienunternehmen, 2023b). As carbon accounting becomes increasingly important and the required processes within family-owned companies have only received limited attention to date (Salvato & Moores, 2010), I contribute to the growing field of research on family-owned companies (Hasso & Duncan, 2013) by answering the following overarching research question within this chapter: "*How and why do family-owned companies account for their GHG emissions along their value chain, and which challenges do they face during this process?*".

To approach this research question, I come up with two core objectives: 1) test whether conceptual frameworks for environmental management developed by past researchers for firms in general also hold for family-owned companies as particular company type and 2) extend this previous research into a new framework by gathering information on the applied methodologies for environmental management, i.e., how do family-owned companies perform their environmental management, identify why family-owned companies account and report carbon emissions besides regulatory guidance as well as identify which challenges family-owned companies face throughout their carbon accounting process. Given that these aspects cover several topics of the environmental management approach, I will divide the overarching research question into multiple research sub-questions later. This analysis has not been performed before for the interface of family-owned companies and their approach to environmental management.

Related to the first objective, various researchers in the past have classified companies into environmental management archetypes based on their level of top-level management involvement, degree of reporting and employee training, as well as the overall importance of environmental matters to management and employees (Carroll, 1979; Henriques & Sadorsky, 1999; Hunt & Auster, 1990; Roome, 1992; Wartick & Cochran, 1985). I, thus, use their developed frameworks as a starting point to test whether the mentioned aspects and categories hold for family-owned companies. A family-owned company can differ from general company archetypes as family-owned companies have been found to be more altruistic than non-family companies (Déniz & Suárez, 2005), cause less pollution (Cennamo et al., 2012) and typically commit to preserving their socioemotional wealth through environmental management (Berrone et al., 2012).

These aspects also influence the second research objective, i.e., applied methodology for environmental management and its motivation to do so as well as the faced challenges during this process. Various methodological approaches exist within environmental management. The most prominent standard used among public corporations is the so-called GHG Protocol, applied by more than 92% of Fortune 500 companies as the accounting standard (WBCSD & WRI, 2023). Other initiatives are, for instance, the SBTi, aiming at enabling companies to set relevant climate targets and provide guidance on how to achieve these targets (Science Based Targets, 2022) or the ISO 14064 standard, which serves as a complement to the GHG Protocol to design, develop, manage, report, and verify a company's GHG inventory (Wintergreen & Delaney, 2007). Furthermore, on behalf of over 680 institutional investors, the CDP collects survey-based data regarding carbon emissions and water consumption from companies, cities, regions, and public authorities in a standardized format (Weiss et al., 2022). To what extent family-owned companies apply each standard has not been discussed in the existing literature, and neither were related factors such as involved resources, calculation methods, or involved software.

The motivation to report such information to outside stakeholders can be manifold and is part of the second research objective. One explanation can be found in a desire to please demands from various stakeholders (Freeman, 1984), while a second explanation can be found in a desire to achieve broad legitimacy in society as their company name and their family name are tied together closely (Cotter & Najah, 2012). The aspects that motivate family-owned companies to account for and report their GHG emissions will thus be analyzed as part of this research chapter.

Besides the motivation behind performing carbon accounting, the literature identifies various general challenges in the carbon accounting process. To name a few, examples involve overall insecurity in reported values (Rypdal & Winiwarter, 2001), uncertainty regarding the mathematical model and chosen parameters (WBCSD & WRI, 2015), as well as undefined calculation standards yielding different data from different suppliers (Olson, 2010). The literature has yet to thoroughly discuss whether these challenges apply to family-owned companies.

Turning towards the research methodology applied for this research chapter, it is crucial to understand that family-owned companies are known for their privacy (Miller & Le Breton-Miller, 2021b), non-disclosure (Poza & Messer, 2001) and preservation of confidential information (Miller & Le Breton-Miller, 2004). As such, public information on family-owned companies is only available to a limited extent. I, therefore, chose a qualitative approach and used a multiple-case study approach (Eisenhardt, 1989). I conducted semi-structured interviews among 13 German family-owned companies, which I further triangulated with external sources to the extent available (Yin, 2009). Cases were carefully selected via a detailed sampling approach (Glaser & Strauss, 1967). Only companies with 100% family ownership, appropriate size in terms of employees and revenue such that the CSRD applies, and companies from industries known for comparably high GHG emissions were chosen. The chosen approach reflects the best opportunity to gather the relevant data, mainly because carbon accounting has yet to become a fully established approach but constitutes an exploratory effort for most companies today. I eventually evaluate the data by precisely transcribing all interviews to then code (Miles et al., 2018) and analyze the generated data within- and cross-case.

Turning to my results, I generally confirm that the classification applied by Henriques and Sadorsky (1999) is also valid for family-owned companies, while most companies either belong to the second or third archetype, which I define as extrinsically-driven reporters and intrinsic sustainability drivers. Additionally, I extend the framework regarding methodology, motivation, and challenges. On the methodological side, I generally confirm the GHG Protocol as the leading standard among family-owned companies. In contrast, most companies have focused on Scopes 1 and 2, and only some have collected Scope 3 GHG data in an exploratory manner. The data collected is used mainly for internal reporting or provided to stakeholders on demand, while only a few companies also report their data externally voluntarily. Customer demand, generational thinking, and an intrinsic will to contribute were identified as the primary motivators for family-owned companies to account for their GHG emissions. Among the main challenges, a need for more sense of urgency among either top-level management or general staff was identified as highly challenging. Additionally, lacking or unstandardized data complicates the accounting process, resulting in high levels of insecurity when modelling the data.

With the achieved results, I contribute to the growing literature related to family-owned companies (Hasso & Duncan, 2013) known for privacy and reservedness (Miller & Le Breton-Miller, 2021b; Stiftung Familienunternehmen, 2023b) by applying an interview-based approach. In contributing to this scientific area, I present a novel and comprehensive scientific framework designed to enhance the understanding of the current state and future potential of carbon accounting within family-owned businesses. This framework will equip researchers and practitioners with the necessary insights to address and improve carbon accounting practices. It is essential to tackle the challenges identified in this context. Consequently, the analysis yields two critical managerial implications: Firstly, the need to raise awareness and address the relatively low sense of urgency regarding carbon accounting among top management and staff across various companies, and secondly, the importance of developing standards for data exchange, both internally within companies and externally between different entities, to mitigate the issues related to carbon emission data accessibility.

After this introduction, I structure this chapter as follows: In the next section, I will cover the theoretical foundations surrounding environmental management frameworks, family-owned companies, environmental regulatory guidelines, carbon accounting methodologies, and theoretical motivations. The third section presents the qualitative multiple-case study methodology applied in this chapter. Section four then presents the results of this scientific work, including the developed company archetypes. Section five summarizes the findings, provides managerial implications, and gives an outlook on potential future research.

2.2 Theoretical Background and Literature Review

As part of the theoretical literature review, I will provide an overview of the literature on environmental management frameworks for companies and discuss past literature on environmental management methodologies, motivations, and challenges. To answer the overarching research question mentioned in the previous chapter, I thus break down my research question into four sub-research questions I will derive in the following four sub-chapters.

2.2.1 General Environmental Management Frameworks

As mentioned, family-owned companies constitute the primary company type in Germany, with over 90% of German companies owned by one or multiple families (Stiftung Familienunternehmen, 2023b). Besides the considerable importance for the German economy, this company type also differs from other corporations in various ways, which I will discuss in the following chapter.

Multiple definitions for family-owned companies have been developed over time. De Massis et al. (2012) have therefore analyzed definitions of family-owned companies for 15 years and identified across 215 studies the most relevant factors for differentiating family from non-family companies. 79% of definitions include family ownership, and 53% include family management as definition criteria. In contrast, only 15% use self-identification and 9% use multiple generations as criteria to define a family business (De Massis et al., 2012). Considering Germany, the German foundation for family-owned companies follows the definition provided by Kirchdörfer (2011), who acknowledges that varying definitions exist, primarily related to equity share and share of control of the family owning the company. He defines a family-owned company as a company of an arbitrary size and legal form where one or multiple families own most of the company. In the case of multiple families owning the company, they must either be directly related to each other or connected via a history within their families of jointly owning the company. Additionally, the families must influence the company sustainably, either via direct exertion of influence within the board of advisors or management or indirect exertion of influence via selected representatives of the families (Kirchdörfer, 2011). The German foundation for family-owned companies further adds to this definition by stating that even public companies listed on a stock exchange can be defined as family-owned companies in case one or multiple families who have founded the company, acquired it, or inherited it, own at least 25% of decision rights (Stiftung Familienunternehmen, 2022).

Family-owned companies are an interesting phenomenon as they differ significantly from public companies (Berrone et al., 2012). In other words, "*family firms are typically motivated by, and committed to, the preservation of the socioemotional wealth, referring to non-financial aspects or 'affective endowments' of family owners*" (Berrone et al., 2012, p. 259). Such non-financial aspects include, for instance, the family's reputation, which is inseparably tied to the family-owned company's actions and sustainable, cross-generational thinking, including the will to hand over the company to future generations. Family-owned companies are more risk-averse than non-family companies (Gomez-Mejia et al., 2011) and are more risk-averse towards socioemotional aspects of their financial performance (Berrone et al., 2012). This trend can also be identified in the literature when looking at ESG-related activities. For instance, family-owned companies have been found to cause less pollution, have built unique stakeholder relationships, and are more altruistic than non-family companies (Berrone et al., 2010;

Cennamo et al., 2012). All these activities primarily explain a great risk aversion towards reputational losses. Moreover, family-owned companies are often situated in rural areas and are economic drivers in their operating region. Thus, they receive special attention from the local population regarding their actions (Déniz & Suárez, 2005).

Whether and how these characteristics influence a family-owned company's environmental management has yet to be determined. To better understand how companies in general can be classified according to their environmental management, various researchers have made schematic definitions of company archetypes (see Table 2.1) to easily understand environmental management efforts (Carroll, 1979; Henriques & Sadorsky, 1999; Hunt & Auster, 1990; Roome, 1992; Wartick & Cochran, 1985). Both Roome (1992) and Hunt and Auster (1990) have clustered companies on a 5-point scale. Roome (1992) starts with the non-compliance level, i.e., companies belonging to this archetype do not adhere to regulatory standards, neither proactively nor cost-driven. Compliant companies, i.e., the second archetype, adhere to regulatory standards while not exceeding them. The third archetype, compliance plus, describes companies that already use environmental information and reporting to their advantage, e.g., by positioning positive aspects in front of customers. The fourth and fifth archetypes describe companies that excel at environmental management and do more than regulators, customers, or society require. While Hunt and Auster (1990) use different wording for these archetypes, i.e., ranging from beginner to proactivist, associated characteristics on every level are similar to those described. Henriques and Sadorsky (1999) linked these two frameworks to a more general framework, i.e., a classification into four archetypes, i.e., reactive, defensive, accommodative and proactive, as more general categories.

Given the individual characteristics of family-owned companies described before on the one hand and the different environmental management classifications applying in general to all companies on the other hand, I make an essential contribution to the existing literature by testing the described framework for family-owned companies. While family-owned companies are known for their risk aversion on one side (e.g., Gómez-Mejía et al., 2007), implying that family-owned companies are hypothetically no frontrunners in environmental management, their high interest in acting sustainably (e.g., Berrone et al., 2010) could imply that no activity at all is also relatively improbable. As explained before, I will use research sub-questions to contribute to the overarching research question stated earlier and, therefore, state this first research sub-question as follows:

Table 2.1 Schematic environmental management company archetypes[2]

Roome (1992)	Non-compliance	Compliance	Compliance Plus	Environmental excellence	Leading edge
Hunt and Auster (1990)	Beginner	Firefighter	Concerned citizen	Pragmatist	Proactivist
Henriques and Sadorsky (1999) Wartick and Cochran (1985) Carroll (1979)	Reactive	Defensive	Accommodative	Proactive	
Overall importance of environmental management	None	Critical issues only	Regarded as relevant function	Top priority function	
Top-level management involvement	None	Partially	From time to time	Full support	
Reporting mode	None	Regulatory minimum	Good internally, Little externally	Fully internal and external	
Employee involvement	None	Little	Some	Strongly preferred	

Do traditional environmental management frameworks for companies in general apply to family-owned companies?

2.2.2 Methodological Approach to Environmental Management

Besides testing the framework, I also aim to extend the framework in terms of the chosen methodological approach. Only limited information exists on family-owned companies today regarding operationalizing the environmental accounting process, its associated accounting methods and involved resources. When discussing the carbon accounting process, it is helpful to understand what it involves. I, therefore, follow the definition provided by Stechemesser and Guenther (2012): "*Carbon accounting comprises the recognition, the non-monetary and monetary*

[2] Adapted from Henriques and Sadorsky (1999).

evaluation and the monitoring of GHG emissions on all levels of the value chain and the recognition, evaluation and monitoring of the effects of these emissions on the carbon cycle of ecosystems" (Stechemesser & Guenther, 2012, p. 35).

Several standards have been established and widely adopted in the industry to perform carbon accounting in companies. First, the so-called GHG Protocol constitutes one of the most widely used standards for carbon accounting, with more than 92% of Fortune 500 companies using it as their accounting standard (WBCSD & WRI, 2023). The GHG Protocol was first established by two NGOs in 2001. It aims to provide a common standard for companies to enable an accurate and fair accounting of GHG emissions. Following the typical financial accounting principles,[3] the GHG Protocol has developed five fundamental principles: Relevance, completeness, consistency, transparency, and accuracy (WBCSD & WRI, 2015). Carbon accounting today is, however, still very much unregulated in comparison to financial accounting (Ioannou & Serafeim, 2017). The GHG Protocol clusters GHG emissions into direct and indirect GHG emissions and classifies these into three different Scopes of GHG emissions: Scope 1, Scope 2, and Scope 3 emissions (see FIGURE 2.1). Scope 1 emissions are direct GHG emissions from a company's sources. Examples here are the operation of a power plant, including its fossil and liquid fuel or company vehicles consuming fuel. Scope 2 emissions are indirect GHG emissions resulting from generating electricity for the company, i.e., the GHG is physically emitted at the electricity power plant instead of the company. Scope 3 emissions are all other indirect GHG emissions from activities outside a company's direct control or ownership. Therefore, a thorough analysis of the company's value chain is required. The GHG Protocol provides separate guidance for Scope 3 emission calculations, breaking Scope 3 emissions into 15 categories categorized into upstream or downstream activities (WBCSD & WRI, 2013).

Besides the GHG Protocol, one noteworthy carbon accounting standard is standard 14,064, published by the ISO. Introduced in 2006, ISO 14064 provides specific minimum standards for how to comply with the defined best practices. As such, the GHG Protocol defines the content to be accounted for, and ISO 14064 defines how to operationalize the process. In this way, both standards complement each other (Wintergreen & Delaney, 2007). Thus, ISO 14064 helps an organization design, develop, manage, report, and verify a company's GHG inventory.

---

[3] Relevance, faithful representation, comparability, verifiability, timeliness, understandability (International Accounting Standards Board, 2018).

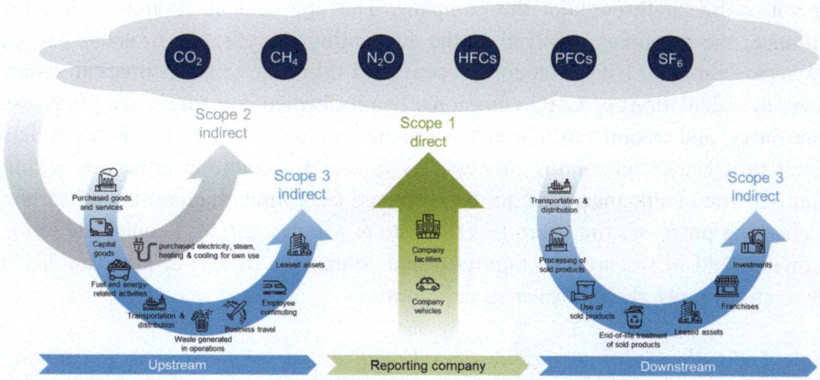

Fig. 2.1 Overview of three GHG Protocol Scopes along the value chain[4]

The third standard mentioned here is the SBTi created by the CDP, the UN Global Compact, the WRI and the World Wide Fund for Nature (WWF) (Science Based Targets, 2022). This initiative aims to enable companies to set relevant climate targets and provide guidance on achieving these targets. Therefore, the SBTi establishes a target validation process along a particular set of criteria to assess and validate a company's climate targets individually and independently. Today, over 2,200 companies covering more than a third of global market capitalization adhere to the SBTi.

Typically, companies would use their annual reporting and integrate their emissions into the annual report (Depoers et al., 2016). Nevertheless, the structure of these company reports differs in terms of reported data and format, which is why another initiative has been launched to overcome this issue, i.e., the previously mentioned CDP. The CDP is an international non-profit charity organization across multiple countries (e.g., Germany, United States of America, United Kingdom, Japan, and China) founded in 2000. On behalf of over 680 institutional investors with over USD 130 trillion in managed assets, the CDP collects survey-based data from companies, cities, regions and public authorities regarding carbon emissions and water consumption. In 2021, over 13,000 companies reported their data voluntarily via the CDP, including 2,400 companies within Europe, equal to 74% of the total market value (Weiss et al., 2022).

In summary, various accounting methods exist for a company's GHG emissions. Nevertheless, it is a question of which standard to use and how to

[4] Adapted from (WBCSD and WRI, 2015).

operationalize it throughout the company. The operationalization includes, for instance, the resources involved in the accounting process, the broadness (e.g., all versus limited GHG Protocol Scopes), and diligence (e.g., estimation versus accurate calculation) of GHG emissions. Family-owned companies are often less innovative, and resource availability is limited (Nieto et al., 2015), which can thus result in a leaner accounting process. As financial accounting processes within family-owned companies have to date received only limited attention and carbon accounting processes thus even less (Salvato & Moores, 2010), I contribute to the growing field of research on family-owned companies (Hasso & Duncan, 2013) by answering my second research sub-question:

How do family-owned companies operationalize their ghg emissions accounting along their value chain?

2.2.3 Motivations to Perform Environmental Management

Besides testing and extending an existing environmental management framework, I aim to contribute to the previously mentioned family-owned company literature on environmental reporting by identifying why family-owned companies collect and report environmental information. Various motivational theories for collecting and disclosing environmental information can be identified. Hahn et al. (2015) cluster such theories into three groups: 1) socio-political theories, 2) economic theories and 3) institutional theories.

First, socio-political theories can be broken down into stakeholder and legitimacy theories. Stakeholder theory was initially introduced by Freeman (1984), who argues that a company's success depends on accounting for the interests of all stakeholders a company has, internally and externally, and not only targeted at the company's shareholders. Gray and Bebbington (2000) argue here, however, that voluntary environmental disclosure results in only sharing information the management is willing to release. As such, the disclosed information only fulfils legitimation purposes, yet there is no accountability for the information shared by the company. Disclosed information can even be used to justify certain decisions, and therefore, companies may use the disclosed information for this purpose while leaving other information aside, thus making it invisible (Broadbent et al., 1994). Another aspect to consider as part of stakeholder theory is the reasoning behind sharing information. Stakeholder theory argues that management will disclose environmental information due to pressure from their stakeholders (Roberts, 1992), yet disclosed information has no completeness guarantee of any kind (Depoers et al., 2016).

In contrast, disclosed information can enhance a company's reputation among stakeholders and increase the perception of the company's brand overall, resulting in a significant impact on employee hiring and retention, creating new business opportunities and assuring better access to external financing (Ioannou & Serafeim, 2017). Another benefit of participating in environmental activities and disclosing environmental information to stakeholders is stakeholder goodwill, almost comparable to insurance preserving corporate financial performance in critical situations (Godfrey et al., 2009). Albertini (2013), for instance, confirms a positive correlation between environmental and financial performance after conducting a meta-analysis across more than 50 studies, underlining that environmental disclosure can safeguard stakeholders as they associate good financial performance with environmental performance.

Legitimacy theory, compared to stakeholder theory, argues that disclosure of information is targeted at an even broader audience and thus aims at society in its entirety. According to this theory, a company's interests are to gain broad acceptance throughout society and, as such, achieve buy-in for its actions and generate a credible image among a broad audience (Cotter & Najah, 2012). Legitimacy theory furthermore argues for environmental disclosure because of pressure from external stakeholders. However, the disclosure does not aim to harm the social contract between the company and the broader society (Deegan, 2002). For climate-related topics, this social contract is firm. Whenever society perceives a company breaches this implicit social contract, society will start to revoke the company's contract by stopping the demand for the product or making public statements against the company. For instance, Aerts and Cormier (2009) found a positive correlation between a company's environmental legitimacy and the quality of disclosed environmental information. Terlaak et al. (2018) argue that companies with a more significant extent of family ownership benefit more from environmental information disclosure as they are perceived to disclose less information than companies with little family ownership.

Economic theories argue that disclosure is merely based on a trade-off between the benefits of disclosing information and the costs of disclosing this information (Clarkson et al., 2008). Shareholders are the focal point here, for which the disclosed information has the potential to reduce the problem of information asymmetries between them and the management, as explained in the principal-agent theory by Jensen and Meckling (1976). This phenomenon is also explained by the signaling theory, where one party communicates with another, and the sending party chooses the content and method of communication. In contrast, the receiving party then chooses how to interpret the received information (Connelly et al., 2011). Thus, the sender can pre-empt scrutiny from stakeholder groups such as political groups. Especially in the case of voluntary disclosures, signaling theory argues that strong emphasis is put on conveying good environmental performance and presenting the company in the best way possible. Nevertheless, the information must be perceived as trustworthy to ensure the integrity of the reporting company.

Lastly, institutional theory constitutes the third cluster of motivation for carbon disclosure presented by Hahn et al. (2015). This theoretical field argues that organizations are driven, similar to economic theory, by profit maximization, yet also by demands from different kinds of (governmental) institutions.

At this point, a quick regulatory digression is helpful to understand the regulatory network family-owned companies operate in today. Most important to mention here is the previously mentioned NFRD, regarded as one of the most impactful directives the EU has enacted to achieve climate targets (Cosma et al., 2022). It limits the company scope to companies with more than 500 employees, net turnover exceeding EUR 40 million or balance sheet volume exceeding EUR 20 million and generally companies of public interest, i.e., credit and insurance institutions and capital market-oriented companies. Within the EU, approximately 11,700 companies fall under the criteria set out in the NFRD (European Parliament & European Council, 2022). Companies to which these criteria apply must report on environmental performance, social and employee matters, human rights performance, corruption and anti-bribery matters in either the management report or a separate non-financial report (CSR Europe & GRI, 2017). Considering the criteria under which companies must comply with the NFRD, it becomes evident that family-owned companies without capital market orientation are outside the scope and, thus, are not obliged to report under the guidelines of the NFRD. To further contribute to the European Green Deal and, as such, achieve the net-zero GHG emission target by 2050, the European Commission has deemed it necessary to further enhance today's reporting guidelines for non-financial matters and, therefore, propose the previously mentioned CSRD (European Parliament & European Council, 2022). Compared to the NFRD, the CSRD will extend the NFRD majorly in terms of company type, reporting scope and reporting format, extending the regulatory scope to more than 50,000 companies (EY, 2022). As such, family-owned companies will, going forward, be regulated under the CSRD and face regulatory pressure to report on environmental information.

Empirically, smaller companies feel regulatory or institutional pressure more strongly, while larger companies are influenced rather by other stakeholder groups (Henriques & Sadorsky, 1999). Larger family-owned companies, especially, will investigate formalized reporting approaches to comply with the needs of their stakeholders (Shields et al., 2018). Smaller family-owned companies are often overwhelmed with the required workload and need more financial or human resources to compile sophisticated carbon accounting and reporting. Nevertheless, institutional pressure is comparably low. Previous authors stated that "despite burgeoning research on companies' environmental strategies and environmental management practices, it remains unclear why some firms adopt environmental management practices beyond regulatory compliance" (Delmas & Toffel, 2004, p. 209).

Moreover, regulatory measures also come with certain drawbacks given the required reporting effort and a need for changing corporate processes. Furthermore, this act of bureaucratization yields a convergence in the disclosure behavior of companies. DiMaggio and Powell (1983) argued that companies are becoming more similar, yet not driven by the need for efficiency but by the need to comply with specific guidelines set by institutions. Thus, companies are becoming more homogenous, which makes them less efficient. Additionally, disclosing environmental information can furthermore be penalized on financial markets or used against the company's interest by competitors (Cormier & Magnan, 1999). Greater exposure to NGOs or other activist groups can lead to negative consequences when the disclosed information is used to attack the company or accuse the company of conducting greenwashing (Lyon & Maxwell, 2008). Lastly, Li et al. (1997) argue that disclosed information could be used as preliminary information for investigators and, as such, increase compliance-related costs.

In summary, various theoretical motivations explain why family-owned companies disclose environmental information voluntarily. Apart from the mentioned motivating factors, which I consider extrinsic, other intrinsic influencing factors, such as the company's values, might exist. Moreover, even if private family-owned companies do not report their GHG emissions externally, an internal accounting might make sense to manage GHG-related risks and identify mitigation and reduction strategies (WBCSD & WRI, 2015). In any case, today, many family-owned companies are at least internally accounting for their GHG emission information and partly already disclose this information externally without being regulated to do so.

I, therefore, motivate the following research question by the broad set of potential motivating factors to disclose environmental information and aim to identify what motivates family-owned companies to do so. I find further support from various authors as research on family-owned companies is regarded as an emerging field of research in the literature (Carrera, 2017), where the amount of research is behind other academic fields today (Prencipe et al., 2014). I therefore state the third research sub-question as follows:

Why do family-owned companies account for their ghg emissions along their value chain?

2.2.4 Challenges in Environmental Management

Many of the required processes in carbon accounting constitute new territory for family-owned companies due to the recency of its introduction. In line with establishing such new processes comes measurable uncertainty. The uncertainty in today's carbon accounting can range between five and twenty percent of the reported GHG emission value (Rypdal & Winiwarter, 2001). This uncertainty can result from several sources, such as uncertainty regarding the mathematical model (Lee et al., 2024), chosen parameters and assumptions (WBCSD & WRI, 2015), as well as undefined calculation standards yielding different data from different suppliers (Olson, 2010). Moreover, the increasing complexity resulting from international and highly flexible supply chains complicates data gathering within a company (Schaltegger & Csutora, 2012). Of course, the previously mentioned limited availability of resources and reluctance to adopt new processes quickly among family-owned companies (Nieto et al., 2015) can also complicate the establishment of new accounting processes. Digital transformation can, in addition, support a smooth carbon accounting process. However, the digitalization of processes depends on the abilities of the family-owned company. Furthermore, the overall transformation effort depends on the individual willingness to transform among the owning family (Heider et al., 2022).

Whether the challenges described above also apply to family-owned companies and to what extent family-owned companies are willing to digitally transform in the carbon accounting space has yet to be discussed thoroughly in the existing literature on family-owned companies. Thus, to better understand which exact challenges family-owned companies face in this regard, the fourth research sub-question of this research chapter shall answer the following question:

Which challenges do family-owned companies encounter when measuring and accounting for GHG emissions along the value chain?

2.3 Methodology

2.3.1 Multiple Case-Study as Methodological Approach

Environmental management is a topic of broad societal interest today, and many companies are willing to speak openly about their approach to measuring and reducing GHG emissions. Nevertheless, family-owned companies often avoid making information public (Miller & Le Breton-Miller, 2021b), are characterized by non-disclosure (Poza & Messer, 2001) and preserve confidential information where possible (Miller & Le Breton-Miller, 2004). Thus, collecting public information on family-owned companies is challenging as it is at least complicated to gather or unavailable. Qualitative data collection is thus most appropriate in this case to collect sufficient data on the one hand and better understand where family-owned companies stand today in their carbon accounting processes on the other hand. In addition, I aim to not only test an existing framework but also extend this into a new framework. Therefore, I deploy a multiple-case study approach to test the existing framework and extend it into a new theoretical foundation following the approach introduced by Eisenhardt (1989). Initially, research questions were defined based on a thorough literature review where I identified today's research gaps. Given the high relevance of carbon accounting and the high complexity involved, case study research is a well-suited method to reflect real-world phenomena (Eisenhardt & Graebner, 2007). As case study research is characterized by using multiple data sources (Yin, 2009), I also triangulate the empirical results where possible.

Conducting research based on a single, extensive case-study research constitutes an exciting approach, yet based on findings in previous literature (Eisenhardt & Graebner, 2007; Yin, 2009), I decided that a multiple-case study approach allows for a more thorough analysis representing the real world more realistically. In addition, this approach allows for a cross-case analysis and thus allows the comparison of different family-owned companies in their approaches instead of a mere within-case analysis (Eisenhardt, 1989). Moreover, I follow Eisenhardt's (1989) replicational logic, i.e., I regard every case as a discrete unit of investigation and thus extend the empirical results with each additional case to eventually develop a new theory.

While the framework testing and extension is focused on a sample of German family-owned companies across multiple industries, generalizability to other family-owned companies in European countries is applicable as other European companies face similar upcoming regulations on a European level. The details of the applied data sampling approach are described in the next chapter.

2.3.2 Data Sampling and Used Resources

Within the focus of this research chapter are German family-owned companies. Germany is Europe's largest economy, and ~ 90% of German companies are family-controlled, resulting in a highly relevant group of companies (Stiftung Familienunternehmen, 2023b). According to Glaser and Strauss (1967), I conducted the sampling to ensure a high-quality sample to select the best cases. I started sampling with German companies with family ownership. To ensure that the results are tied to family ownership, I only focused on companies owned 100% by one or multiple families related to each other. I thus avoid the influence of other shareholders as many examples within Germany exist with partial family and partial public ownership (e.g., Volkswagen AG, Wacker Chemie AG). Furthermore, many private companies today are not regulated by the NFRD. However, they might fall under the CSRD regulations when relevant criteria are met. To ensure that regulatory aspects also influence company decisions, I reduced the sample to companies exceeding two of the following three criteria, thus falling under the regulation of the CSRD: 1) More than 250 employees, 2) more than EUR 40 million net turnover or 3) more than EUR 20 million balance sheet. Such companies face reporting requirements as part of the new CSRD and are thus assumed to have already considered carbon accounting to some extent. Family-owned companies in scope were limited to, at most, a net turnover of EUR 5,000 million to differentiate the sample sufficiently from large public corporations. These sampling boundaries, on the one hand, helped to interview companies which are sufficiently large and, therefore, are assumed to have proper carbon accounting in place and, on the other hand, differentiate themselves sufficiently from DAX-40 companies where ~ 80% of companies exceed the upper net turnover level. The industry focus was set on companies belonging to the industrial and consumer goods sectors and the transportation industry due to their comparably high GHG emissions across all three Scope levels as defined in the GHG Protocol. Due to the comparably high GHG emission levels, companies are likely to have considered carbon accounting more thoroughly. Lastly, I only considered companies with public communication regarding their activities towards fighting the climate crisis for this sample as I assumed a genuine interest in this topic among those companies and presumably employees responsible for carbon accounting. Based on this multi-step sampling process, I was able to identify a set of 13 cases (Table 2.2) which I reached through either one of the following methods: 1) reach-out via e-mail or social media, 2) personal network or 3) introduction via the interviewed family-owned company. I contacted 29 companies, resulting in a 45% response rate. I mainly conducted the interviews with one interview partner per company, i.e., the CEO, the head of sustainability or the sustainability manager. In two cases, I spoke to multiple interview partners in multiple interviews to generate a further in-depth understanding. In all other cases, the relevant information was sufficiently captured in one interview. All interviews were conducted in May, June, and July 2022 and lasted between 43 and 78 min, using virtual telecommunication methods involving cameras. Towards the last interviews, I identified a convergence of interview results, assuring that further interviews would yield only a little insight. Thus, the interview procedure was stopped after the described cases (Eisenhardt, 1989). For the previously mentioned data triangulation (Yin, 2009), I extended the empirical interview-based results with publicly provided company information in press releases and company websites. In addition to the described cases, three expert interviews were conducted with a senior manager from a leading consulting company, the CEO and founder of a start-up focusing on carbon emission accounting, and the sustainability manager from an international family-owned company located outside Germany to further triangulate the findings. To ensure a high level of validity, I assured the interview partners of the complete anonymity of the collected data before the interview. Furthermore, the interviews were semi-structured, i.e., a deviation from the interview guideline was possible. The interview guide involved multiple open questions to avoid suggestive questions (see Appendix A) and it was designed per the guidance Yin (2009) provided.

2.3.3 Data Analysis

According to the approach described by Eisenhardt (1989), I initially developed each case individually and conducted the within-case analysis. I then compared the results across cases to test the existing framework (Henriques & Sadorsky, 1999) and extend it. Initially, all interviews were precisely transcribed. Transcripts were then coded and analyzed using the MAXQDA[5] tool. The coding was inspired by the approach Miles et al. (2018) described, and I, therefore, diligently assigned individual codes to each transcript passage. In total, a set of 708 individual written codes were coded. I grouped the developed codes into first-order categories in a second coding round. Afterwards, I was able to divide these

[5] Software program developed by German software company usually deployed for mixed methods and qualitative data analysis. Supports researchers in coding and visualizing text-based data input.

Table 2.2 Overview of interviewed companies

Company	Industry	Revenue [EUR M]	Employees	Interview partner(s)
Alpha	Healthcare	1,800	8,000	Sustainability Manager
Beta	Industrial Goods	3,400	13,000	Head of Sustainability & Sustainability Manager
Gamma	Industrial Goods	2,100	15,000	Group Director Quality & Environment, Sustainability Manager and Team Manager Environmental Protection
Delta	Agriculture	200	500	CEO
Epsilon	Paper	1,000	2,500	Sustainability Manager
Zeta	Industrial Goods	600	1,500	Sustainability Manager
Eta	Industrial Goods	200	1,500	CEO
Theta	Logistics	4,000	12,000	Senior Project Manager Sustainability
Iota	Construction	125	650	Sustainability Manager
Kappa	Industrial Goods	250	2,000	CEO
Lambda	Industrial Goods	250	1,500	CEO & Head of Sustainability
Mu	Industrial Goods	300	4,000	Member of the Executive Board
Nu	Industrial Goods	250	1,000	Quality Manager

categories into higher-level categories in a third round to thus derive the second-order categories resulting in a three-level coding approach. The overall approach was conducted iteratively, and thus second-order categories also influenced first-order categories during the coding process. With the generated evidence, initial hypotheses were revised and shaped further to create additional internal validity.

I could thus identify specific patterns as part of the cross-case analyses to derive categories with generalizability beyond the discussed cases. Finally, additional validity was built by comparing the results with conflicting and similar literature and further triangulation with company-provided public information and expert interview input to eventually reach closure in a tested and extended framework.

2.4 Results and Discussion

The empirical analysis of the qualitative data allows me to find answers to the defined research objectives and questions. I can test whether the previously developed frameworks (Carroll, 1979; Henriques & Sadorsky, 1999; Hunt & Auster, 1990; Roome, 1992; Wartick & Cochran, 1985) apply to family-owned companies and extend their conceptual frameworks into a new framework in terms of methodological approach towards carbon accounting, motivation to perform carbon accounting and reporting beyond regulatory guidance as well as challenges family-owned companies face throughout their reporting journey. I aggregated the data to a meaningful level for all research questions to contribute to current research with meaningful result clusters. While writing this chapter, I was challenged whether a difference between family-owned companies and large public corporations (e.g., DAX-40) exists several times. Therefore, I will also answer this question in the results section. Lastly, I critically discuss the results in a broader economic context.

2.4.1 Carbon Accounting: Company Archetypes

As described in the methodology, I have performed within-case and cross-case analyses. The cross-case analyses and the derived framework are the most considerable contributions to the literature on carbon accounting and family-owned companies. Therefore, I focus the results on the findings from the cross-case analysis, allowing me to answer my defined research questions holistically. Where applicable, I additionally provide information from the within-case analyses.

Based on my analyses, I derive an extended framework for carbon accounting among family-owned companies. While some aspects of previous frameworks still apply (Henriques & Sadorsky, 1999), I extend the framework into a new one (see Table 2.3). I, therefore, cluster the interviewed companies into archetypes and present the results for each along five relevant categories concerning carbon accounting: 1) overall importance, 2) motivation, 3) methodology, 4) challenges and 5) company size. As such, categories two, four and five are entirely new, while the third category not only comprises top-level management involvement, reporting mode and employee involvement (as used by previous authors, e.g., Carroll, 1979; Henriques & Sadorsky, 1999; Wartick & Cochran, 1985) but is furthermore extended to also comprise the applied carbon accounting standards (e.g., GHG Protocol), used software, calculation method and measurement years. Four archetypes are sufficient to describe the different family-owned company types. I, thus, generally stick with the categorization used by previous authors (Carroll, 1979; Henriques & Sadorsky, 1999; Wartick & Cochran, 1985) while renaming them into the, from my point of view, more specific archetypes: 1) Sustainability laggards, 2) extrinsically-driven reporters, 3) intrinsically-driven realists, and 4) sustainability frontrunners which I briefly describe in the following:

I specify the first identified archetype as sustainability laggards. Companies of this archetype need to show more urgency in working on carbon accounting. Moreover, the motivation to measure GHG emissions is generally low and will eventually only result from regulatory pressure. Shifting towards the applied methodology, standards such as the GHG Protocol still need to be discovered. Thus, no internal reporting nor external collection or reporting of data is taking place, and no employees are assigned to accounting tasks related to GHG emissions. In selected cases, external support is requested to collect the first set of GHG emission data. However, calculations are equal to a back-of-the-envelope calculation instead of a profound analysis. Most challenging for this archetype is the shallow sense of urgency and the general missing mindset towards reducing carbon emissions. Family-owned companies of this archetype are comparably small, thus ranging below EUR 250 M in revenue.

Second, I identified extrinsically-driven reports as an archetype for family-owned companies regarding carbon accounting. They differentiate themselves substantially from the previous archetype in various categories. First, they show at least low urgency when measuring GHG emissions among top-level management. Motivation results mostly from external pressure, i.e., customer demand, regulatory pressure, and sometimes pressure from financial institutions. As such, this company archetype measures Scope 1 and 2 GHG emissions according to the GHG Protocol to adhere to the accepted minimum amount of data, while Scope 3 data is not measured. Data reporting only occurs on demand, i.e., no regular reporting mechanisms are established, and top-level management needs to request the data regularly. In line with the reduced reporting efforts, a limited number of employees is involved. On average, less than two employees are involved in carbon accounting, mainly not located in a separate sustainability

Table 2.3 Four archetypes of carbon accounting among family-owned companies

Archetypes / Categories		Sustainability laggards	Extrinsically-driven reporters	Intrinsically-driven realist	Sustainability frontrunners
Overall importance & sense of urgency		None	None to low	Low to medium	High
Motivation		Fully driven by upcoming regulatory changes	Regulatory and customer pressure as main drivers	Motivated to act sustainably & generational thinking	Feel obligated to contribute to society
Methodology	Standard & Scopes	No use of standards	GHG Protocol Scope 1–2	GHG Protocol Scope 1–2, Scope 3 exploratory	GHG Protocol Scope 1–3 and additional method (e.g., SBTi)
	Reporting mode	No internal or external reporting	Internal reporting on demand	Regular internal reporting	Full external and internal reporting
	Management involvement	No interest among top management	Sporadic interest among top-level management	Interest in some management meetings	High and regular agenda item
	Employee involvement	No dedicated sustainability employees	< 2 employees integrated into other department (e.g., Quality Management)	2–5 employees integrated into other department (e.g., Quality Management)	> 5 employees in dedicated sustainability department
	Software	No software used	E-mail and regular spreadsheet software (e.g., Microsoft Excel)	E-mail and regular spreadsheet software (e.g., Microsoft Excel)	E-Mail, spreadsheet software and dedicated GHG measurement software

(continued)

Table 2.3 (continued)

Archetypes / Categories		Sustainability laggards	Extrinsically-driven reporters	Intrinsically-driven realist	Sustainability frontrunners
Overall importance & sense of urgency		None	None to low	Low to medium	High
	Calculation method	Back-of-the-envelope calculations, if at all	Mere backward calculation via financial information	Mix of GHG and financial data backward calculation	Actual measurement of GHG data wherever possible
	Years measured	Exploratory only, no full measurement of any kind	One-time effort only	1–3 years in annual effort	> 3 years in annual effort
Challenges		Low sense of urgency and missing mindset among management and owners	Limited personnel and unestablished data reporting processes and interfaces	Insecurity regarding internal and external data accuracy	Limited data availability from external suppliers
Company size [M EUR]		< 250	> 1,000	All	> 250

department but within another department, e.g., the quality management department. Using e-mail and spreadsheet software (e.g., Microsoft Excel), a rather unestablished process is applied to collect the data. Data is mainly calculated backwards, i.e., derived from financial data instead of actual emission measurement, and to date, only one full year has been calculated. The most challenging aspects for this company type are limited personnel on the one hand and unestablished processes on the other. Interview results showed that larger family-owned companies with revenue beyond EUR 1,000 M belong to this archetype.

Third, I identified the intrinsically-driven realists as an archetype describing family-owned companies in their carbon accounting behavior. The sense of urgency is higher among top-level management yet still close to a low to medium level compared to the fourth archetype. The general staff's sense of urgency is still relatively low throughout the organization, while top-level management perceives higher importance in reducing carbon emissions. Intrinsic factors now constitute the main motivating factors paired with generational thinking and a strong will to contribute to society. Some extrinsic motivating factors are also coming into play, e.g., customer demand, creating a competitive advantage or being attractive to future employees, yet intrinsic motivating factors are predominant. Regarding carbon accounting standards, Scopes 1 and 2 are measured with confidence following the GHG Protocol, yet Scope 3 data is collected using an exploratory approach with limited data confidence. In line with this confidence, external reporting does not occur, while internal reporting is regularly performed and sometimes discussed in management meetings. On average, around two to five full-time employees oversee carbon accounting and reporting, mostly still integrated into an existing department, e.g., quality management. The software used is comparable to the second archetype, while data is calculated based on financial backward calculation and some actual GHG data measurement. Companies of this archetype have established relevant processes within the last three years.

Thus, processes are no longer a real challenge, but limited data availability from internal and external sources still yields high uncertainty regarding the accuracy of achieved calculation results. In terms of revenue, no tendency can be observed, i.e., revenue does not indicate whether a company is intrinsically motivated to account for its GHG emissions. Again, a sense of urgency among top-level management is the main driver for this archetype. Nevertheless, carbon accounting and reduction are not top priorities, resulting in reduced speed of setting up holistic carbon accounting processes.

Lastly, I determine sustainability frontrunners as a company archetype where a high sense of urgency among top-level management and general staff driving the sustainability efforts is the case. As such, measuring and reducing carbon emissions is essential and is perceived as a task for everyone. A lack of urgency constituted an overarching challenge among previous archetypes, yet not among this company archetype anymore. The motivation to measure and reduce GHG emissions is highly intrinsic, i.e., family-owned companies belonging to this archetype are driven by their will to contribute to society and their generational thinking and show a strong will to improve themselves constantly through benchmarking against other companies. This company archetype is far advanced in standards, applies the GHG Protocol across all three Scopes, and further enhances the achieved results with additional standards, e.g., SBTi. Data is calculated with high confidence and reported externally and internally regularly. Reporting data in such a diligent way requires substantial resources. Family-owned companies in this archetype have at least five full-time employees working on carbon accounting and reporting, supported mainly by further part-time employees. A dedicated sustainability department, including defined processes, is set up. While e-mails and spreadsheet software are still used regularly for data collection and calculation, dedicated GHG emission measurement software is also used where applicable. Processes were set up several years ago, and wherever possible, actual GHG emission data is measured instead of using a financial backward calculation. Data availability among external suppliers is the most challenging aspect for this company type. International suppliers apply different standards, especially in a globalized world, making calculations difficult. Although substantial resources are required, it cannot be generalized that only companies of significant size in terms of revenue belong to this archetype. Instead, companies with revenue above EUR 250 M already belong to this archetype. In conclusion, the main driving force behind belonging to the sustainability frontrunners can be identified in a high sense of urgency among the top-level management and the family owners.

In summary, I identify four different archetypes. Although no significant number of companies were interviewed to generalize from this population to all family-owned companies, I see that most companies either belong to the second or third archetype with a slight tendency towards the third archetype (see Appendix B, for an allocation of interviewed companies to archetypes). Companies falling under archetypes one or four are only observed rarely. In the next three sub-chapters, I elaborate on the exact methodology, motivation, and challenges faced when performing carbon accounting to answer research sub-questions two, three, and four.

The How—Methodology and Processes of Carbon Accounting

Measuring and accounting for GHG emissions is not trivial and constitutes a new approach for most family-owned companies. Much of the required data points have never been collected before, and processes for collecting such data still need to be implemented. Nevertheless, family-owned companies have found different approaches to collecting and synthesizing the data meaningfully. I will highlight which standards are used by family-owned companies, to which degree these standards are already implemented today and how family-owned companies calculate the GHG emission data. Moreover, I will shed light on the experience in this field regarding how many years companies have already measured such data, how many resources they invest, and which software companies use to support their calculations. I will then conclude by shedding light on the used reporting methods.

Starting with the applied standards, I introduced the GHG Protocol as the leading standard for carbon accounting among companies in general, which also applies to family-owned companies. While it is not mandatory to use this standard, it is the most holistic and, at the same time, most detailed approach for measuring GHG emissions. Moreover, companies stated that a set standard is helpful to avoid further discussions, e.g., "*Ultimately, it is about comparability, and it is about the fact that we are always in competition and have to make sure that we are also comparable and everything that offers a definition in the market and thus actually one where we do not have to discuss with the people, is of course simply taken with the palm of our hand*" (Gamma, Pos. 26). All but one company reported an accounting approach based on this standard. Besides the GHG Protocol, only one company has applied the SBTi, and no companies have reported participating in the CDP. Furthermore, family-owned companies do also not adopt the ISO 14064 standard. However, some mentioned using other ISO standards, such as ISO 50001, i.e., a norm for an energy management system related to carbon accounting. As part of the carbon accounting, most companies reported focusing on all six GHGs instead of CO_2 only and thus report so-called CO_2-equivalents where all GHGs are converted into CO_2. As mentioned earlier, the GHG Protocol splits GHG emissions into Scopes 1,2 and 3. However, most family-owned companies only focus on Scopes 1 and 2, which are far more trivial to measure and calculate than Scope 3. Only two interviewed companies fully report on their Scope 3 emissions with confidence. Companies who have already performed their first calculations on Scope 3 still hesitate to publish these figures to avoid justifying significant changes in reported numbers in the following years due to potential changes in the calculation method.

Zooming in on the calculation method, various approaches can be applied, varying from a mere spend-based approach, e.g., deriving transportation-related GHG emissions from total logistics costs, to a direct measurement of consumed energy.

The chosen approach again varies across Scopes. While Scopes 1 and 2 are comparably easy to calculate, e.g., by collecting data from the electricity meter and multiplying it with a specific CO_2 factor, Scope 3 is far more complex to calculate and frequently only possible via a spend-based approach. Another way to facilitate such calculations is via databases, which allow family-owned companies to multiply their input materials with certain CO_2 factors. One example mentioned during the interviews was the so-called Product Environmental Footprint (PEF) database, which allows companies from the agricultural sector to find the right CO_2 factors for their input materials.

Nevertheless, specific GHG emissions must be calculated via a spend-based approach, reducing data correctness as more assumptions are involved. The calculation process in most family-owned companies interviewed was reported to be highly manual and based on data collection via e-mail and aggregation via Excel. Beta stated, "*I am not giving away any secrets here, but currently, our climate management is an Excel hell, but we have currently mapped that* via *Excel because we simply cannot collect the data in any other way yet because it is simply not available in this granularity from the production control systems*" (Beta, Pos. 16). Specific software tools to collect, aggregate, and report the data is not used by any of the interviewed companies. Nevertheless, it is essential to highlight that the main issue for companies today is not internal data collection itself. Instead, the issue lies with collecting data from suppliers, as this kind of data was never requested from suppliers before or captured otherwise.

In terms of effort and resources involved, family-owned companies reported an average number of employees involved of two to four full-time equivalents. Half of the interviewed companies had already set up a specific sustainability department, and the other half had integrated these employees into their quality management departments. Data collection started for most companies in 2019 or 2020, while only two companies reported a data collection start for Scopes 1 and 2 before 2019 in an annual format. Lastly, family-owned companies reported using annual data analyses primarily for internal top-level management reporting. Very few companies publish public sustainability reports and only provide data to external parties when specifically asked for, e.g., by customers. As most data analyses still contain a relatively high degree of uncertainty due to missing data points and data calculated based on a broad set of assumptions, reluctance to share data with the public prevails.

In summary, the methodology of measuring and accounting for GHG emissions in family-owned companies is dominated by the GHG Protocol as an overarching framework. Nevertheless, most companies focus on Scopes 1 and 2 in a manual instead of a software-driven approach and need more insight into their Scope 3 emissions. Nevertheless, Scope 3 typically accounts for most of the total emissions.

For instance, considering the sustainability report published by Wacker Chemie AG, a German company majorly (~70%) yet not fully family-owned, > 80% of GHG emissions pertain to Scope 3 emissions (Wacker Chemie AG, 2020). I will elaborate on the challenges associated with Scope 3 emission accounting later in this chapter.

The Why—Motivation for carbon accounting

I aim to extend previous frameworks on carbon accounting and thus deliberately asked for the motivation behind carbon accounting among family-owned companies. This question originates from the fact that family-owned companies in Germany, when conducting the interviews, were not required to disclose environmental information and, as such, did not face regulatory pressure (European Parliament & European Council, 2022). Nevertheless, it can still make sense for family-owned companies to account for their GHG emissions, e.g., to improve the management of GHG-related risks and develop strategies to mitigate such risks. At the same time, a higher degree of bureaucracy and more personnel and financial resources correlate with the measurement and accounting of GHG emissions.

Based on the performed analyses, the motivating factors to measure and account for GHG emissions can be clustered into four intrinsic and six extrinsic categories. The intrinsic motivating factors are generational thinking, the will to contribute, benchmarking, and employee demand. The extrinsic motivating factors are customer demand, competitive advantage, attractiveness for future employees, regulatory pressure, pressure from financial institutions and access to financing, and social pressure. Both intrinsic and extrinsic motivating factors are ordered by the degree to which the factors motivate family-owned companies from high to low.

The first and highest intrinsic motivating factor is generational thinking. As seen earlier, family-owned companies are characterized by general long-term thinking and a strong will to ensure the company's persistence over decades. These characteristics are underlined by the results achieved in the interviews. For example, Lambda highlights that "*we are now more than 100 years old as a company. As a family business, we think not only of quarters but also of decades and generations. Moreover, if this is to continue for another 100 years, let us say. There must also be a planet that is still supposed to exist*" (Lambda, Pos. 18). This is consistent with statements from other companies such as Iota: "*Especially when you see the third generation already growing up in the family business, which is a completely different motivation (for carbon accounting)*" (Iota, Pos. 101). Across all cases, this factor was most significant among most companies.

The second intrinsic motivating factor points in the same direction as the first motivating factor, i.e., the will to contribute to society. Family-owned companies feel a special responsibility to contribute to society. For example, Delta raises the following statement: "*Because we are also a family business, decisions are made at the lunch table, and our children are increasingly involved here. Nevertheless, not only because of the children, we say, we companies must optimize, reduce, or avoid resources, and then compensate*" (Delta, Pos. 34). A particularity for family-owned companies here is that their will to contribute is frequently paired with a strong regional focus. Again, Delta frames this precisely stating that "*we do not want to stand in a corner and say, well, now we have compensated, and 100,000 trees will be planted. We want projects we can touch and follow*" (Delta, Pos. 90).

Benchmarking constitutes the third most important intrinsic motivating factor mentioned during the interviews. Alpha stated, "*You cannot control what you cannot measure, i.e., we cannot say we want to get better somehow if we do not know where to start*" (Alpha, Pos. 44). It becomes evident that data transparency is an essential basis to reducing GHG emissions going forwards. Nevertheless, only around half of the family-owned companies interviewed are already setting targets, stating, for instance, that "*we have targets for all three Scopes. We have set specific targets for 2045 and 2050, and they are in place*" (Epsilon, Pos. 83). In contrast, other companies state that target setting will be "*the cherry on top, i.e., we set the targets afterwards and then expand our system*" (Theta, Pos. 45). As only half of the companies are already setting targets, it becomes clear that benchmarking constitutes a motivating factor of medium importance.

Lastly, demand from currently active employees has been mentioned as a motivating factor for family-owned companies. In this regard, Alpha stated that "*the recording of our GHG emissions has arisen bottom up. Out of our team, that we must do it in any case*" (Alpha, Pos. 42). Yet only one company stated that carbon accounting is driven bottom-up rather than top-down. Thus, this motivating factor is of relatively low intrinsic importance.

Extrinsic motivating factors constitute the other large category of motivating elements for family-owned companies to measure and account for their GHG emissions. Customer demand has been mentioned the most and thus constitutes the highest motivating extrinsic factor for family-owned companies as their customers increasingly request information on GHG emissions of the entire company or specific products. Most interviewed companies supply to their customers in a business-to-business relationship. Often, their customers are large corporations mandated to account for their GHG emissions. Thus, they also request the information from the family-owned companies. High pressure was especially mentioned in the automotive industry as this industry receives much attention and pressure from many angles to reduce GHG emissions. While many customers directly request GHG emission information, such requests are also included in requests from organizations such as EcoVadis. This French organization, for instance, supports companies in managing a company's business relationships, upstream and downstream, by requesting and managing sustainability information. For instance, Mu states, "*For some time now, we have also been experiencing increased interest from suppliers in the form of questionnaires sent to us*" (Mu, Pos. 69).

The second extrinsic motivating factor comes from the will to gain a competitive advantage in the market. As seen before, customers demand environmental information from their suppliers, i.e., family-owned companies. This information is then used to make supplier decisions. Family-owned companies state that disclosing GHG emission information, ideally presenting low GHG emissions, can yield more signed contracts. Gamma stated that "*the further up the value chain I am, the more I can differentiate myself with these topics, even to an end customer*" (Gamma, Pos. 68). Other companies even stated that they are already aware of their advantage in terms of low GHG emissions over their competitors. Nevertheless, correctly measuring and accounting for their GHG emissions underlines this advantage with precise data. Epsilon states, "*We know we are better than the competition with our energy supply. Moreover, we can score points with that […]. Moreover, here we need concrete tools that we can use to demonstrate that we can help our customers reduce their footprint and that we can do this as a very, very effective tool*" (Epsilon, Pos. 75).

Attractiveness for future employees was the third most important extrinsic motivating factor. The younger generation, especially those who are now finishing their educational journey and entering the job market, show an increased interest in sustainability. Looking at movements such as Fridays for Future, where many young students fight to prevent climate change, it becomes clear that environmental aspects are at the top of many young people's minds when entering the job market. Family-owned companies often have disadvantages in the job market as they are perceived as more conservative, change-resistant, and inflexible, resulting in a reduced attractiveness in the eyes of young talent entering the job market (Duran et al., 2016; Hauswald et al., 2016). Thus, family-owned companies must increase attractiveness through several factors, including a strong sustainability mindset. Measuring and accounting for GHG emissions and using this to reduce GHG emissions actively can be a differentiating factor in the job market. Nu described this in their interview: "*It is becoming increasingly common for applicants to ask: What is your company's position on sustainability? What do you do? Furthermore, of course, you want to attract applicants, but you also want to retain employees. So, these are the crucial areas for us, so we also address sustainability issues and account for GHG emissions*" (Nu, Pos. 36).

As mentioned, family-owned companies are not obliged to disclose their environmental information under the NFRD, as this regulation only applies to capital market-oriented corporations and credit and insurance institutions. Nevertheless, the upcoming CSRD pressures family-owned companies, so I identified this as the fourth most important extrinsic motivating factor. Family-owned companies will need to report their GHG emissions based on the CSRD starting in 2026, but the pressure is still perceived as low. However, a genuine will to prepare for the reporting and thus perform several trial runs before the first official reporting is desirable to pre-empt reporting issues. Nu stated, "*It is also the case that legal requirements will, of course, have to be met. It is not urgent for us now* per se, *but we want to prepare ourselves for everything coming. Be it the CSRD revision, i.e., reporting requirements that we must fulfil by 2026 at the latest for the financial year 2025. [...] So, all these legal requirements are coming our way. We want to prepare ourselves and do our work so that we do not have to create something just before the deadline that can no longer be achieved*" (Nu, Pos. 36). Yet customers of family-owned companies are partly already under pressure from the NFRD which explains why regulatory pressure exerts lower pressure and yields lower motivation than customer demand and the ability to achieve a competitive advantage.

Closely related to regulatory pressure is the access to financing and the pressure exerted via financial institutions as a motivating factor. When performing their credit assessment, credit institutions increasingly consider the environmental information of their debtors. Looking at this from the perspective of a credit institution, it makes sense to associate higher environmental performance with a higher probability of a company's successful future, resulting in lower risk and, thus, lower interest rates for companies (Healy & Palepu, 2001; Plumlee et al., 2015). To disclose this information to credit institutions, family-owned companies must measure and account for their GHG emissions, thus complying with their requirements. Lambda states that "*purely from a financial point of view, based on the rating, I either get the better or worse interest rate. If I am sustainable, I get a better one; if not, I get the worse one. This, too, is now common practice*" (Lambda, Pos. 72). Nevertheless, this appears to be a smaller motivating factor. In turn, companies started with carbon accounting driven by other motivating factors such as customer demand or generational thinking. They only afterwards used the generated data to access green financing.

Lastly, pressure from society strongly related to legitimacy theory (Suchman, 1995) introduced earlier builds an extrinsic motivating factor for family-owned companies. The German society has shifted increasingly towards a more sustainable way of thinking and expects sustainable acting from German companies (O'Riordan & Hampden-Turner, 2021). Here, measuring and accounting for GHG emissions can be used to showcase in a data-based approach how a company actively manages and reduces GHG emissions. For instance, Beta reported that they were accused of product greenwashing and are even facing a lawsuit from an NGO due to their carbon offsetting projects. However, only one family-owned company throughout the research project reported societal pressure, presumably driven by their business-to-consumer focus. In contrast, most other companies are business-to-business companies and appear less in public, resulting in less societal attention and attacks. Thus, this constitutes the most negligible extrinsic motivating factor in this research. When focusing on pure business-to-consumer companies, the research might yield different results.

In summary, I identified intrinsic and extrinsic motivating factors for family-owned companies to measure and account for their GHG emissions. While some factors result in a low motivation for family-owned companies, generational thinking and the will to contribute to society as intrinsic motivation and customer demand as extrinsic motivation are the factors especially driving the need for measuring and accounting for GHG emissions. After analyzing why family-owned companies account for their GHG emissions without regulatory obligations, I now shift to their challenges when performing their carbon accounting.

The Which—Challenges German family-owned companies are facing

Measuring and accounting for GHG emissions is a comparably new field for family-owned companies. As with establishing all new processes, many are performed for the first time, resulting in company challenges. Thus, I have targeted the challenges of measuring and accounting for GHG emissions as the fourth and last research sub-question. I identified five challenge areas: two constitute overarching challenges, and three are processual challenges. The two overarching challenges are a lack of urgency and limited personnel availability. In comparison, the three processual challenges range from data collection and aggregation over data modelling to reporting and controlling.

Starting with the first overarching challenge, i.e., needing more sense of urgency, almost all companies report needing more sustainability awareness among employees and partly among top-level management. Eventually, GHG emissions and sustainability affect all employees' ways of working. Nevertheless, not all employees are aware or want to be aware of the upcoming challenges and the need to reduce GHG emissions as a company. While this is a general challenge, especially for the older generation of employees, it needs a sense of urgency towards carbon accounting. For instance, Lambda states, "*It is an issue just to get that into the understanding of older colleagues. The generation coming in now has a lot more focus on these issues. It is a holistic issue. It does not just affect the quality or the sustainability department; it affects every single area of our company, e.g., how do I plan an air travel, how do I get to work, how do I drive home from work*" (Lambda, Pos. 60). This is also represented in statements from other companies, e.g., Alpha who reported that "*there are some people in the company who have completely understood the topic and have a complete grasp of it and are also intrinsically motivated to tackle the issue. However, there is also a completely different side that can hardly grasp the topic. Moreover, in my opinion, it is a generational issue*" (Alpha, Pos. 82). Reducing GHG emissions and acting sustainably is a topic every employee needs to contribute to. Thus, creating an overall sense of urgency among employees is crucial and needs to be overcome by family-owned companies to achieve GHG emission targets. This image also needs to be portrayed by the top-level management. Around half of the interviewed companies reported a high sense of urgency among top-level management, while the other half lacked top-level management buy-in and support. For instance, Alpha accounts for Scopes 1 and 2 carbon emissions in line with the GHG Protocol. Nevertheless, data has not been reported to the top-level management as this group has no interest. Without sufficient top-level management interest, measuring and reducing GHG emissions throughout the company will be impossible.

The second overarching challenge consists of limited personnel availability. Carbon accounting involves many manual process steps for data collection, modelling, and reporting, especially as it is a comparably unestablished field. Family-owned companies are typically smaller in terms of number of employees. Thus, they can shift resources slower than large public corporations or even free up the budget for hiring additional resources. Around half of the interviewed companies thus have integrated carbon accounting into their quality management departments, where resources work only part-time on carbon accounting. Nevertheless, additional resources will be required with an increased workload in the future, especially when companies start focusing on Scope 3 GHG emissions as well. The other half of the companies have already set up dedicated sustainability departments. However, hiring the right people is more challenging than initially anticipated for various companies. For instance, Gamma reported to "*have advertised two positions for more than a quarter of a year, and we cannot fill them*" (Gamma, Pos. 2). At the same time, Beta says, "*In general, finding good people in the field is very difficult, especially with the upcoming changes*" (Alpha, Pos. 32). Family-owned companies are frequently located in rural areas which makes it even more complicated to hire young talent in this area of expertise. Some companies have, therefore, established offices in attractive locations to attract young talent, yet finding the right employees is still challenging. Nevertheless, this challenge was expected to eventually be solved by interviewed companies through more talent entering the job market and a comparably low number of employees needed. Leading companies have reported that around five to six full-time employees can collect, aggregate, and report GHG emission data across all three Scopes of the GHG Protocol.

Besides the fundamental challenges described, processual challenges range across the entire carbon accounting process, from data collection and aggregation over data modelling to reporting and controlling. Starting with the first step in this process, i.e., data collection and aggregation, I further break down this process step into data collection and aggregation from external and internal sources. External data collection means receiving data from suppliers providing the family-owned company with specific parts or materials with a particular carbon footprint. The family-owned company purchasing the good then accounts for the supplied product's carbon footprint within the Scope 3 upstream GHG emissions typically in the purchased goods and services category. However, receiving the correct data in a suitable format from the suppliers is a significant challenge for family-owned companies. Mu, for instance, states that they "*see fewer challenges in the calculation than in the data provision from suppliers and its quality*" (Mu, Pos. 100). Other family-owned companies reported that working with international suppliers is even more challenging in this regard due to different data formats or a different understanding of the product carbon footprint calculation. While this might not be too challenging for one supplier, it becomes a considerable challenge when hundreds or thousands of goods are supplied for a manufactured product. Ultimately, a supplier providing such data has an additional effort for which additional financial resources are required. This additional investment must be charged again to the family-owned company and their customers. Nevertheless, customers expect data transparency at no additional costs. Lambda reflects this: "*For the data transparency, you pay the surcharge. Moreover, there, of course, we are also dependent on our customers, because many do not yet want to pay these surcharges, especially not in current times as they already have surcharges in current times*" (Lambda, Pos. 42).

The second step after receiving the correct data in the suitable format from the suppliers is to collect the data internally within the family-owned company. Interviewed family-owned companies frequently have global and decentralized setups. Collecting the data from all subsidies and geographical locations is, on the one hand, very time-consuming and, on the other hand, very challenging without clear and strict data standardization. Iota summarized this as "*our problem is actually that the data is available, but somehow rather organized in a decentral way or often also available but in the wrong unit*" (Iota, Pos. 83). A clear definition of relevant key performance indicators (KPIs) and how to calculate these is frequently missing resulting in different calculation methods and thus differing results. Also, many of the interviewed family-owned companies have grown fast via acquisitions. Many of these acquisitions have never been properly integrated, which is also reflected in unstructured IT systems, making data aggregation even more challenging. Gamma states, "*This is also important, i.e., uniform IT structures. I would say that groups of a certain size have this and can aggregate in this way. However, I would say that we have grown structures through smaller acquisitions, which we have had, and they are not fully integrated. That is exactly what we are seeing now in aggregation, where problems keep coming up*" (Gamma, Pos. 27). Lastly, not only the internal IT structures need to be coherent, but also the internal structures among departments. Central data aggregation departments, e.g., the sustainability department, do not yet have interfaces established into all relevant departments for holistic data collection, making the data aggregation process more difficult. Zeta, for instance, stated that "*there are so many contact persons for the individual topics, for the individual Scopes as well. That is somewhat difficult in this corporate structure*" (Zeta, Pos. 31). Ultimately, this again results in a time-consuming effort which is challenging to manage without automation.

The second processual challenge is situated in data modelling. Data modelling depends on data collection and aggregation as higher quality data inputs make data modelling much more manageable. Nevertheless, data collection and aggregation are challenging, resulting in comparably poor data inputs for data modelling, which is the second big processual challenge. The three main drivers of data modelling challenges are 1) poor data quality, 2) high data granularity and 3) difficulties in making the correct assumptions. Poor data quality makes data modelling incredibly challenging, as confidence in calculated results still needs to be higher for most companies. For instance, Mu stated this as their biggest challenge: "*The currently biggest challenge is the data quality. Data is not available in the desired quality yet, so in some cases, we must use the worst-case scenario as a basis, which means that the calculation of the emissions is slightly more negative for us*" (Mu, Pos. 91). Thus, poor data quality leads to companies applying a conservative calculation method yielding potentially worse results than required. Other companies reported data quality issues, especially among Scope 3 emissions, which are far more complex to collect than Scope 1 & 2 data. This aspect is also closely connected to the second challenge of data modelling, i.e., high data granularity. Scope 3 emissions come from many data sources, making the data very granular. These many data sources and input formats make the modelling exercise incredibly challenging. Iota framed this as "*so, if you want to calculate Scope 3 in a manufacturing company and all the materials used, including these upstream chains, it is a huge amount of work*" (Iota, Pos. 81). Lastly, making the correct assumptions is challenging when it comes to data modelling. These challenges are, on the one hand, the result of poor data quality, which requires making assumptions, but on the other hand, emission factors are required for specific data inputs where assumptions are required. Considering power consumption, not all electricity is the same, i.e., it can be generated from various sources, and thus, GHG emissions are different. Iota reflects this in another example: "*Not all concrete is the same. Depending on its strength class, for example, whether it contains more or less cement. So C2025 concrete naturally has a completely different carbon footprint than a C5060 or even a stronger concrete*" (Iota, Pos. 55). Eventually, this leads to uncertainty when calculating GHG emissions and results in a trade-off between investing the correct number of resources performing the calculations sufficiently granular on the one hand and on the other hand pragmatically calculating GHG emissions without being too conservative or opening the door for being accused of greenwashing.

Lastly, reporting and controlling constitute the third big processual challenge in the carbon accounting process. The data collected, aggregated, and modelled in the previous process steps are only a means to an end. Eventually, family-owned companies aim to measure and reduce their GHG emissions. Reducing GHG emissions, however, requires changes in current processes for which data-based prioritization and steering is needed. Thus, controlling processes must steer each company's GHG emission reduction efforts. Nevertheless, family-owned companies just started collecting data and still need to establish transparent reporting or controlling processes, making it especially challenging now.

Looking first at the reporting, transparent reporting formats need to be improved, and as most family-owned companies only started with Scopes 1 and 2 measurements, reporting is still evolving. Moreover, the uncertainty in the modelled results creates reluctance among companies to report their data publicly. Nu summarized this: "*No uniform granular standard exists in the industry yet. That is the reason why we do not publish it. Because once a number is fixed, then you are measured by it without having this explanation behind it*" (Nu, Pos. 34).

Besides the mere reporting of data, controlling is even more challenging as companies are facing a plethora of data points when accounting for Scopes 1, 2 & 3 across various locations and departments. Thus, prioritizing the GHG emission reduction efforts where the impact is significant and the effort is low is not as trivial as it might seem. Zeta described this challenge: "*What I still see as a challenge is actually: What do we do with the data? How do I get a roadmap from it now? Reporting is one thing, but as I said, I also want to do something with the figures. I do not yet have a clear picture of how we will approach this*" (Zeta, Pos. 69). In financial controlling, detailed steering concepts have been developed over decades, which are now also required for GHG emission controlling. Such concepts were also referenced in an interview with Beta, who is comparably far advanced in carbon accounting, yet still stating that for "*a real carbon footprint that I can then control, similar to what I do in cost controlling where I can control my supply chain costs, is still a long way off, and it is tough at this moment*" (Beta, Pos. 26).

In summary, two fundamental challenges, a lack of urgency and personnel availability, and three processual challenges along the carbon accounting process were identified. While the fundamental challenges are expected to resolve comparably fast, clear data standards for data collection, which enable proper data modelling and clear controlling concepts building upon the data, will take more work. This results from many interlinks within and across companies, often even cross-border, which must be overcome in the long term.

2.4.2 Carbon Accounting Differences Between Family-Owned Companies and Large Public Corporations

GHG emissions generally do not differ by company type, i.e., a family-owned company might have similar GHG emissions compared to a large, public corporation, and thus, it also measures those similarly. During the interviews, however, I explicitly focused on this difference with a specific set of questions. Results are highly valid as several sustainability managers had work experience in large public corporations and thus could provide valid comparisons. With this approach, two main differences have been identified from the perspective of family-owned companies: resource scarcity and long-term thinking.

Resource scarcity refers to financial resource scarcity, which results in personnel resource scarcity. Lambda states, "*A DAX company has more resources to deal with these issues than we do. We must find smart solutions because setting up large departments would not be supported by the cost structure and the structure of the company*" (Lambda, Pos. 64). Especially in these relatively early days of carbon accounting, transparent processes have not yet been established resulting in a low degree of automation and as such a high amount of manual process steps for which personnel resources are required. Family-owned companies' sustainability managers reported that from their point of view, large public corporations can shift resources more short-term and flexibly due to higher resource availability. Alpha stated in this regard that it is more complicated for them to receive the budget for personnel resources as "*every decision still goes more or less through the board of directors*" (Alpha, Pos. 100). However, other companies also reported the reduced bureaucracy and accelerated release of budget for personnel resources in case something matters to the family owner. Gamma reported even a challenge with finding the right resources, stating, "*The market has been grazed for two years. Everyone dealing with the subject of sustainability, the big players have hired all those resources, and now it is even harder for us*" (Gamma, Pos. 4). However, this statement also does not hold for all companies as some family-owned companies are trying to circumvent this issue through office locations in larger cities attracting young talent. In summary, resource scarcity is a more significant challenge for family-owned companies than large public corporations, reducing access to currently required talent.

Long-term thinking is the other factor identified as the main difference between family-owned and large public corporations. Family-owned companies, for instance, are not obliged to report every quarter to their shareholders. This is underlined by Epsilon stating that this "*is, of course, a great advantage that we have, because the family can, of course, plan a bit longer term than if they were to move from one quarterly report to the next*" (Epsilon, Pos. 27). This also means that family-owned companies are not pressured right now to deliver GHG emission figures but rather still have time to assure that numbers are as correct as possible once they are published for the first time. This long-term thinking also stems from a long-term responsibility towards the company's future and future generations. Lambda's CEO summarizes this as "*I then have to justify myself to my children in several decades, in doubt as to why I did or did not do certain things*" (Lambda, Pos. 66). This, of course, is a different incentive for these family-owned company managers than mere financial long-term incentives a board member of a large, public corporation would have. These fundamentals may influence the approach to carbon accounting and the actions taken resulting from the captured data.

2.4.3 Critical Discussion of Results

This research chapter investigates the measurement and accounting of GHG emissions in German family-owned companies. Therefore, I tested an existing framework on environmental management in companies for family-owned companies and extended it in terms of motivation, methodology and challenges related to carbon accounting.

First, I can generally confirm that the previously developed 4-level framework also applies to family-owned companies (Carroll, 1979; Henriques & Sadorsky, 1999; Wartick & Cochran, 1985). The overall importance of environmental management to family-owned companies, top-level management involvement, reporting mode, and employee involvement is similar for general and family-owned companies. As I extended the applied methodology to family-owned companies, I saw that the GHG Protocol constitutes the predominant standard for carbon accounting, similar to Fortune 500 companies where adoption is above 90% (WBCSD & WRI, 2023). Regarding the motivation for carbon accounting, previous authors found that family-owned companies are risk-averse (Gomez-Mejia et al., 2011), want to preserve socioemotional wealth (Berrone et al., 2012) and are more altruistic than non-family companies (Berrone et al., 2010; Cennamo et al., 2012). These aspects also translate into carbon accounting, as most family-owned companies are motivated intrinsically to measure and reduce carbon emissions rather than extrinsically. Still, extrinsic motivation is essential for less active companies, i.e., extrinsically-driven reporters and sustainability laggards. Their motivation can be found in socio-political theories such as stakeholder theory (Freeman, 1984), where companies disclose environmental information due to stakeholder pressure (Roberts, 1992). Previous researchers found that disclosed information has no guarantee for completeness (Depoers et al., 2016), which I also saw during the interviews: most family-owned companies only partly apply the GHG Protocol. In addition, carbon accounting is used for legitimation purposes. Family-owned companies also seek buy-in for their actions from society and aim to generate a credible image among a broad audience (Cotter & Najah, 2012).

Regarding the challenges in carbon accounting, I have seen previously that actual carbon emission data can range between five and twenty percent from the reported GHG emission values (Rypdal & Winiwarter, 2001). Due to unestablished and new processes, the perceived uncertainty among family-owned companies appears even more extensive. Of course, mathematical models still need to be established (Lee et al., 2024), and accurately choosing parameters and assumptions is challenging (WBCSD & WRI, 2015). On top of this, receiving different data from different suppliers and collecting accurate data internally is incredibly challenging for family-owned companies today (Olson, 2010). In addition, limited personnel availability makes carbon accounting furthermore challenging (Nieto et al., 2015). The need for standardization of carbon emission data across companies makes it especially hard to translate data from one company to another. Going forward, clear guidelines would facilitate the carbon accounting process paired with overcoming today's challenges of resource scarcity and unestablished processes.

2.5 Conclusion

This chapter investigates the measurement and accounting of GHG emissions in German family-owned companies. The world is facing increasing energy prices, and companies and governments are struggling to meet the goals agreed upon in the Paris Agreement to limit the global temperature increase to 1.5° Celsius above pre-industrial levels. Achieving these targets was once more doubted at the UN climate conference, COP27, in Egypt in November 2022 (Ward, 2022). Reducing GHG emissions, however, will only be possible based on a solid data basis for which carbon accounting is essential. Within Germany, the largest economy in Europe, family-owned companies account for 90% of all German companies and constitute the backbone of the German industry, the fourth largest economy in the world in 2020 (International Monetary Fund, 2021). Considering the importance of reducing GHG emissions, paired with the relevance of German family-owned companies for Germany and the world while also keeping the lack of regulations in mind, I felt the need to investigate this research area further.

I have therefore tested and extended previous frameworks on environmental management for German family-owned companies and identified four archetypes. Carbon accounting among family-owned companies is in a solid state as most companies fall under the second or third archetype with a tendency towards the third archetype, i.e., intrinsically-driven realists. I have identified generational thinking and the will to contribute to society as the main intrinsic motivating factors pushing carbon accounting forward. Customer demand, in addition, is the primary extrinsic motivating factor. Although family-owned companies face upcoming regulations for measuring and accounting for GHG emissions, I could not identify regulatory factors as a primary motivating factor. Family-owned companies stick to globally agreed standards, i.e., the GHG Protocol, yet most companies have only implemented Scopes 1 and 2 measurements. Scope 3, however, constitutes the most complicated measurement category and accounts for most GHG emissions.

Nevertheless, more than intrinsic motivation alone will be required. A higher sense of urgency among company leaders is required, proper processes must be set up, investment in personnel is needed, and better data integration across companies is incredibly challenging. Thus, further work will be required to measure carbon emissions thoroughly and eventually reduce carbon emissions. Given their relevance, family-owned companies can be a significant driver in Germany.

2.5.1 Scientific Contributions and Practical Implications

Carbon accounting has, to date, only received limited attention (Salvato & Moores, 2010). Furthermore, the research on family-owned companies is regarded as a growing field in the existing literature (Hasso & Duncan, 2013). Thus, I contribute to this strand of literature through the new and extended scientific framework, which shall help researchers and practitioners better understand where family-owned companies stand today in carbon accounting and what could be done to improve and facilitate carbon accounting processes going forward. It will be essential to, therefore, overcome the identified challenges. Thus, two managerial implications are most important as a result of the analyses: 1) increasing awareness to overcome the still comparably low sense of urgency among top-level management in some companies and general staff overall in most companies, as well as 2) creating standards for data exchange both within and across companies to overcome the data availability challenges.

Increasing awareness is vital among top-level management and employees. The awareness among top-level management is the first step towards reducing GHG emissions throughout the company. Reducing GHG emissions requires top-level management support. If top-level management acknowledges carbon accounting and reduction as top priorities, it can become a central part of the company's strategic goals. A few interviewed companies even reported that although carbon accounting is already taking place, the aggregated data is of no interest among the top-level management. As such, no regular reporting is taking place. However, increasing the awareness among this target group can mostly be achieved externally, e.g., via even more regulatory or customer pressure. One alternative way to achieve this could be to exert pressure via educational events of family organizations such as the Stiftung Familienunternehmen. The second step is then to increase awareness among general staff. As mentioned earlier, employees partly do not consider GHG emission reduction or sustainability in general as a top priority. Alpha, for instance, quoted from a training session where an employee stated, "*We need to be careful not to focus too much on the sustainability trend*" (Alpha, Pos. 86). Thus, increasing awareness even more among employees from all functions and age groups is essential for a successful GHG emission reduction journey. A mix of top-level management communication and educational events is required to create a mindset towards GHG emission reduction. A lasting impact will only be possible if all employees live and communicate this mindset throughout the company. Beta summarizes this: "*It (GHG emission reduction) is not the function of a staff unit. It is not the function of a compliance team, but it is the function of everyone in the company to think about this in their respective area of expertise*" (Beta, Pos. 34). As such, it needs to become part of a company's culture and DNA.

The other managerial implication is creating standards for data exchange within and across companies. A company must collect GHG emission information from suppliers regarding the materials they purchase to calculate their GHG emissions. Today, information is transmitted in multiple ways, in multiple data formats and includes different information. For instance, sometimes a supplier would provide Scope 1, 2 and 3 GHG emission information at the company level while another supplier provides Scope 1 & 2 data at the product level. For each family-owned company receiving the data, finding a common denominator when dealing with hundreds or thousands of suppliers becomes overly complicated. The global setup of many companies makes this even more challenging. A typical data standard is an indispensable basis for correct carbon accounting, as upstream calculation errors or missing data will follow through to customer reports. Moreover, calculations based on such inconsistent data will be inaccurate and can eventually lead to wrong decisions. Thus, onboarding all companies to a common ground where data is shared in the same data formats will rigorously facilitate data collection and calculation processes while at the same time making the results more accurate and reliable.

2.5.2 Limitations and Areas for Future Research

Within this chapter, I have asked why and how family-owned companies measure and account for their GHG emissions and which challenges they face when accounting for their GHG emissions. I answered all research questions via a multiple-case study approach, including within and cross-case analyses among 13 family-owned companies. These cases were selected via a detailed sampling approach to only include companies with 100% family ownership, appropriate size in terms of employees and revenue such that the CSRD applies and industries known for comparably high GHG emissions. With this approach, relevant results could be achieved, and interview results started to show substantial overlap after the first few interviews, justifying the termination of interviews after the identified set had been interviewed. Nevertheless, the results are subject to certain limitations addressed in the following.

First, the chosen data set is still comparably small and thus does not allow for statistically significant statements. Nevertheless, interview results were triangulated with external experts, e.g., from a leading consulting company and a start-up building software for carbon accounting, mainly confirming the results.

Second, only family-owned companies from comparably CO_2-heavy industries were considered. Moreover, I focused on companies communicating certain sustainability activities in either sustainability reports or their website, leading to a bias towards companies where GHG emissions play, by nature, already a specific role within the company. Nevertheless, it is impossible to conclude to what extent family-owned companies generally care about carbon accounting, as family-owned companies not accounting for their GHG emissions were omitted in this case study setup. Third, I compared the carbon accounting approach of family-owned companies with that of large public corporations. The results achieved here, however, are solely based on perspectives from employees in family-owned companies reported during the interviews. I did not collect a direct view from employees in large public corporations. Nevertheless, statements from employees in family-owned companies were based on work experiences in large, public corporations. Results were further enhanced with a literature review, which added validity to the generated results.

As an avenue for future research, I suggest a cross-sectional survey design with a much higher number of participating family-owned companies. Thus, verifying or falsifying the identified company archetypes would be possible. On top of that, I suggest focusing on all family-owned companies of appropriate size without focusing on CO_2-heavy industries only, thus generating a more holistic view of the actual status of carbon accounting among German family-owned companies.

Alternative research for future researchers could stem from investigating how the current approach among German family-owned companies compares to other nationalities. Identifying whether specific findings are solely a German phenomenon or whether these findings also hold for other nationalities can enhance the findings and increase their external validity and generalizability.

Appendix

Appendix A. Case Study Guideline and Interview Questionnaire

Topic: Measurement and accounting of GHG emissions in family-owned companies.

Objective of this work: Understand why family-owned companies account for their GHG emissions, how they measure and account for their GHG emissions and which challenges they face when measuring and accounting their GHG emissions along their value chain.

Research team: Julius Baumgart (PhD Researcher), Prof. Dr. Gunther Friedl (Supervisor).

Research questions:

How do family-owned companies operationalize their GHG emissions accounting along their value chain?
Why do family-owned companies account for their GHG emissions along their value chain?
Which challenges do family-owned companies encounter when measuring and accounting for GHG emissions along the value chain?

Interview guidance:

Personal introduction of researcher and interviewee (personal background, prior experiences)
General information (objectives of the interview, information about recording, next steps after the interview)
Questions Part I: General information about the family-owned company, e.g., industry, age, size, culture, etc.
Questions Part II: Understanding reasoning behind GHG emission accounting, how it is performed, and which challenges the company has faced so far
Questions Part III: Future GHG emission accounting

Questions Part I:

Objective of this section is to gather basic information about the family-owned company and learn about the company's culture and the role sustainability plays within the company
Part I.I: Basic information
Company's industry:

In which industry is the company active?

Company's founding date:

When was the company founded?

Company size:

What is the current company revenue [in EUR]?
How many employees work for the company?

Company ownership:

What does the current ownership structure look like?
Is the company fully owned by family members?

Part I.II: Company culture & role of sustainability overall
Involvement of the owner family:

Do family members work for the company? If yes, in which positions do family members work?
Has the family always owned the company?

Company identity:

Does the company identify itself as a family-owned company?
If yes, how is this image portrayed throughout the company?
If yes, what impact does this have on the employees?
If no, why is that the case?

Role of sustainability within the company:

How does the company value non-financial / sustainability goals compared to financial goals?
How has this changed over the past years?
Does the firm have a sustainability department? If no, who is in charge of sustainability initiatives?

Questions Part II:

Objective of this part is to understand the reasoning behind performing the GHG emission accounting, the method how it is performed, and the challenges involved in the GHG accounting which the company has faced so far
General check:

Do you currently measure GHG emissions (CO_2 equivalents)?

Reasoning behind GHG emission accounting:

Why do you measure GHG emissions (CO_2 equivalents)?

- Is the data used for internal reporting or external reporting?
- Do you feel pressure from external stakeholders to report such data?
- Do you do it in preparation of future reporting obligations, e.g., Corporate Sustainability Reporting Directive (CSRD)?
- Do you set CO_2 emission targets and track your performance against these targets (SBTi)?

Method of performing GHG emission accounting:

How do you currently measure & account for your GHG emissions, i.e., which standards do you use (GHG Protocol, ISO 14064, SBTi, etc.)?
Why have you decided to use this standard?
Do you measure GHG emissions along all Scopes, i.e., 1–3?
Do you include all kinds of GHG emissions or CO_2 only?
How often have you measured your GHG emissions already?
Will this be an annual effort going forward?
Are you developing the accounting fully in-house or together with external service providers?
Do you use specific software or tools for the GHG accounting?
How do you report your GHG emissions currently (e.g., company reports or Carbon Disclosure Project)?

Challenges when measuring GHG emissions:

What effort is required to account for your GHG emissions in terms of time, workload and employees involved?
Which challenges have you faced so far in measuring your GHG emissions?

How did you overcome these challenges, if at all?
What level of confidence do you have in the correctness of your accounting?

Questions Part III:

Objective of this part is to understand how the ghg accounting within the company will change & improve over the next few years
Effort:

Do you think that the GHG accounting going forward will be more effort or less effort than what it has been in the past? Why?
Do you think that the current level of data granularity is sufficient for the next years?
How much potential do you see in automating GHG emission accounting for your company?

Family-owned company versus public corporation:

Do you see a particular difference why GHG accounting for you as family-owned company might impact your business differently than a public corporation going forward?
Do you see a difference in how you might use the measured data in comparison to a public corporation?

Any other remarks:
Are there final thoughts you want to share regarding measurement and accounting of GHG emissions?

This chapter investigates how family firms balance tensions between economic and environmental goals arising in the course of decarbonization. Goal tensions and their resolution are particularly relevant.

Appendix B. Matching of Cases to Identified Archetypes

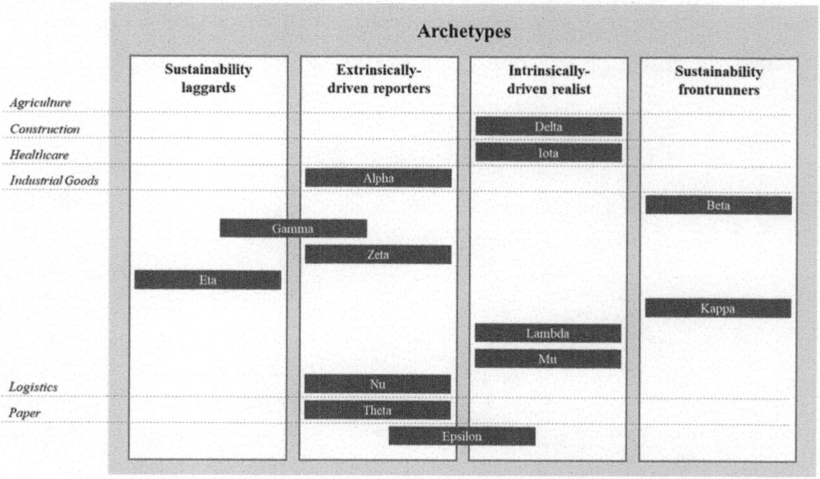

Management of Goal Tensions in Strategic Decision-Making

3

Managing Goal Tensions in Strategic Decision-Making—The Case of Decarbonization

Johanna C. Schulze-Berge and Gunther Friedl

This chapter investigates how family firms balance tensions between economic and environmental goals arising in the course of decarbonization. Goal tensions and their resolution are particularly relevant in family firms due to the overlap between the family and the business. Employing the attention-based view, we conduct a multiple case study with eleven German firms and derive a model that connects a firm's motivation and attitude toward decarbonization with a strategy for balancing economic and environmental goals. We contribute through concrete, implementable strategies for multiple goal management. We further reveal that the motivation for environmental behavior in family firms stems not only from non-economic, intrinsic firm goals but also extrinsic goals. Moreover, we elaborate the attention-based view by illustrating how firms' organizational attention yields heterogeneous goal management strategies.

This chapter has been accepted and presented at G-Forum 2022 in Dresden and the 43rd USAEE/IAEE Conference in Houston.

Author contributions: RE performed the interviews and data analysis and wrote the first draft. AK supported the development of the research idea and significantly contributed to the revision of the chapter.

J. C. Schulze-Berge (✉) · G. Friedl
TUM School of Management, Technical University of Munich, Munich, Germany
e-mail: Johanna.Schulze-Berge@whu.edu

G. Friedl
e-mail: gunther.friedl@tum.de

G. Friedl (ed.), *Decarbonizing German Family Firms*, Familienunternehmen und KMU, https://doi.org/10.1007/978-3-658-47801-8_3

3.1 Introduction

Due to increasing climate change concerns, decarbonization[1] is perceived as one of the greatest challenges of our time. At the UN Climate Change Conference in 2015, Chancellor Angela Merkel emphasized the unique role decarbonization would play in this century: "We must now agree on a binding review mechanism under international law so that this century can credibly be called a century of decarbonization" (Fereday, 2019, p. 5). Since then, the urgency for firms to decarbonize has increased rapidly through the introduction of binding climate regulations such as the European Union (EU) Green Deal (European Commission, 2022b) and the German Climate Change Act (Die Bundesregierung, 2022). In Germany, one-fourth of all greenhouse gas (GHG) emissions originate from the activities of manufacturing firms (German Environmental Agency, 2023), of which 90% of firms are owned by families (Altenburger & Bachner, 2020). Yet, at the same time, especially family firms have earned a reputation for investing substantial efforts into decarbonization in recent years. For instance, in 2022, the family firm *Alfred Kärcher* received the German sustainability prize as they launched a program called "Reduce, reuse, recycle", mitigating carbon emissions through the usage of recyclates and low-carbon packaging alternatives (Familienunternehmen im Fokus [FIFo], 2022). According to the chief executive officer (CEO), decarbonization investments are made "because it is in the genes of the family" (FIFo, 2022). The firm further proclaims it decarbonizes to act responsibly (FIFo, 2022). However, at the same time, family firms are challenged by the high costs of investments in decarbonization. For instance, the German family firm *Schlagmann Poroton*, a brick manufacturer, has led an industry initiative that ascertained that 2.3 billion euros in investments will be required by 2050 for the German brick industry to reach climate neutrality (Knitterscheidt, 2021).

According to behavioral theory, future-oriented firms simultaneously pursue economic and non-economic goals (Argote & Greve, 2007; Cyert & March, 1992). Nonetheless, due to the requirement of significant investments for effective decarbonization, economic and decarbonization goals can be perceived as conflicting in the short term (Hahn et al., 2010; van der Byl & Slawinski, 2015), and tensions between managers may arise (Cespa & Cestone, 2007).

Family-firm researchers have repeatedly stressed the urgency to resolve tensions between multiple firm goals to avoid severe consequences for the firms

---

[1] Decarbonization refers to "the process by which countries, individuals or other entities aim to achieve zero fossil carbon existence. Decarbonization refers to a reduction of the carbon emissions associated with electricity, industry, and transport" (Intergovernmental Panel on Climate Change, 2022, p. 546).

and their managers (e.g., Kammerlander et al., 2015). However, concrete, differentiated strategies for balancing economic and environmental targets along the entire strategic decision-making process are missing (Engert & Baumgartner, 2016; Lozano, 2015; Margolis & Walsh, 2003; van der Byl & Slawinski, 2015). This gap in the literature is specifically significant for family firms, as not only the presence of multiple goals but also the tensions between economic and non-economic goals are particularly strong in the family firm context due to the imbrication of the family and the business (Chrisman et al., 2014; Diaz-Moriana et al., 2022). A lack of analysis of how family firms can manage economic and environmental goals can lead to detrimental consequences for relationships within family firms as well as the family firms' long-term survival (Diaz-Moriana et al., 2022; Kammerlander & Ganter, 2015). Therefore, family firms are a specifically interesting context to study strategies for multiple goal management within decarbonization.

Hence, we analyze the following research question: *"Why and how do family firms manage economic and environmental goals in their strategic decision-making processes?"*

This research question intentionally considers multiple goals in the context of strategic decision-making processes. Within this study, we define strategic decisions according to Eisenhardt and Zbaracki (1992) and Wilson (2015). Strategic decisions are often linked to other decisions in an organization and can be complex, based on limited, contradicting information, and may entail trade-offs and risks (Wilson, 2015). Strategic decisions are "important, in terms of the actions taken, the resources committed, or the precedents set" (Eisenhardt & Zbaracki, 1992, p. 17). They are made by top management and impact the firm's survival (Eisenhardt & Zbaracki, 1992).

Furthermore, we will use decarbonization goals, expressed through carbon dioxide, in short, CO_2, as a representation of environmental goals in this study (Delmas et al., 2015; Trumpp & Günther, 2017). The need to focus research on CO_2 is manifested by a new EU regulation, the Corporate Sustainability Reporting Directive (CSRD), which obligates 50,000 firms in the EU to report and externally assure their carbon footprint (European Commission, 2023). Firms will be required to publicly announce forward-looking information on decarbonization targets, enhancing the pressure to pursue environmental next to economic goals.

To answer the research question, we conduct a multiple case study incorporating an inductive case analysis method, similar to other authors in this field (Diaz-Moriana et al., 2022; Strike & Rerup, 2016). Through the qualitative analysis of interviews with eleven German family firms, enriched with archival firm data from 2018-2021 and ten expert interviews, an inductive model is derived based on the attention-based view by Ocasio (1997), answering *why* and *how* economic and environmental goals are managed in strategic decision-making processes. Going beyond previous research, the attention-based model not only provides four concrete strategies (*presence of environmental information (incl. innovation), designated capital expenditures (CapEx), artificial CO_2 price, and no integration*) for balancing economic and environmental goals but also explains why strategies are heterogeneous among family firms based on different motivations, firms' goals, and attitudes toward decarbonization, firms' goal systems.

Our study offers three theoretical contributions. First, our findings inform the literature on multiple goal management (Diaz-Moriana et al., 2022; Epstein et al., 2015; Ivory & Brooks, 2018) by presenting strategies for how firms balance economic and environmental goals. Thus, we are answering calls for concrete, implementable strategies (Engert & Baumgartner, 2016; Lozano, 2015; van der Byl & Slawinski, 2015), and we are the first to investigate strategies for goal tensions during firm decarbonization, representative of other environmental firm activities. In addition, our findings show that strategies for multiple goal management should consider firms' goals and goal systems (Chua et al., 2018).

Second, we reveal that the motivation for environmental behavior in family firms stems not only from non-economic, intrinsic firm goals but also extrinsic goals such as pressure from regulatory institutions, client demand, or a competitive advantage in tender situations. Third, we connect the research on multiple-goal management with the attention-based view (Ocasio, 1997). We advance the attention-based view by illustrating how firms' organizational attention regarding diverse goals and goal systems yields heterogeneous strategies.

In terms of managerial implications, the insights of this chapter serve as an inspiration for practitioners in balancing economic and environmental goals. We hope to increase the presence and pursuit of decarbonization activities at family firms.

3.2 Theoretical Background

3.2.1 Family Firm Goals

Tensions between economic and non-economic goals

Family firms play a crucial role across Germany since 90% of all firms are family firms (Altenburger & Bachner, 2020; Stiftung Familienunternehmen, 2019a). However, an indisputable and commonly aligned definition of the term family business does not exist (O'Boyle et al., 2012; Posch & Speckbacher, 2012). Despite the vagueness surrounding the term "family firm", there are two central themes that this study regards as relevant criteria for being classified as a family firm. First, we consider a family firm as governed by a dominant coalition, expressed through ownership of the majority of property rights by one or a small number of families as well as family members forming part of the firm's executive management or supervisory board (Chua et al., 1999). Second, a family firm is characterized by personalized control over the firm with the intention of transgenerational firm ownership (Chua et al., 1999; May, 2012; P. Sharma, 2004). This chapter will focus on private family firms and exclude publicly listed family firms from the analysis, as ownership is less dispersed in private family firms, and the interests of family owners become more apparent (Cruz et al., 2015).

Furthermore, the connection of the family with firm ownership will empower the family to determine firm goals (Mitchell et al., 1997). Family firms are known for pursuing a wider set of goals than just economic goals, as non-economic goals are also highly important to them (Berrone et al., 2010; Brundin et al., 2014; Chrisman et al., 2012; Gómez-Mejia et al., 2011; Sharma et al., 1997). Non-economic goals are clustered around five dimensions. Non-economic goals of family firms include transgenerational value (Brundin et al., 2014; Chua et al., 1999; Zellweger et al., 2012), family reputation (Berrone et al., 2012; Chrisman et al., 2012; Kammerlander & Prügl, 2016), power and control (Carney, 2005; Chua et al., 1999; Zellweger et al., 2013), enduring ties (Brundin et al., 2014; Kammerlander & Prügl, 2016; Miller & Le Breton-Miller, 2005; Zellweger et al., 2013), and affect and emotion (Berrone et al., 2012; Chrisman et al., 2012).

By adhering to their non-economic goals, family firms preserve their socioemotional wealth (SEW) (Berrone et al., 2012; Berrone et al., 2010; Gómez-Mejía et al., 2007; Zellweger et al., 2012). The phenomenon SEW can be described as "the non-financial aspects of the firm that meet a family's affective needs such as identity, the ability to exercise family influence, and the perpetuation of the family dynasty" (Gómez-Mejía et al., 2007, p. 106). The five dimensions of SEW match with the five types of non-economic goals previously described (Berrone et al., 2012; Gómez-Mejia et al., 2011). As such, the protection of SEW serves as a non-economic point of orientation that can encourage the firm to make decisions that are not backed up by economic considerations (Berrone et al., 2010; Zellweger et al., 2012). The preservation of the SEW is "the single most important feature of a firm's essence" (Berrone et al., 2012, p. 260) and distinguishes it from other organizational firm types.

The desire to reach non-economic goals and protect a firm's SEW has also been identified as the main driver of environmental behavior at family firms (Berrone et al., 2010; Block & Wagner, 2014; Garcés-Ayerbe et al., 2022; P. Sharma & Sharma, 2011). Family firms even prioritize environmental topics across corporate social responsibility topics to protect their SEW (Campopiano & Massis, 2015). Non-economic goals like transgenerational value and power and control exerted by the family are closely linked to the desire to achieve excellent environmental performance in family firms (Dangelico et al., 2019).

However, pursuing environmental behavior does not diminish the relevance of economic aspects at family firms (Argote & Greve, 2007; Brundin et al., 2014). Due to the imbrication of the family and the business, the costs of deficits in managing economic and environmental goals weigh particularly high in family firms (Aparicio et al., 2017; Chrisman et al., 2012; Chua et al., 2018; Habbershon et al., 2003; Kotlar & Massis, 2013; Moores, 2009). A lack of analysis of how family firms can manage economic and environmental goals can lead to detrimental consequences for relationships within the family firm as well as the family firm's long-term survival (Diaz-Moriana et al., 2022; Kammerlander & Ganter, 2015). At the same time, a desire for SEW protection and a long-term mindset might serve as strategic assets unique to family firms that could help them to find adequate strategies to reconcile economic and environmental goals (Craig & Dibrell, 2006; Garcés-Ayerbe et al., 2022). Therefore, family firms are a specifically interesting context to study strategies to simultaneously manage economic and environmental goals.

An attention-based view on goal tensions

A highly relevant theory regarding the understanding of firms' strategic decision-making processes is the attention-based view (Ocasio, 1997). For instance, in 2015, Kammerlander and Ganter applied the attention-based view to family firms' decision-making on discontinuous technological change.

Ocasio (1997, p. 187) points out that "firm behavior is a result of how firms channel and distribute the attention of their decision-makers." He provides a theory that can help to explain why and how a firm makes certain strategic decisions, which he refers to as the structural distribution of attention (Principle 3) (Ocasio, 1997). The strategic decision made is a result of the focus of attention (Principle 1) and the situated attention (Principle 2) of the decision-maker because each decision-maker can only adhere to a limited number of issues and answers (Ocasio, 1997).

One particular part of the attention-based view that has gained scholarly attention is attention breadth, which is the number of topics a decision-maker adheres to at the same time (Pringle et al., 2001). In 2020, Ahn argued that sustainability requires a pronounced attention breadth, as economic and non-economic goals need to be considered simultaneously. While Ahn (2022) focuses on the influence of the CEO's attention breadth on the resulting sustainability performance, we want to detail the strategies that lead to this performance instead. We propose that analyzing organizational attention's influence on strategies for managing multiple goals can yield new insights. For this purpose, we will conceptualize decision-makers' attention through goals that drive the pursuit of environmental behavior as well as goal systems (Chua et al., 2018) between economic and environmental goals. We will assess the decision-making processes that cope with economic and environmental goals in detail without consideration of the sustainability performance thereafter.

3.2.2 Multiple Goal Management

The behavioral theory of firms states that firms pursue a variety of non-economic and economic goals (Argote & Greve, 2007; Cyert & March, 1992), which are sometimes even conflicting (Meyer & Gupta, 1994; Unsworth et al., 2014). Yet, when trade-offs exist between multiple goals and variables are unclear, no purposeful decisions are likely to be made because managers do not always behave rationally or well-purposed (Jensen, 2000). They are boundedly rational and have cognitive limits (Eisenhardt & Zbaracki, 1992). Hence, higher decision-making complexity also leads to a longer required decision time (Astley et al., 1982). The performance in decision-making declines with each additional goal pursued simultaneously (Obloj & Sengul, 2020). Managerial actions are paused and downtime is created when goals point in different directions (Ethiraj & Levinthal, 2009). However, organizations can accomplish multiple goals if effective strategies are derived and implemented (Ethiraj & Levinthal, 2009; Obloj & Sengul, 2020).

Multiple firm goals may be in alignment, independent, or in conflict (Obloj & Sengul, 2020). While the win-win approach tries to reconcile environmental with economic goals, the trade-off approach highlights tensions and demands the choice for one of these goals (van der Byl & Slawinski, 2015). On the one hand, in the course of the win-win approach, Elkington (1998) introduced the "triple bottom line approach" (p. 22), an attempt to balance social, economic, and environmental goals. Similarly, Edmans (2020) introduced the "pie-growing mentality", in which a firm's primary objective is the creation of social value rather than profits (p. 3). Thus, long-term payoffs can be positive, although the projects leading up to this value creation would not have been approved by applying a classical shareholder value framework (Edmans, 2020). Furthermore, there is abundant literature pointing out that "it pays to be green" (Hang et al., 2018, p. 738) via a positive link between environmental behavior and profitability (Busch et al., 2020; Fujii et al., 2013; Hang et al., 2018).

On the other hand, with adherence to the trade-off approach, T. Hahn et al. (2010) describe a trade-off between economic, environmental, and social organizational outcomes. Economic and environmental initiatives can benefit each other in the long run while they strive for the same resources in the short term (Margolis & Walsh, 2003; van der Byl & Slawinski, 2015). Hence, environmental initiatives can potentially prevent managers from reaching their short-term profitability goals (Gaba & Greve, 2019; Sarkis & Cordeiro, 2001).

Family-firm researchers have repeatedly stressed the urgency to resolve tensions between multiple firm goals to avoid severe consequences for the firms and their managers (e.g., Kammerlander et al. 2015). However, research developing strategies for resolving goal tensions in family firms is scarce. In 2022, Diaz-Moriana et al. demonstrated that family firm decision-makers apply sense-making and sense-giving mechanisms when they face goal tensions. While the study sharpens the understanding of sense-making in family firms, it does not provide concrete, implementable strategies that practitioners can apply in their firms to balance economic and non-economic tensions in the future. The study covers non-economic goals in general without focusing on environmental or decarbonization goals, potentially disregarding peculiarities in goal tensions and structures in this context.

In summary, there is a call for concrete, implementable strategies for balancing economic and environmental targets (Engert & Baumgartner, 2016; Lozano, 2015; van der Byl & Slawinski, 2015), especially for family firms (Aparicio et al., 2017; Chrisman et al., 2012; Chua et al., 2018; Habbershon et al., 2003; Kotlar & Massis, 2013; Moores, 2009).

3.3 Methodology

3.3.1 Research Design and Setting

To adequately answer the research question, we will pursue an exploratory, inductive qualitative study on the basis of multiple cases (Eisenhardt, 1989; Yin, 2018). Not only is public information about decarbonization limited (Martin & Moser, 2012), but family firms are also known for their unwillingness to disclose information (von Stietencron, 2013). Moreover, internal firm processes, such as strategic decision-making, are not externally accessible. Last, there is "limited extant knowledge about how and why non-economic goals affect adaptation processes" (Kammerlander & Ganter, 2015, p. 364) and a scarcity of research spanning the fields of environmental behavior, strategic decision-making processes, and family firms. Therefore, we pursue an inductive, qualitative study that allows for the exploratory analysis of multiple cases (De Massis & Kotlar, 2014). A multiple case study enables authors to build stronger theory, in contrast to a single case study (Yin, 2018), by conducting within- and cross-case analyses (Eisenhardt, 1989). Furthermore, case studies are useful for *why* and *how* questions (Yin, 2018), such as the research question of this work. Last, it is a commonly applied research strategy in the analysis of processes at family firms (De Massis & Kammerlander, 2021) and for studying "contradictions, tensions, paradoxes and dualities in family firms" (Fletcher et al., 2016, p. 2), which often underlie strategic decision-making based on environmental goals in the short term (Gaba & Greve, 2019; Margolis & Walsh, 2003; van der Byl & Slawinski, 2015).

We will examine data from family firms with headquarters in Germany. The observation unit is the strategic decision-making process within the family firm. We will follow the definition of strategic decisions provided in the introduction. Mintzberg et al. (1976) point out that a strategic decision-making process starts with strategic decision identification, passes a development phase, and ends with the selection phase. Based on Glaser and Strauss (1967), we pursue a theoretical four-step sampling approach to select the most suitable cases, as indicated in Fig. 3.1. This is especially relevant for family firms that are known for their heterogeneity (Chua et al., 2012; Dibrell & Memili, 2019; Miller & Le Breton-Miller, 2021a). Cases were chosen to replicate or extend the theory (Eisenhardt, 1989).

The focus lies on firms headquartered in Germany since Germany is the largest economy in the EU and Germany has passed decarbonization targets early on (Die Bundesregierung, 2022). Additionally, family firms are the dominant organizational firm type in Germany (Stiftung Familienunternehmen, 2019a; von Stietencron, 2013). Furthermore, we will apply the definition of family firms from the theoretical background section of this chapter. Publicly listed firms will be excluded, as existing research on large or publicly listed companies in Germany partially exists already (Günther & Günther, 2017; Günther et al., 2018) and ownership is less dispersed (Cruz et al., 2015). Publicly listed family firms are commonly defined by a threshold of 20% control by family members (La Porta et al., 1999) in contrast to the 50% dominant influence definition in this chapter.

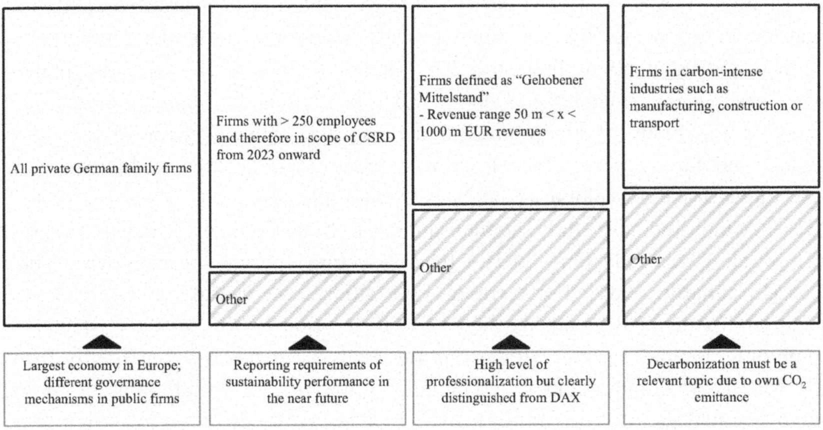

Fig. 3.1 Sampling process. *Source* Own figure

This finding is supported by Foss et al. (2021), who state that ownership competence will have a much higher effect if there is high ownership concentration. Similarly, Schulze and Zellweger (2021) point out that a high ownership creation enables the owners to personally create value based on their decision-making and business judgment. Moreover, we will consider only firms with more than 250 employees, as these are obliged to report their decarbonization performance from 2024 onward as part of the CSRD (European Commission, 2023). In addition, a range between 50 million euros and one billion euros in revenue is applied. This group is referred to as "Gehobener Mittelstand" in Germany (Venohr & Langenscheidt, 2015, p. 5). The group "Gehobener Mittelstand" is unique to the world, as this group of medium-sized, industrial companies accounts for 68% of all German exports (Venohr & Langenscheidt, 2015, p. 5). This procedure ensures a high level of professionalization to derive relevant learning while still establishing a clear distinction in size from publicly listed companies in the DAX, the German benchmark index, via a limit to one billion euros in revenue. All firms are in carbon-intensive industries, such as the manufacturing, construction, or transport sector, as decarbonization must be a relevant topic to these firms due to their emittance of CO_2.

The final sample consists of eleven family firms (see Table 3.1). The firms are affiliated with seven different industries, earned an average of ~500 million euros in revenue and employed an average of ~2,000 employees. We talked to family firm owners and sustainability managers who were directly involved in strategic decision-making and formed part of the top management team, as suggested by the definition of a strategic decision by Eisenhardt and Zbaracki (1992). If the family firm owner was not available, he was replaced by a leader and close advisor of his team, who also serves as a reliable source of knowledge according to Walker (1997). A sufficient level of variance in the sample is ensured by differing degrees of sophistication of decarbonization reporting among the selected firms, which was derived based on publicly available information and validated in the interviews.

3.3.2 Data Collection

The primary source of data within this research will be semi-structured interviews conducted with the eleven selected firms. For the interviews, word-by-word interview transcripts are created in preparation for a subsequent coding process in MAXQDA[2].

The case study protocol according to Yin (2018) and the abbreviated interview guide can be found in Appendix A. The interviews took place in January and February 2022 and lasted on average 60 min per firm. Overall, we collected 660 interview minutes and more than 220 pages of transcripts. All interviews were performed virtually for both the interviewer's convenience and circumstances arising from the COVID-19 pandemic. To ensure the validity of the interview data, several steps were followed (Eisenhardt, 1989). Each interview was extensively prepared with desk research and a review of archival data, which enabled in-depth conversations. We started the interviews by reassuring our interviewees that all interview contents would be subject to confidentiality to ease the interview atmosphere and encourage deeper, more trustful conversations. To further relax the situation, we always asked for explicit permission to record the interview before the actual interview started (Eisenhardt, 1989).

After each interview, we reviewed the answers and refined the questions slightly if necessary. For instance, the section "Deep Dive strategic decision-making process with integration of CO_2 emissions" was enriched during the interviews, as decision rules were part of the theory-building process and could not have been formulated via a literature review (see Appendix A). Eisenhardt (1989) confirms that building theory from case studies allows for adjustments

[2] MAXQDA is a software used for qualitative and mixed-methods research, and it primarily supports researchers in coding and visualization of data.

Table 3.1 Profiles of the organizations in the sample

Characteristics of the firms							Characteristics of the interviews				
Company	Industry	Firm age[1]	Generation[1]	Revenues[1] (in m EUR)	Employees[1]	Sophistication sustainability reporting	Interviews[2]	Interview minutes	Interview partners	Years with the firm	
Alpha	Waste / transport	120	4	200	1,200	High	1	61	CEO (family); Project Manager Sustainability, Climate, Innovation	25 4	Press releases, annual reports and company websites from 2018 - 2021
Beta	Consturction	70	2	285	1,520	High	1	52	Leader Environment and Security	25	
Gamma	Paper / Packaging	215	8	940	2,500	High	2	62	Head of Sustainability	4	
Delta	Mechanical engineering	110	3	210	1,800	High	2	90	Former CEO (family), currently advisory board; Head of Quality and Sustainability	34 6	
Epsilon	Consumer goods	70	3	890	1,100	High	1	46	Head of Sustainability; Head of Corporate Communication	4 14	

(continued)

Table 3.1 (continued)

Characteristics of the firms							Characteristics of the interviews			
Company	Industry	Firm age[1]	Generation[1]	Revenues[1] (in m EUR)	Employees[1]	Sophistication sustainability reporting	Interviews[2]	Interview minutes	Interview partners	Years with the firm
Zeta	Consumer goods	260	9	520	6,500	High	1	60	VP Engineering and Sustainability	7
Eta	Consumer goods	140	4	760	2,350	Medium	1	49	Head of Sustainability and Assistant to Board	5
Theta	Automotive supplier	30	2	130	300	Medium	1	60	CEO (family)	7
Jota	Automotive supplier	170	5	270	1,350	Basic	1	60	Vice President Quality; Head of Sustainability & Employee Security	3 22
Kappa	Chemicals	180	5	860	1,260	Basic	1	56	Head of Sustainability	25

(continued)

Table 3.1 (continued)

Characteristics of the firms							Characteristics of the interviews			
Company	Industry	Firm age[1]	Generation[1]	Revenues[1] (in m EUR)	Employees[1]	Sophistication sustainability reporting	Interviews[2]	Interview minutes	Interview partners	Years with the firm
Lambda	Chemicals	50	2	640	1,730	Basic	1	55	CEO (non-family) Head of Production and Technology (incl. ESG)	8 10
Not-case specific	Experts from various industries	-	-	-	-	Not applicable	-	-	Advisors from consultancies in the field of sustainability, representatives of family firm foundations, researchers in the field of decarbonization and family firms, German firms that are not part of "Gehobener Mittelstand"	

Note 1. Based on the latest available year (2021/22); 2. Count of the interviews conducted
Source Own table

concerning new emerging topics. Finally, we sometimes exchanged relevant documentation with the interview partners, such as past sustainability reports, before entering the analysis phase. After marginal, newly gained insights decreased, we did not conduct any further interviews in line with the recommendation from Eisenhardt (1989).

While the interviews of the selected family firms serve as our primary source of data, we triangulated all findings by incorporating two additional data sources (Kotlar & Massis, 2013; Theißen et al., 2014). First, archival data from the firms' websites and past press releases served as empirical evidence for the family firms' decarbonization activities, which not only benefitted the data analysis but also helped us to familiarize ourselves with the firms in preparation for the interviews (Diaz-Moriana et al., 2022). Second, ten expert interviews with advisors from consultancies in the field of sustainability, family firm foundations, and other researchers in the areas of environmental behavior and family firms, as well as German family firms that are not part of "Gehobener Mittelstand" (Venohr & Langenscheidt, 2015, p. 5) complemented the data. For instance, the exchange with a representative from a family firm foundation provided additional insights into how goal tensions are discussed in family firm plenaries, helping to calibrate the perceptions from our private conversations with family firms. Furthermore, the exchange with advisors from sustainability consultancies helped distinguish and formulate the goal management strategies based on the interview input.

3.3.3 Data Analysis

Our data analysis combined two methods—the multiple case study approach (Eisenhardt, 1989) and the in-depth inductive case analysis method (Gioia et al., 2013), similar to other authors that conduct qualitative research on processes in family firms (Diaz-Moriana et al., 2022; Strike & Rerup, 2016). As already illustrated by Diaz-Moriana et al. in 2022, the multiple case study approach by Eisenhardt enables the comparison within and across cases (Eisenhardt & Graebner, 2007), while the inductive analysis allows the analysis of systematic similarities and differences across cases and reveals comprehensive strategic decision-making processes (Corley & Gioia, 2004). As such, our data analysis comprised three key steps.

First, we performed a within-case analysis based on the compiled data from interview transcripts, archives, and expert interviews. Initial key themes were identified (Miles et al., 2014) and first-order categories were established by focusing on materials covering decarbonization, goals and goal systems, as well as strategic decision-making. Triangulation between the data sources was crucial at this stage. While the support of findings among the data sources made the results more robust, discrepancies between data sources required us to approach the interviewees again (Theißen et al., 2014). The within-case analysis yielded eleven detailed case descriptions after repeatedly reducing, displaying, and concluding the data (Miles et al., 2014).

Second, we performed a cross-case analysis to seek similarities and differences among the findings from single case studies and draw overarching patterns (Eisenhardt, 1989; Eisenhardt & Graebner, 2007), enabling us to aggregate the assigned codes into second-order themes (Gioia et al., 2013). In line with inductive qualitative research, we remained open to any concepts that appeared from the data, resulting in continuous iterations regarding the correct inferring, grouping, and labeling of the data.

Third, we started to search for theories that would be able to bind our second-order themes into aggregate dimensions. It became apparent that there are systematic differences in the strategies for multiple goal management, the *how*, and the reasons for pursuing decarbonization, the *why*. Hence, we searched for theories linking the findings of the *why* and the *how* questions. The strong relevance of the attention-based view by Ocasio (1997) became explicit at this stage because the focus and situation of attention (*why*) will influence the structural distribution of attention (*how*). We did not consider the attention-based view at the start of this research project but explored its value for our research throughout the analysis phase.

Last, through various rounds of iterations, we improved our themes and finally derived our final data structure (see Appendix B). We collected explanatory examples to facilitate external observers to comprehend our inferences (see Appendix C).

3.4 Results

3.4.1 An Attention-Based Model for Managing Economic and Environmental Goals

Building on case-based evidence and the attention-based view of Ocasio (1997), this chapter introduces an inductive model of family firm adaptation to decarbonization and arising firm decarbonization goals that exist in parallel to economic firm goals (see Fig. 3.2). The framework exhibits why and how family firms have developed strategies to manage economic and environmental goals simultaneously. Next, we will guide successively through our model. The rich evidence from the cross-case analysis can be reviewed in parallel in Appendix C.

In our derived model, the strategic decision-making process starts with the decarbonization timeline postulated by scientists and policymakers, which serves as the stimulus to which family firms react and which is external to all firms. As the first step and following Ocasio's first principle, the firm's "focus of attention" is represented by the motivation that encompasses intrinsic and extrinsic goals for decarbonization. While intrinsic goals drive all firms in the sample, some family firms are additionally driven by extrinsic goals on their decarbonization journey. Intrinsic goals observed reflect relevant categories of non-economic goals of family firms in the literature (Berrone et al., 2012; Gómez-Mejia et al., 2011). The observed intrinsic goals include transgenerational value (Chua et al., 1999; Zellweger et al., 2012), family reputation (Berrone et al., 2012), power and control (Carney, 2005; Chua et al., 1999), and enduring ties (Miller & Le Breton-Miller, 2005; Zellweger et al., 2013). Extrinsic goals are client demand, pressure from regulatory institutions, and a competitive advantage in contrast to other market participants when pursuing decarbonization successfully. Subsequently, Ocasio's second principle, "situated attention", is represented by the firm's attitude toward decarbonization. Attitudes vary enormously between firms arising from different goals, as discussed in terms of "the focus of attention", as well as from different goal systems, as to how the link between economic and decarbonization goals is perceived. Some firms regard decarbonization as an entrepreneurial opportunity irrespective of their market environment, while others perceive it as a comparative chance for their firm in contrast to other market participants, a sole necessity, or are unaware of whether decarbonization poses a chance or challenge for their firm. Together, the motivation and attitude toward decarbonization answer the question of *why or why not* firms manage economic and decarbonization goals in their strategic decision-making.

As the last step, the strategic decision-making process ends with Ocasio's "structural distribution of attention", illustrating strategies for *how* family firms manage economic and environmental goals. They purposefully integrate or do not integrate decarbonization, expressed through the key performance indicator (KPI) CO_2, in their strategic decision-making process driven by their motivation and attitude toward decarbonization. The first strategy of CO_2 integration is depicted by the *presence of environmental information (incl. innovation)*. CO_2 is deeply integrated into a firm's culture, and employees are naturally accustomed to considering CO_2 in various processes. These include portfolio adaptation and innovation processes, where CO_2 serves as a relevant KPI to be improved with

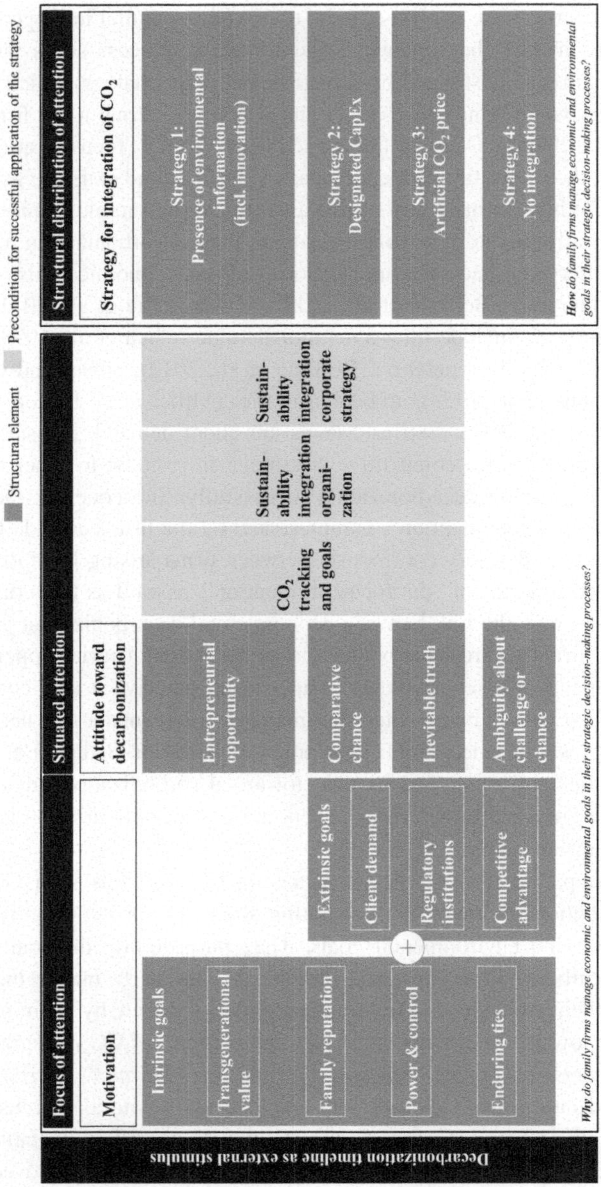

Fig. 3.2. An attention-based model for managing economic and environmental goals. *Source* Own figure

each new product. Furthermore, CO_2 is considered throughout the entire strategic decision-making process, e.g., via the presence of managers from specific departments or similar representation of economic and environmental information in a firm's balanced scorecard or other decision tools. Firms applying this strategy regard decarbonization as an entrepreneurial opportunity and pursue it solely based on intrinsic goals. The second strategy is a *designated CapEx*, where the budget size is determined top-down based on the list of activities required for a firm's successful decarbonization, also referred to as the decarbonization roadmap. Available funds are compared with the decarbonization roadmap and assigned to decarbonization projects accordingly. Firms applying a designated budget adopt the attitude that decarbonization is a comparative advantage for their firm in competition with other market participants, so they assign the required funds to decarbonize more effectively than the competition. A third strategy is the introduction of an *artificial CO_2 price* as a variable in a firm's investment calculations. This artificial CO_2 price can, for instance, be derived based on an expectation of future CO_2 prices as well as compensation costs. In contrast to the *designated CapEx* strategy, this is a calculation approach to be applied by employees across the firm and not mainly by top management. Firms using this strategy regard decarbonization as an inevitable, scientific truth to which they necessarily need to adhere. Therefore, this factual, numerical strategy enables the firm to make forward-looking investment decisions, which are still costly at this point but are likely to pay off in the future. Finally, as a fourth strategy, some firms show a case of *no integration* in their decision-making and are unaware of their goal system, whether decarbonization poses a challenge or a chance to the firm's financial performance.

As our cross-case analysis shows, strategies to reconcile economic and environmental goals are deployed. Furthermore, there is no "one size fits all approach". The introduced strategies fit the divergent motivations and attitudes toward decarbonization of the corresponding firms. Additionally, no firm expressed the opinion that it would not want to integrate CO_2. Instead, a lack of deeper integration was due to internal capability gaps in emission tracking, integration of sustainability in the organization, or the corporate strategy, which are necessary preconditions to be fulfilled.

3.4.2 Representative Case Study per Strategy

In the following, we will describe four case studies representing the four strategies introduced in the attention-based model in Fig. 3.2. Following the advice of Eisenhardt and Graebner (2007), we summarize all cases applicable to each strategy in Fig. 3.3 and only describe representative cases in detail to limit the richness of our qualitative data. We observe that the allocation of the cases to strategies shows no systematic differences arising from the industry, size, age, or current generation of firms. Subsequently, the case-by-case description will help to better understand the motivation, attitude, and preconditions under which the selected strategies emerged and how they function within the family firm business.

The presence of environmental information (incl. innovation). *Delta* sells advanced machinery and is therefore mainly active in business-to-business (B2B) markets.

Motivation *Delta's* decarbonization achievements stem from its strong intrinsic goals. *Delta* is an energy-positive company, as it has various forms of renewable energy generation installed on its production site. It has further received prices for its sustainable performance and takes part in relevant consortia for climate change in Germany. *"The topic is in the genes of the family."* Transgenerational value has a high priority for the owner family. *"We adopt a long-term perspective, we want to be successful in the long term, we want to hand over a good and healthy company to our children in the long term."* Family reputation is also important. *"We want to take personal responsibility. We want to act sustainably."* The firm holds strong personal ties to the local community and nature and wants to show its gratitude by protecting the local circumstances.

Attitude toward decarbonization *Delta* believes that sustainability and decarbonization are entrepreneurial opportunities. *Delta* believes that economy and ecology are not in contrast to each other if one works with a long-term orientation across generations. *"If one does a good job—it does not get more expensive—definitively not. In the long run, it rather becomes cheaper."* For the firm, decarbonization is more than a competitive advantage. Instead, the firm adopts an entrepreneurial spirit. *"You might find areas where we have invested, although we could not calculate it exactly [...]. If it serves the bigger purpose, one also has to accept a certain level of risk."* However, most of the time, sustainability initiatives are only pursued if a payoff is backed up by in-depth analysis. Due to its strong sustainability orientation, the firm even receives applications from personnel who are intrinsically motivated in the topic and want to work for a sustainable employer. In addition, all employees are specifically trained in the area of sustainability at the start of their job, and sustainability ambassadors can be found in all departments. The sustainability

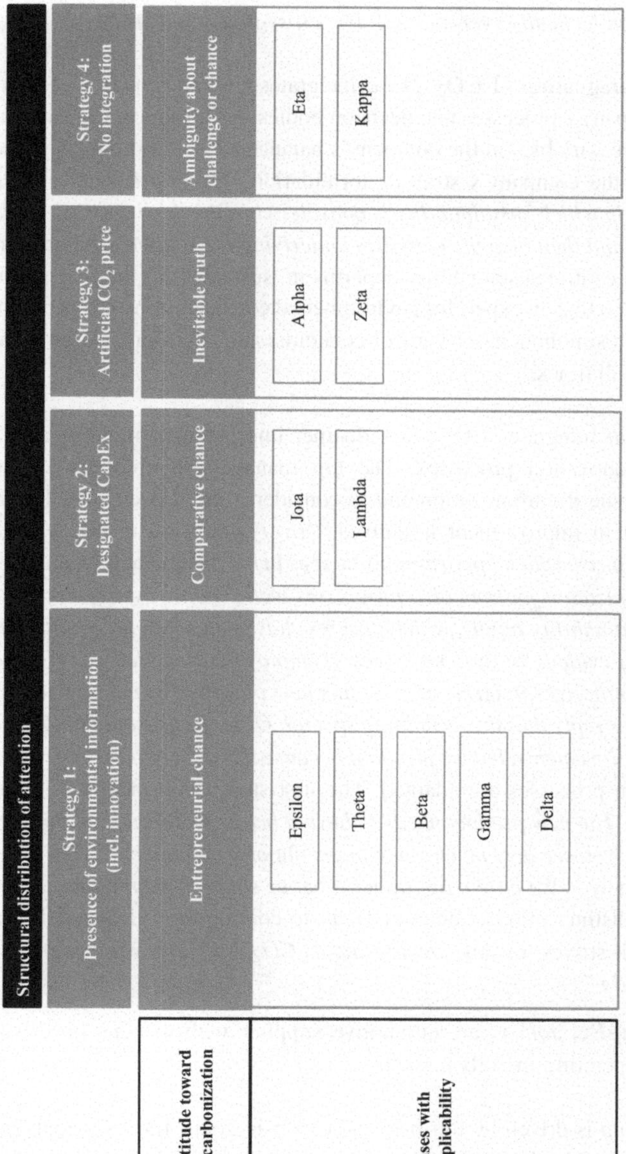

Fig. 3.3. Case allocation to the attention-based model. *Source* Own figure

strategy is cross-functionally integrated into the corporate strategy. *"Sustainability has an impact on basically everything. It is a cross-functional strategy."*

Strategy for integration of CO_2 *Delta* integrates CO_2 information consistently within the company's processes and decision bodies. For instance, CO_2 and energy consumption are variables in the company's balanced scorecard, which is the key instrument for the company's strategy formulation. *"We work with a balanced scorecard [...] in which sustainability is considered in the departments' goals, the strategic goals and then also the activities underlying the roadmap."* Furthermore, in addition to a central sustainability department, sustainability has been assigned per department so that an expert for environmental considerations forms part of any discussion and a simultaneous review of economic and environmental information is facilitated at all times.

Moreover, *Delta* integrates CO_2 via a distinct improvement mindset and adaptation of its innovation processes. The top management enforces a spirit to continually pursue decarbonization and to consider it in all decisions. The whole firm takes part in improvement initiatives. *"Everyone needs to take part and if everyone recognizes, which opportunities he sees in his direct environment, then the whole decarbonization journey also progresses well. We always review, also outside of the sustainability report, which progress has been made. In addition, this is natural and self-evident for our employees. If employees are asked about some new sustainability initiatives in terms of what this new initiative is and how it is calculated, employees reply that this is nothing special. Other firms would hold speeches about these improvements, but we just do it because it is part of our DNA."* In addition, innovation processes are adapted. The first step was to adopt an important decision rule. *"The new product needs to have a better footprint than the previous one. Over time, you see how much you can get out of it in numbers."* The firm also acts pragmatically. *"We care more about a better solution than about the way to get there."* A distinct mindset enables *Delta* to continuously decrease its carbon footprint, and it strives toward *"decreasing its CO_2 emissions while increasing its revenues steadily."*

Designated CapEx. *Jota* is an automotive supplier with a focus on drive-train technologies operating in B2B markets.

Motivation *Jota* is driven by intrinsic and extrinsic goals. Intrinsic goals include the transgenerational value of the firm, power and control, enduring ties, and family reputation. For instance, transgenerational value and family reputation mean for

Jota not only that the firm shall be made future-proof for future family generations but also that the management team consists of family fathers who feel personally responsible and want to take ownership for making the company sustainable for the future. In line with this perception, CO_2 compensation is not an option, as *"it would not be truly sustainable."* Meanwhile, *Jota* is also strongly driven by two extrinsic motives. First, *"we are also a little bit pushed ahead by our clients"*, as the supplier selection criteria become increasingly stricter with regard to decarbonization. *"If clients visit us, it happens often that they do not want to talk to us about the product or the price, but instead review the sustainability systems."* A second extrinsic motive is also linked to this. *Jota* perceives its decarbonization performance as a *"USP"* in comparison to other market players. *"If one can shine with Scope 3*[3]*, which is something that many suppliers do not have on the agenda yet, this serves as an advantage on the market."*

Attitude toward decarbonization *Jota*, therefore, adopts the attitude that decarbonization is a competitive advantage compared to its competitors. *Jota* believes that the short-term, economic, and environmental goals could be in conflict. *"However, in the long term, there is no such conflict."* It constitutes a win-win situation for *Jota* that being sustainable helps to win clients and contracts. *"We also participate in benchmarks from firms or service platforms, and the regular result is that we are from our size and industry always in the upper midfield—sometimes even leaving large, publicly listed companies behind."* The progress in sustainability and decarbonization *"is fully supported by the owner-manager."* A new sustainability department was recently founded, carbon-neutral products are planned for 2035, and a decarbonization roadmap was established for this purpose.

Strategy for integration of CO_2 *Jota* experiences that it is increasingly difficult to make assumptions about CO_2 prices and energy costs for the future, which has also resulted in selected firm investments from the past not performing as expected. Despite these uncertainties, *Jota* is strongly convinced that the CO_2 price will rise and that it will imply high costs to not decarbonize effectively. Hence, *Jota* developed a CO_2 decarbonization roadmap with underlying decarbonization activities. At the end of the year, all funds that are available from firm profits are assigned to the decarbonization activities of this roadmap. Therefore, annual capital expenditures emerge. In contrast to larger firms, *Jota* does not have a designated percentage of

[3] GHG emissions that "are a consequence of the activities of the company but occur from sources not owned or controlled by the company" are referred to as Scope 3 (Greenhouse Gas Protocol 2004, p. 25).

CapEx that is invested every year, but instead the firm follows the rule to invest *"as many funds as required and available for the decarbonization activities."* The only restriction is that *"we want to be independent of financial institutions"*, so only the self-earned, available funds are invested and no external funds are added.

Artificial CO_2 price. *Zeta* sells stationery products and is, therefore, active in the business-to-consumer (B2C) business.

Motivation *Zeta* is driven by intrinsic and extrinsic goals concerning decarbonization. Intrinsic goals comprise transgenerational value, power and control, and most importantly family reputation. The last family firm generation was represented by a family CEO who died a few years ago. He was intrinsically interested in sustainability and regarded the sustainability of products as a requirement at the firm, which is known for high quality. He further perceived it as a prerequisite of *"a good merchant"* to take responsibility for the environmental impact of the firm. Therefore, he decided to invest in forest projects in South America in the 1980s. These projects simultaneously served as a source of raw materials and as a form of CO_2 compensation. *"The topic of the forest projects and certified wood, was for the brand, as well as for the company and the family owner [...] extremely important."* In recent years, sustainability was not only an established firm value due to the firm's early sustainability investments in the past, but extrinsic goals such as a new EU taxonomy and consumer demand for green products were the key drivers for the firm's decarbonization efforts.

Attitude toward decarbonization Zeta sees decarbonization as an inevitable, scientific truth to which it necessarily needs to adhere. *"We realize that progress in sustainability is also in the interest of the consumer and legal requirements and that making progress is nothing that can be done at the side without asking some bigger questions. The low-hanging fruits have been collected, the quick fixes have been fixed and now we have reached a stage where we have to ask ourselves the question of how to allocate our capital. Otherwise, it will be difficult to progress."* *Zeta* is convinced that investments in decarbonization are inevitable. *"These are costs or investments, which we carry out today, but that is value protecting. If we would not do it, my firm value will eventually erode."* Last, *Zeta* also stresses that its attitude has slightly changed over the last years. *"Back then, colleagues at the firm were probably not aware, of what challenges this world would face, if we would sincerely like to work toward the 1.5-degree goal."* The firm had technical and operational sustainability and decarbonization goals for its employees for years. Climate neutrality on the firm level was reached early due to the firm's own compensation projects in South America. However, in the last year, *Zeta's* decarbonization goals were publicly announced, and since then, stricter goals have also lived at the employee level.

Strategy for integration of CO_2 *Zeta* is implementing a new strategy for the integration of CO_2 in its strategic decision-making process. It will introduce an artificial CO_2 price in its investment calculations, e.g., based on assumptions of expectation of future CO_2 prices or CO_2 compensation costs. *"We will set a price once a year and then apply it for the economic efficiency calculations of investments."* By applying this new strategy, the firm hopes to make future-proof decisions. *"If we only consider the extra costs of switching to green alternatives, we would never be able to do it. However, we believe that we will save CO_2 via this approach. If we would source compensation externally in the future, we would have to pay much more money for it."* *Zeta* believes that this is the only feasible way to make a switch. *"I regard this as the absolutely right way to change the processes because otherwise, we will never leave the old economic management."* *Zeta* also has specific examples, where the strategy worked very well. *"For instance, recently in our Malaysia business, they wanted to switch to green electricity, but this would have led to increased electricity costs. From a classical investment viewpoint, this switch would have not been feasible."* This strategy of CO_2 integration enables *Zeta* to calculate the case for future-oriented investments, which are still costly at this point but are likely to pay off in the future.

No integration. *Eta* offers toys and books and can therefore be classified as a B2C company.

Motivation *Eta* is similarly driven by intrinsic and extrinsic goals. Non-economic goals have always had high importance for the family and firm. For instance, enduring ties to employees who are keen on making progress with regard to sustainability and decarbonization is an intrinsic goal, which drives sustainability and decarbonization efforts. Meanwhile, the firm is also extrinsically driven to strive for decarbonization since licenses, new partnerships, and collaborations are offered based on firms' sustainability performance. *Eta* is aware of regulatory requirements but does not perceive them as pressure.

Attitude toward decarbonization *Eta's* attitude toward decarbonization is not clear. The firm believes that a lack of sustainable performance poses a risk of firm value destruction. Meanwhile, *Eta* is still discussing whether sustainable performance is also an opportunity for the firm in the form of value creation. Currently, the tendency is that whether sustainability and decarbonization represent a risk or a chance needs to be decided per product. Furthermore, the firm does not perceive itself as one of the largest emitters. *"We as a consumer goods industry are aware that we do not spin the biggest wheel in terms of total emissions."* Thus far, decarbonization has always been a cost topic for *Eta*. However, *Eta* also puts this into context by stating that *"we are still relatively new in the game."* A sustainability strategy was developed from scratch in 2019 as part of a larger strategic project. However, the sustainability strategy is still separate from the corporate strategy. As part of this new strategy, CO_2 has also been tracked since 2018, and a decarbonization roadmap was top-down derived. However, the roadmap only covers the footprint of operations. A small sustainability department exists, but it is the plan to establish sustainability ambassadors across the organization. Trust in the sustainability department and its calculations are to be established in traditional departments such as purchasing, controlling and research and development, where CO_2 has not yet become a target variable. *"We have the idea that each firm department will live this topic and understand it, but there we are still at the beginning."*

Strategy for integration of CO_2 *Eta* has not yet integrated CO_2 into its strategic decision-making process. CO_2 is mainly considered a cost topic, e.g., via an assigned budget for CO_2 compensation that was derived with a high-level approximation of CO_2 costs. The CO_2 approximations here are not primarily technical or strategic but were mainly used for an employee involvement initiative. *Eta* wanted to specify a rough amount of its CO_2 to enable a poll where employees could vote on which CO_2 initiatives the firm should pursue. Otherwise, CO_2 is mainly measured and considered after a strategic decision is made. *"It is measured subsequently and then reduction measures are derived accordingly. However, the decision we make is not based on CO_2 at the highest level."* New investment decisions, e.g., into renewable energy assets, are based on an assessment of cost, resilience, and CO_2. However, *Eta* does not have a fixed system for how it weighs these aspects against each other. *Eta* believes that internal firm processes will likely have to be transformed severely, impacting the core firm's DNA. CO_2 will have to be prioritized as a target variable to pursue certain reduction initiatives despite hurdles such as increased complexity. *"That we become much more agile in product development [...]. That we say we are open to new materials and will test new suppliers for qualification, which are smaller. This makes the supplier management generally more complex."* In summary, *Eta* is still *"in a phase of radical change."* The limited CO_2 integration does not arise from a lack of willingness but instead is rooted in a lack of prerequisites, e.g., the integration of the firm's sustainability strategy into the corporate strategy. Furthermore, the firm has just started its decarbonization journey in 2019, thus many processes are still in development.

3.5 Discussion

3.5.1 Contribution

Theoretical implications

Our findings entail theoretical implications concerning multiple goal management, family firm goals, and the attention-based view. Insights were derived by observing the tensions and their reconciliation between economic and environmental goals arising through decarbonization.

First, we contribute through three strategies for CO_2 integration, providing evidence that economic and environmental goals can be reconciled, even in the short term. These findings extend the research on multiple goal management (Diaz-Moriana et al., 2022; Epstein et al., 2015; Ivory & Brooks, 2018) and follow the call for concrete, implementable strategies to address goal tensions (Engert & Baumgartner, 2016; Lozano, 2015; van der Byl & Slawinski, 2015). According to the behavioral theory of the firm, it is clear that modern firms will tend to pursue multiple goals in the future (Cyert & March, 1992), which manifests the value of these research findings.

We are among the first researchers (Diaz-Moriana et al., 2022) that not only state goal tensions and their consequences at family firms but also investigate mechanisms and strategies to overcome these. Beyond existing contributions, our attention-based model presents differentiated strategies for firms depending on their motivation and attitude toward decarbonization. These can also be referred to as firms' goals and goal systems. Some firms are mainly driven by intrinsic goals and perceive economic and decarbonization goals as a chance to pursue relatively unsystematic forms of CO_2 integration through the *presence of environmental information (incl. innovation)* or a *designated CapEx.* In contrast, other firms that are driven by both intrinsic and extrinsic decarbonization goals and perceive decarbonization to be a threat to their profits, at least in the short term, deploy a systematic, fixed approach for CO_2 integration in the form of an *artificial CO_2 price.* It seems that the closer a firm perceives economic and environmental goals to be in alignment, with the propensity to a win-win relationship (Porter & van der Linde, 1995), the less systematic is the design of the multiple goal strategy. In contrast, firms that are instead rather proponents of the trade-off theory (Andersson et al., 2018; Friedman, 1970; Levitt, 1958) reconcile environmental and economic goals through more clearly defined, strict methods. Thus, we elaborate the research on multiple goal management by illustrating that strategies should be assessed considering firms' goals and goal systems (Chua et al., 2018). In addition, unlike previous research (e.g., Diaz-Moriana et al. 2022), the derived strategies are concrete and implementable as they entail specific and practical mechanisms, such as introducing an artificial CO_2 price. Despite their increasing prevalence, no research of which we are aware investigates strategies to overcome goal tensions arising during firm decarbonization.

Second, based on the SEW theory and in line with previous literature (Berrone et al., 2010; Chrisman et al., 2012; Gómez-Mejia et al., 2011; Hüseyin et al., 2017; Kammerlander & Ganter, 2015; Sharma & Sharma, 2011), we show that non-economic goals, here so-called intrinsic goals, have an impact on organizational behavior of family firms such as the strategic decision-making. To protect a firm's SEW, they serve as a motivation for family firms to decarbonize (Berrone et al., 2010; Campopiano & Massis, 2015; Sharma & Sharma, 2011). However, we also reveal that the motivation for environmental behavior in family firms stems not only from non-economic, intrinsic firm goals but also extrinsic goals such as regulatory pressure, competitive advantage, and client demand. These findings contrast previous family firm research that stated that family firms are driven by the desire to pursue internal, non-economic firm goals through environmental behavior (Altenburger & Schmidpeter, 2018; Dangelico et al., 2019). In contrast, non-family research has previously highlighted the relevance of extrinsic goals and pressure (Böttcher & Müller, 2015; Garcés-Ayerbe et al., 2012; Sangle, 2010). An explanation for the enlarged applicability of extrinsic goals to family firms could be that regulatory decarbonization pressure has recently increased, e.g., through the European Climate Law in 2020 (European Commission, 2022b) and the announcement of the CSRD in 2021 (European Commission, 2023). Further, non-governmental stakeholders like investors (Blanco et al., 2017; Boukherroub et al., 2017; Li et al., 2020), customers (Hartmann & Moeller, 2014; Jira & Toffel, 2013), and society (Boukherroub et al., 2017; Eggert & Hartmann, 2021) also increasingly request decarbonization progress from family firms. Future research should investigate whether external goals continue to drive environmental behavior in family firms and whether internal or external motivation prevails.

Third, the contributions of this chapter are related to the attention-based view (Ocasio, 1997). Like Kammerlander and Ganter (2015), this chapter confirms that the connection of research on attention with the family firm literature is essential for an improved understanding of family firm behavior. We are among the first to contribute to the connection of research on multiple goal management and the attention-based view (Ahn, 2022). However, instead of assessing the antecedents of organizational attention (Ahn, 2022; Kammerlander & Ganter, 2015), this study shows how organizational attention, in terms of diverse goals and goal systems (Chua et al., 2018), can explain heterogeneous strategies for managing economic and environmental goals in strategic decision-making processes. As an extension, we still encourage an in-depth exploration of the antecedents of organizational attention in the context of family firms and decarbonization. Firm founders' imprint has been proven as highly relevant in strategic decision-making (Baron et al., 1999; Tripsas & Gavetti, 2000), which could be particularly interesting for family firms, as the family and the business are strongly intertwined (Habbershon et al., 2003).

Managerial implications

This work goes beyond the extant knowledge of concrete goal management strategies to be applied by practitioners at family firms. We show that economic and environmental goals can be reconciled through the usage of an effective strategy and accordingly hope to incentivize firms to pursue decarbonization goals next to their economic goals.

For firms to apply the findings of this chapter, we propose the following *guidelines of application* based on Fig. 3.2: 1) definition of a firm's goals for decarbonization; 2) evaluation of the attitude of the firm toward decarbonization based on a firm's goal system; and 3) application of the related multiple goal management strategy. Meanwhile, all firms interested in the proposed strategies should work on fulfilling the preconditions outlined in Fig. 3.2.

3.5.2 Limitations and Future Research

Despite the abovementioned contributions, our study has a few limitations, which should also be regarded as an impetus for future research.

Although most family firms demonstrate similar values, they are heterogeneous in their nature (Chua et al., 2012; Dibrell & Memili, 2019; May, 2012), which might endanger the applicability of findings to other family firms. We are aware of these idiosyncrasies, and through awareness and a theoretical sampling strategy, heterogeneity was purposefully limited.

Furthermore, the study is limited to the context of large German family firms, so it cannot be immediately transferred to non-family firms, although the attention-based view (Ocasio, 1997), as well as the phenomenon of decarbonization, are relevant across firm types. We, therefore, call for future research to conduct a comparative study between family and non-family firms to validate that multiple goal management strategies are not different.

The study only considers firms for which decarbonization is a relevant topic, not considering firms that do not engage in decarbonization. For building theory, any form of decarbonization reporting was required, so the sample serves this purpose. As the number of firms that do not engage in decarbonization will shrink rapidly in the coming years due to the CSRD, it will be interesting to test how often the derived strategies occur in a larger sample via a survey.

Moreover, this study does not assess the decision quality regarding family firms' effectiveness resulting from the three CO_2 integration strategies. The current focus is instead to understand which strategy is suited to which type of family firm than to assess which strategy leads to the best results. Given that many firms have been tracking carbon emissions only for a few years now, this might be an interesting topic to investigate in the future when more firms for analysis and prolonged empirical evidence are available.

Although environmental aspects weigh the highest among ESG considerations for many companies (Adams & Frost, 2008; Adu et al., 2022), environmental goals are only one form of non-economic ESG goals. Therefore, this study could be repeated with an alternate non-economic goal.

3.6 Conclusion

Given the urgency to decarbonize, it is necessary to sharpen the theoretical and managerial knowledge of strategies for balancing economic and environmental goals in firms. Through evidence from multiple case studies in the German family firm context and the application of the attention-based view (Ocasio, 1997), we provide a model that offers concrete, implementable strategies for multiple goal management and connects these to a firm's goals and goal system. While the findings entail theoretical implications regarding multiple goal management, family firms' goals, and the attention-based view, they shall aid practitioners in operating profitably while decarbonizing efficiently.

3.7 Appendix

3.7.1 Appendix A. Case Study Protocol, Interview Guide and Interview Questions

The **case study protocol** is based on the recommended structure of Yin (2018):

Objective of the research study:
Understand which strategies family firms deploy to manage economic and environmental simultaneously

Research team:
Johanna Schulze-Berge; Gunther Friedl

Research question:

- Why and how do family firms manage economic and environmental goals in their strategic decision-making processes?
- Which family firm goals or goal systems lead to different strategies?

Interview guide

- Personal introduction of the researcher (background and prior experience, research interests and objective) as well as personal introduction of the interviewee (educational and professional background)
- Information on interview (explanation of recording practice and interviewee's active consent to record, clarification of next steps after the interview)
- Interview questions Part 1: Background of the family firm, family essence and economic and non-economic goals (incl. environmental)
- Interview questions Part 2: Integration of decarbonization in the strategic decision-making process
- Interview questions Part 3: Outlook (incl. questions interviewee)

Interview questions (abbreviated version)

Part 1: Background of the family firm, family essence, and economic and non-economic goals (incl. environmental)

This part of the interview intends to

a.) **complete the basic information on the firm** *[only if not publicly available]*
b.) **learn about the essence of the family firm**
c.) **identify the key goals of the firm (incl. environmental)**

Part 1.a.)

Firm industry:

- In which industry does the firm operate?
  ☐ Manufacturing
  ☐ Construction
  ☐ Transport (incl. waste disposal services)
- If manufacturing, what is the focus of the business?
  ☐ Automotive supplier
  ☐ Consumer goods
  ☐ Chemicals
  ☐ Paper/packaging
  ☐ Other

Firm age:

- When was the firm founded?

Firm size:

- What has been the revenue in euro in the last year?
- How many employees does the firm currently employ?

Firm owner:

- What is the ownership structure of the firm?
- Is there a dominant business-owning family? Which ownership share of the firm is held by this family?

Part 1.b.)

Firm identity:

- Does the firm consider itself a family firm? If so, how are firm identity and family identity linked?

Family involvement:

- How many family members from the business-owning family are active in the top management? Which positions do family members fill? Are the successors involved yet and how?

Family values & vision:

- What are the most important non-economic goals and values of the business-owning family? Have they changed over time? How strongly are they lived at the firm level?
- How does the family's vision (aspirational picture of the firm in 10 years) for the family firm look like and did it change over time?

Part 1.c.)

[Only if relevant—Definition: Decarbonization refers to "the process by which countries, individuals or other entities aim to achieve zero fossil carbon existence. Typically refers to a reduction of the carbon emissions associated with electricity, industry and transport" (Intergovernmental Panel on Climate Change, 2022, p. 546)]

Attitude toward decarbonization:

- What does the firm aspire as the most important economic and environmental goals? How are they considered in the firm's strategy?
- How would you describe the relation of the economic and environmental goals over time? Has it changed? If so, why?
- How does the business-owning family judge the market environment/ impact of decarbonization and which potential options for decarbonization does it consider for the firm?

Current environmental behavior:

- Does the firm have a sustainability department? Where is it located in the organization and who does it report to?
- Do you measure CO_2 emissions Scope 1,2 and 3 (in t CO_2 equivalent)?
- Do you currently report your CO_2 emissions internally (e.g., with employees) or externally (e.g., website/business partners)? If so, how?

Future environmental behavior:

- Does the firm have decarbonization targets?
- How did the firm derive these firm decarbonization targets (e.g. regulatory framework, Science-Based Targets Initiative, competitors, etc.)? Did you publicly announce them? If so, how?

Motivation:

- Do you feel pressure from stakeholders such as customers, suppliers, and the local community to implement CO_2 reductions?
- Do you expect to be obliged to report your emissions externally? If yes, when?

Progress:

- How would you rate your current progress with regard to decarbonization?
- Which decarbonization activities did you already carry out and which do you plan for the future?

Part 2: Integration of CO_2 emissions in the strategic decision-making process

The part intends to understand why and how the strategic decision-making processes were or will be adapted concerning decarbonization and the management of multiple goals.

[Only if relevant—Definition: A strategic decision is "'important, in terms of the actions taken, the resources committed, or the precedents set" (Eisenhardt & Zbaracki, 1992, p. 17). A strategic decision is made by top management and impacts the firm's long-term organizational health and survival (Eisenhardt & Zbaracki, 1992). Wilson (2015) confirms these aspects and adds that strategic decisions can be complex or need to be based on limited, contradicting information. He further states that strategic decisions often entail trade-offs and risks and are linked to other decisions (Wilson, 2015). The strategic decision-making process starts with a strategic decision identification and ends with the strategic decision selection (Mintzberg, 1976).]

- Do you integrate decarbonization in your strategic decision-making process? -> *depending on the answers different follow up questions*

  a) ***No adaptation to decarbonization*** *in the strategic decision-making process:*

Why did you decide to not integrate decarbonization (CO_2 emissions) in your strategic decision-making?
How was your firm performance at that point in time?
Who was involved in the decision not to integrate decarbonization (CO_2 emissions) into the firm's strategic decision-making?
What would change your mind with regards to this decision?
Do you have a perspective on how your approach for the integration of decarbonization (CO_2 emissions) could look like?

b) ***Adaptation to decarbonization*** *in the strategic decision-making process:*
Do you integrate decarbonization (CO_2 emissions) in your strategic decision-making process?
For which type of decision is it useful to consider decarbonization (CO_2 emissions)?
Why did you decide to integrate decarbonization (CO_2 emissions) in your strategic decision-making process for these decisions (see above question)?
Who was involved in the decision to integrate decarbonization (CO_2 emissions) in strategic decision-making?
How was your firm performance when you made the decision to integrate decarbonization (CO_2 emissions)?

Deep Dive strategic decision-making process with integration of CO_2 emissions:

- Please describe the decision-making process in detail and provide an example decision illustrating how it works. -> *depending on answer different follow up questions*

Decision-makers:

- Who makes the strategic decisions? How is the business-owning family involved and which other employees/departments are involved?

Decision-making process:

- Is there a standardized approach for making strategic decisions or does it always differ?
- What are the start and the end of the strategic decision-making process?
- Since when do you apply this approach for decision-making?

Information basis & decision rules:

- Based on which set of information do you make decisions (financial and non-financial)?
- Do you have decision rules?
  - Do sustainable investments have to pay off? If so, after which time?
  - Do you have a strategy to make environmental and financial aspects comparable (e.g. via a common unit, weighting system, etc.)?
  - Does your company consider an internal or external CO_2 price? If so, how do you calculate it and how do you apply it?
  - How relevant is managerial judgment in these decisions (incl. entrepreneurial risk)?

Part 3: Outlook

This part of the interview intends to provide some perspective on how the firm's decarbonization strategy and decision-making process could change in the future. Moreover, the aim is to give the interviewee the opportunity to mention any important point referring to the interview topic that had not been addressed before and exchange relevant documentation.

Distinction family firm:

- In your opinion, would your business have adapted its strategic decision-making differently if it had not been owned and/or managed by a family (e.g. in comparison to publicly listed companies)?

Future decision-making:

- Are you planning to change/enhance the decision-making process in the future? If so, why?

Additional remarks & information:

- Are there any other thoughts and considerations which you would like to share with regards to the interview topic?
- Do you have any documentation supporting the above findings (e.g., family charter, decision-making process requirements, etc.)?

3.7.2 Appendix B. Data structure

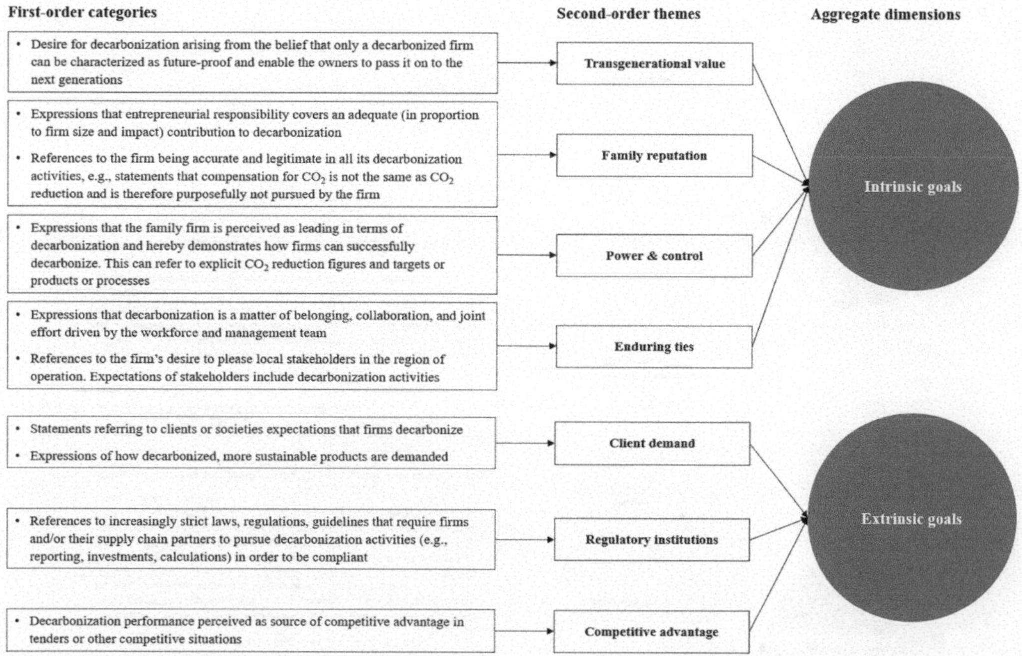

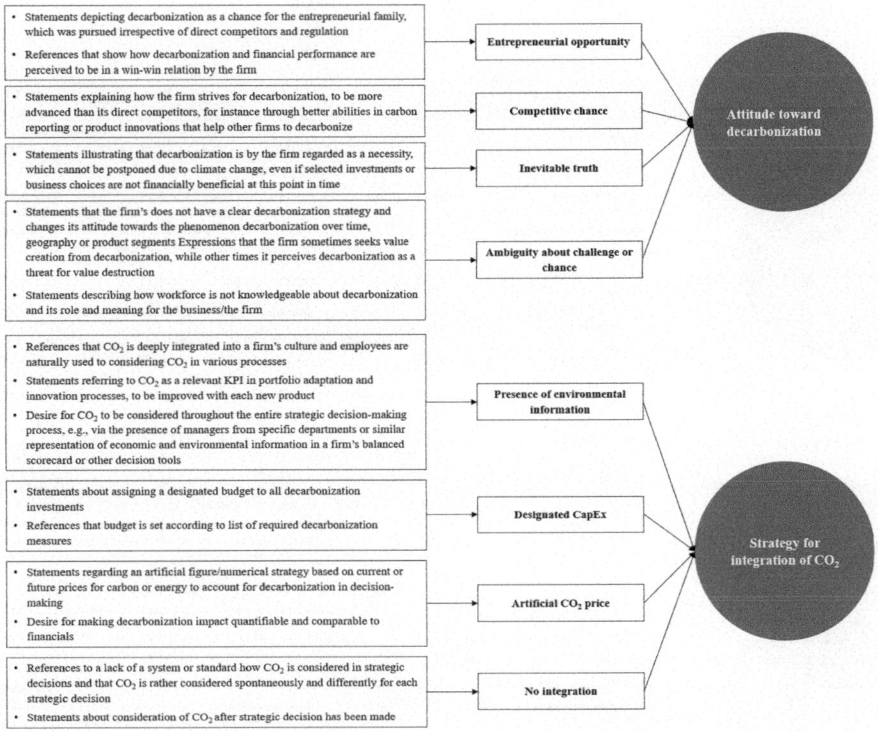
Statements depicting decarbonization as a chance for the entrepreneurial family, which was pursued irrespective of direct competitors and regulation
References that show how decarbonization and financial performance are perceived to be in a win-win relation by the firm
Entrepreneurial opportunity
Statements explaining how the firm strives for decarbonization, to be more advanced than its direct competitors, for instance through better abilities in carbon reporting or product innovations that help other firms to decarbonize
Competitive chance
Statements illustrating that decarbonization is by the firm regarded as a necessity, which cannot be postponed due to climate change, even if selected investments or business choices are not financially beneficial at this point in time
Inevitable truth
Statements that the firm's does not have a clear decarbonization strategy and changes its attitude towards the phenomenon decarbonization over time, geography or product segments Expressions that the firm sometimes seeks value creation from decarbonization, while other times it perceives decarbonization as a threat for value destruction
Statements describing how workforce is not knowledgeable about decarbonization and its role and meaning for the business/the firm
Ambiguity about challenge or chance
Attitude toward decarbonization
References that CO_2 is deeply integrated into a firm's culture and employees are naturally used to considering CO_2 in various processes
Statements referring to CO_2 as a relevant KPI in portfolio adaptation and innovation processes, to be improved with each new product
Desire for CO_2 to be considered throughout the entire strategic decision-making process, e.g., via the presence of managers from specific departments or similar representation of economic and environmental information in a firm's balanced scorecard or other decision tools
Presence of environmental information
Statements about assigning a designated budget to all decarbonization investments
References that budget is set according to list of required decarbonization measures
Designated CapEx
Statements regarding an artificial figure/numerical strategy based on current or future prices for carbon or energy to account for decarbonization in decision-making
Desire for making decarbonization impact quantifiable and comparable to financials
Artificial CO_2 price
References to a lack of a system or standard how CO_2 is considered in strategic decisions and that CO_2 is rather considered spontaneously and differently for each strategic decision
Statements about consideration of CO_2 after strategic decision has been made
No integration
Strategy for integration of CO_2

3.7.3 Appendix C. Selected case-based evidence

Aggregate dimension: Intrinsic goals	
2nd-order codes	Selected evidence on 1st-order codes
Transgenerational value	"It is important to build the company sustainably, that we make it future-proof, and we do this for future family generations." (*Delta*) "It is important that the focus is on the family business that we build up this family business sustainably, that we build it up for the future and position ourselves in such a way, also that we do it for the next generations." (*Epsilon*)
Family reputation	"Yes, the issue of sustainability has always been very important to the family, which has always actually been there to act as a very responsible company, and there we refer to this concept of the ordinary businessman." (*Zeta*) "but we are really concerned about our impact as a company, what carbon footprint we leave behind, we would like to keep that as low as possible, because we would like to do all which is in our power for climate protection." (*Alpha*)
Power & control	"And that we also manage to keep up this momentum, so that we don't get left behind, I would say, because we've come so far as pioneers and so much is happening now, and I think it's important that we keep on track and continue to implement it as well as we have so far." (*Delta)* "So in this respect, we already have the claim to be number one. That's not just size, but we want to, we invest a lot in technology. We want to be sustainable because casting has been around for 5,000 years and without that technology, men will not be able to sustain the way of living on earth right now." (*Kappa*)

(continued)

(continued)

Enduring ties	"Two main factors: One came from within, namely employees and the management team. I would say that our employees have a very strong penchant for sustainability issues in general. I would even go so far as to say that most of them live or want to live very sustainably." (*Eta*) "In terms of the environment, there are very high expectations from the neighborhood, which need to be seen and considered." (*Gamma*)
Aggregate dimension: Extrinsic goals	
2nd-order codes	Selected evidence on 1st-order codes
Client demand	"So, we have to make the product carbon neutral and with that we have noticed very clearly in the last two years that there was a lot of pressure from outside that we have to move, and that is, I think, within the consumer goods industries or products especially strong." (*Zeta*) "because for the last year and a half, they've all been coming around the corner with their questionnaires... and if you can also show corresponding certifications, then you definitely have plus points." (*Theta*)
Regulatory institutions	"If we, as a small business, wait now until the regulation does apply to us and everyone is sharp, then we will be too late. And then we will no longer be able to catch up. That means we always have to be a little bit ahead of the wave." (*Jota*) "Yes, that, one does not come to it like the virgin to the child, but is yes already in such a way, that the topic has rolled over us in the last 2 years actually by the legislation and by the requirements, which come then, so that one is also forced." (*Lambda*)
Competitive advantage	"But of course, so for us sustainability is a big, a competitive factor." (*Delta*) "We partly leave the biggest, big stock companies behind us—and that's a USP for us." (*Jota*)

(continued)

(continued)

Aggregate dimension: Attitude toward decarbonization	
2nd-order codes	Selected evidence on 1st-order codes
Entrepreneurial opportunity	"We have been doing this for 25 years by now, even if it was sometimes unpleasant, some stories were sometimes more effort, that was worth it in the end. What many companies are upset about right now, we've have mastered for a long time." (*Beta*) "that's the beauty of it, that if we, if we find value creation that can make an ecological contribution on top of it." (*Gamma*)
Competitive chance	"If one can shine with Scope 3, which is something that many suppliers do not have on the agenda yet, this serves as an advantage on the market." (*Jota*) "I think the big opportunity we see now is that all the black sheep will be forced out of the market and in the other countries, where you might think environmental protection has never played a role, they will now take huge steps to do so as well. And then, of course, our technological leadership helps...with technologically leading products, where we help customers to achieve CO_2 neutrality." (*Lambda*)
Inevitable truth	"We realize that progress in sustainability is also in the interest of the consumer and legal requirements and that making progress is nothing that can be done at the side without asking some bigger questions. The low-hanging fruits have been collected, the quick fixes have been fixed and now we have reached a stage where we have to ask ourselves the question of how to allocate our capital. Otherwise, it will be difficult to progress." (*Zeta*) "Yes, we have also come to the conclusion that we should and must take responsibility for our own activities." (*Alpha*)

(continued)

(continued)

Ambiguity about challenge or chance	"So, if at some point in five years it turns out that the firm's product does not comply with the practices of sustainability, then it will very strongly and seriously reduce the market value, but then also represent a breach of trust. This is value protection, and we agree on that. Value creation in the sense of a clear USP or unique selling proposition, also vis-à-vis competitors. We are not yet in agreement on that. However, this will probably be viewed in a more differentiated way in the business unit or portfolio segments." (*Eta*) "That was the Green Deal once, that was also the trigger, why I said, I have to raise my hand here for a moment, something is happening here ... But the second is also things like taxonomy. Yes, the taxonomy regulation. Green bonds, yes, advantageous criteria to get and so on." (*Kappa*)
Aggregate dimension: Strategy for integration of CO_2	
2nd-order codes	Selected evidence on 1st-order codes
Presence of environmental information (incl. innovation)	"Sustainability is integrated into all processes, so that the sustainability manager is always involved in upcoming topics, e.g. new product development or packaging." (*Epsilon*) "The new product needs to have a better footprint than the previous one. Over time, you see how much you can get out of it in numbers." (*Delta*) "There are corporate performance indicators that are included in the balanced scorecard. There we have in a classical way anyway 4 dimensions. There are finances, processes, personnel and or what it's called, I think potential and what's the fourth one called? I can't think of it right now, and we've added a fifth dimension, namely energy and environment." (*Theta*)

(continued)

(continued)

Designated CapEx	"Okay, so the decision-making process: We look at which measures are needed to get the CO_2 footprint controlled and they are financed." (*Jota*) "We always have 10 to 20 million capital expenditures per year... 15–20% always ESG investments, …they bring us really forward in the environmental ... we can invest the cash flow sensibly, and for decades there has always been something going into ESG, in particular environmental protection." (*Lambda*)
Artificial CO_2 price	"We will set a price once a year and then apply it for the economic efficiency calculations of investments." (*Zeta*) "That means that the responsible managing directors now also have a cost factor. This is the only way how they can calculate that if I invest in something that incurs less CO_2, then I will have a positive effect and save money. So, that means that many things can be calculated." (*Alpha*)
No integration	"It is measured subsequently and then reduction measures are derived accordingly. But the decision we make is not based on CO_2 at the highest level." (*Eta*) "That is different from product to product. We have to look in detail." (*Kappa*)

4 Reporting of Sustainability Information Under the CSRD

Multiple Case Study Analysis on the Consequences of Mandatory Sustainability Reporting in Private German Family Firms

Ralf Ebner and Alexandra Knoth

This chapter explores the consequences of the Corporate Social Responsibility Reporting Directive (CSRD) on family firms. The European Commission (EC) extends under the CSRD the number of reporting companies from approximately 12,000 to 50,000, with the greatest increase in Germany. For 2025, around 13,000 German private family firms must disclose a sustainability report for the first time. Preparing a sustainability report that meets the requirements of the CSRD involves its own consequences. Based on a multiple case study of ten German private family firms, we develop a framework that illustrates implementation challenges and provides guidance to unlock business opportunities. Building on family business research, we contribute to the literature by differentiating family firms based on their sustainability strategy and maturity of sustainability reporting. This allows us to derive three archetypes facing varying implementation challenges. The analysis reveals direct and indirect opportunities along a firm's value chain. After introducing a reporting process, all archetypes can benefit from

This chapter has been accepted and presented at the 18th EIASM Workshop on Family Firm Management Research in Naples, Italy in 10/2023.

R. Ebner · A. Knoth (✉)
TUM School of Management, Technical University of Munich, Munich, Germany
e-mail: alexandraknoth@gmail.com

R. Ebner
e-mail: ralf.ebner@volkswagen.de

G. Friedl (ed.), *Decarbonizing German Family Firms*, Familienunternehmen und KMU, https://doi.org/10.1007/978-3-658-47801-8_4

direct opportunities, whereas a proactive sustainability strategy needs to unlock indirect opportunities.

4.1 Introduction

> *"Without a sense of purpose, no company, either public or private, can achieve its full potential. It will ultimately lose the license to operate from key stakeholders."*
>
> Larry Fink, CEO of BlackRock (Forbes, 2018)

The continuous rise and record high of global carbon dioxide (CO_2) emissions in 2022 (World Economic Forum, 2023), the growing development of social inequality across countries (The Economist, 2023) or the increased fossil-fuel extraction due to the invasion of Ukraine has accelerated the importance of how to improve sustainable performance among corporate stakeholders (Pérez et al., 2022). Companies' actions and their linked externalities have considerable effects on sustainability issues, governments impose rules and use regulatory instruments like reporting directives to modify economic behavior (Christensen et al., 2021; Pérez et al., 2022). Organizations that fail to comply will face penalties (DiMaggio & Powell, 1983) or may even lose their license to operate (Gunningham et al., 2003).

The regulatory landscape on sustainability led to a "wave of regulation" in the European Union (EU) (Lykkesfeldt & Kjaergaard, 2022). The membership of all EU Member States (MS) in the United Nations influences the development of sustainability legislation in the EU (United Nations, 2007). Several cooperations arise from this alliance, including the field of sustainable development. Especially the binding 2030 Agenda for Sustainable Development and the Paris Agreement transformed the sense of purpose for sustainable change and climate action around the globe (Bauer et al., 2021; Olsen et al., 2019). To implement the agreed goals of the United Nations and transmit this purpose to the EU, the European Commission (EC) published the European Green Deal in 2019 (European Commission, 2019). Its implementation and, thus EU's sustainability transition requires one trillion euros (European Commission, 2020). To facilitate financing and direct investment decisions into sustainable funds, the EU taxonomy calls for the disclosure of sustainability information from public companies that fall under the Non-Financial Reporting Directive (NFRD) (Action 9, COM (2018) 97 final) (European Commission, 2018). In 2018, the NFRD was the EU's starting point for mandatory sustainability reporting (Hummel & Jobst, 2021). In 2022, the Corporate Sustainability Reporting Directive (CSRD) succeeds the NFRD

(European Commission, 2022a). The most drastic change relates to the extended company scope, which will apply from 2025 (Art. 5, CSRD) (European Union, 2022) and increases the number of reporting companies regardless of their capital market orientation from 12,000 to 50,000, with a much larger increase in Germany (Baumüller & Grbenic, 2021).

German reporting companies increased from 500 to 15,000 (DIHK, 2023). The resulting delta of 14,500 corresponds to the number of companies required to disclose a sustainability report according to EU guidelines for the first time. Among them, around 88% are private family firms since this is the share of companies privately owned by families in Germany (Stiftung Familienunternehmen, 2023a). The former German Federal Ministry for Economic Affairs and Climate Action further underlines the importance of family firms: "*Our economic model is based on medium-sized, family-owned firms. Quite appropriately, they are described as the "engine" of our national economy*" (Handelsblatt, 2019).

Research on mandatory sustainability reporting has shown that first-time reporting companies (Hoffmann et al., 2018; Pedersen et al., 2013) and private small and medium-sized enterprises (SMEs) (Campopiano & Massis, 2015; Parker et al., 2009) have difficulties in implementing a sustainability reporting mandate. Hoffmann et al. (2018) analyzed the change from voluntary to mandatory non-financial reporting in German companies based on the NFRD. They concluded that introducing a reporting mandate led to decreased reporting quality due to the number of new reporters, indicating implementation challenges. Private SMEs have obstacles to coping with a reporting mandate, as they have little experience with norm-based sustainability reporting due to missing pressure from financial markets (Campopiano & Massis, 2015) or limited financial resources (Parker et al., 2009). Specifically, family firms differ in their sustainability disclosure behavior due to their socioemotional wealth (SEW) (Arena & Michelon, 2018; Aureli et al., 2020; Biswas et al., 2019; Campopiano & Massis, 2015; Gavana et al., 2017; Terlaak et al., 2018; Venturelli et al., 2021). Losing the license to operate for a family firm would hurt its SEW, as one key goal of families is passing the business to future generations (Berrone et al., 2012; Zellweger et al., 2010). However, research on voluntary sustainability reporting has shown that such a report and the underlying processes can also serve as an opportunity.

It is difficult for those firms to learn from research or previous lessons learned since the consequences of integrating a sustainability reporting mandate are highly context specific (Gulenko, 2018). Both in terms of institutions' motivation to impose a sustainability reporting mandate (Christensen et al., 2021) and the firm-specific context (Micco et al., 2021). Thus, we cannot extrapolate the findings on the research of listed companies under the NFRD (Fiechter et al., 2022; Ottenstein et al., 2022) to the effects of the new CSRD. Beyond that, research on family firms' sustainability reporting refers only to voluntary reporting in listed firms (Arena & Michelon, 2018; Gavana et al., 2017; Terlaak et al., 2018).

Given the importance of family firms for the German economy, the motivation of our study is to build an inductive framework for German private family firms (PFF) that shows the potential challenges and opportunities of implementing a sustainability reporting mandate based on the new CSRD. Thus, our chapter analyzes the following research question: *What challenges do private family firms face regarding the introduction of a sustainability reporting mandate, and how can a standard framework provide guidance to meet or even exceed the legal requirements and unlock business opportunities?*

To answer the research question, we conducted an exploratory, inductive qualitative study with multiple cases (Eisenhardt, 1989; Yin, 2018). Our study is based on the theoretical sampling approach (Glaser & Strauss, 1967). The sample selection criteria include (1) German PFF, (2) family ownership of at least 50%, and (3) the firm's operation in the business-to-business (B2B) market. The final sample consists of ten PFF from seven industries. As a primary data source, we interviewed one sustainability expert or board member in each case of our sample. The data analysis relied on the inductive method of Gioia et al. (2013). The resulting data structure of the within- and cross-case analysis formed the basis for creating an inductive framework. We confirmed our findings by a sustainability expert from a sustainability expert from a leading advisory firm. The chapter refers to the status quo of family firms' heterogeneous sustainability strategies as a theoretical basis. Thus, our analysis relies on the SEW concept (Gómez-Mejía et al., 2007) to explain the unique behavior of family firms, in addition to Lee's (2011) theoretical framework combining institutional and stakeholder theory. Lee's configurational concept, which is also a proven approach in family business research (Hsueh et al., 2023), helps to classify the cases according to their sustainability strategy as a response to a sustainability reporting mandate.

Our findings and the derived framework show theoretical and practical relevance. First, we contribute to research of family firm's heterogenous sustainability strategy (Campopiano & Massis, 2015; Cennamo et al., 2012; Déniz, María de la Cruz Déniz & Suárez, 2005; Hsueh et al., 2023; Sharma & Sharma, 2011) and reporting behavior (Arena & Michelon, 2018; Aureli et al., 2020; Biswas et al., 2019; Campopiano & Massis, 2015; Gavana et al., 2017; Terlaak et al., 2018; Venturelli et al., 2021). Going beyond existing findings, we differentiate family firms based on their sustainability strategy and maturity of sustainability reporting. This allowed us to derive three PFF archetypes (i.e., conservative sustainability denier, cautious first-time reporter, visionary early adopter) that face varying degrees of the identified sustainability reporting implementation challenges. Regarding the second part of our research question, we identified direct and indirect or "locked" opportunities in different business functions. Irrespective of the archetype, all firms can benefit from direct opportunities (e.g., process transparency) that arise after the introduction of a reporting process. In contrast, the indirect opportunities (e.g., product innovation) need to be unlocked through a proactive sustainability strategy. Hence, our study contributes to the knowledge about how configurations of SEW and external influences (i.e., the imposition of a sustainability reporting mandate, including stakeholders' expectations for meeting these legal requirements), shape family firms' sustainability strategy. We show that PFFs' sustainability strategy indicates the type and degree of reporting challenges and the possibility of gaining a more comprehensive set of opportunities. Second, we extend the literature on the impact of mandatory sustainability reporting in general (Christensen et al., 2021; Ioannou & Serafeim, 2017) and on the EU's disclosure directives in particular (Fiechter et al., 2022; Ottenstein et al., 2022), as our findings contribute to the sparse research on the CSRD. Our framework highlights the challenges and opportunities associated with the new directive. Therefore, our framework also highlights practical implications for family and non-family firms by supporting them on their path to preparing for one of the most pivotal milestones of sustainability reporting[1] in the EU.

Our study encompasses five further chapters, starting with the theoretical background. We provide a brief overview of research on family firms' sustainability strategy and reporting behavior, followed by the theory of Lee (2011). An outline of the EU sustainability disclosure directives, including the status quo on their impact, continues stressing the need for building theory in this field. Chapter three explains the methodological approach for our inductive framework, which is illustrated and described in chapter four. The fifth chapter discusses our results, which will be concluded in chapter six.

[1] This chapter refers to the term "sustainability reporting", which aligns with the CSRD. Previous studies often use the term "non-financial reporting", which refers to the predecessor, the NFRD. Due to the vagueness of the term "non-financial," the EC changed the name with the amendment of the new directive (Baumüller & Grbenic, 2021).

4.2 Theoretical Background

4.2.1 Definitional Dilemma and Family Firms' Heterogenous Behavior

Academia's interest in family firms is constantly increasing (Pieper, 2010), which is underlined by the fact that over 70% of the world's gross domestic product is generated by family firms (UNCTAD, 2021). Despite this high momentum, the ambiguity of the term "family firm" confronts researchers with a definitional dilemma (Brockhaus, 2004; Lansberg, 1988). There is no consensus among the concepts to define family firms (Harms, 2014). For this reason, Chrisman, Chua & Sharma (2005) recommend focusing on a particular definition before proceeding with research. Although a family's involvement in the firm through management or ownership appears to be the most evident characteristic, the real essence of a family firm is rather captured by its specific behavior and corresponding vision (Chua et al., 1999). Hence, Chua et al. (1999, p. 25) developed a definition that considers both the family's involvement and the family firm's essence:

> *"The family business is a business governed and/or managed with the intention to shape and pursue the vision of the business held by a dominant coalition controlled by members of the same family or a small number of families in a manner that is potentially sustainable across generations of the family or families."*

The dominant coalition of a family firm is composed of family members, or a mix of family and non-family members nominated by the controlling family, ensuring the family's influence in determining members' composition and the business strategy (Chua et al., 1999; Sharma & Sharma, 2011). Therefore, family members mostly hold top management positions or sit on the board (Chen et al., 2008). As we analyze family firm-specific consequences induced by a sustainability reporting mandate that aims to change a firm's behavior (Christensen et al., 2021), it was reasonable for this chapter to choose a definition based on a behavioral approach. In this vein, the SEW concept (Gómez-Mejía et al., 2007), which extends the behavioral agency theory (Gómez-Mejia et al., 2000; Wiseman & Gomez-Mejia, 1998), has become the key differentiating factor for family firms (Berrone et al., 2012). The initial behavioral agency theory assumes that a firm's dominant principals make choices based on their reference point to preserve accumulated endowment. In contrast, the SEW concept is based on the notion that family principals instead care about their socioemotional endowment or wealth, which captures non-economic utilities like the enjoyment of family influence (Berrone et al., 2012; Berrone et al., 2010; Gómez-Mejía et al., 2007). Hence, for any issue that could negatively impact the SEW, such as introducing a sustainability reporting mandate, a family principal is even willing to bear financial losses or put the business at risk to preserve its SEW (Berrone et al., 2012; Berrone et al., 2010; Gómez-Mejía et al., 2007). Consequently, family firms pursue a set of economic and non-economic goals (Berrone et al., 2010; Kotlar & Massis, 2013) with a higher risk aversion to SEW (Berrone et al., 2012a).

However, as emotions vary within the family of the controlling firm (Berrone et al., 2012; Hoy & Sharma, 2010), SEW as a psychologically anchored concept (Berrone et al., 2010) implies heterogeneity in family principals' reference frames and, therefore also in family firms' behavior (Cennamo et al., 2012). Going one step further, as emotions emerge from situation-specific activity (Pugh et al., 2022), looking from a socioemotional lens would therefore mean that family firms' behavior also depends on its specific context (Lumpkin et al., 2011; Wright et al., 2014). Within family business research, Wright et al. (2014) distinguish between an organizational context, which refers to internal firm factors like goals or governance, and an institutional context, which refers to external political and legal institutions. Given the fact that stakeholders are defined as "*any group or individual who can affect or is affected by the achievement of the organization's objectives*" (Freeman, 1984), including governmental officials (Gómez-Mejia et al., 2011), these external institutions (Wright et al., 2014) can be attributed to family firms' major stakeholder group. Family firms are more responsive to external stakeholders (Cennamo et al., 2012; Gómez-Mejia et al., 2011), especially regarding sustainability demands (Vardaman & Gondo, 2014). Therefore, how would PFFs respond to an external demand from an institution such as the EC to disclose a sustainability report?

Considering this context-affected and heterogeneous behavior within the SEW framework, researchers developed sub-dimensions of SEW (Berrone et al., 2012; Venturelli et al., 2021). These dimensions serve as instruments to measure and validate the belief that non-economic goals can lead to positive performance outcomes (Berrone et al., 2012). Berrone et al. (2012) refer in their model to five dimensions which were condensed into the FIBER acronym that includes (1) ***f****amily control and influence*, (2) ***i****dentification of family members with the firm*, (3) ***b****inding social ties*, (4) ***e****motional attachment*, and the (5) ***r****enewal of family bonds to the firm through dynastic succession*. Family firms prioritize these dimensions differently, which results in company-specific behavior (Berrone et al., 2012). The isolated consideration of these dimensions allows to derive characteristics of family firms. For instance, (1) *family control and influence* are exerted over the dominant family coalition (Berrone et al., 2012) and desired by family members (Zellweger et al., 2012). The main derived attribute is family members' preservation of control over strategic decisions (Chua et al., 1999) and day-to-day operations (Vardaman & Gondo, 2014). (2) *Identification of family members with the firm* describes the strong connection between the family and the firm (Berrone et al., 2012) that results in one unique identity (Berrone et al., 2010). This is mainly due to the frequent coincidence of family and firm names, which is also a reason why stakeholders perceive the family and the firm as one entity (Berrone et al., 2012). (3) *Binding social ties* refer to a family firm's social relationships (Berrone et al., 2012). The existing social bonds and inclusion within the family can also extend to non-family members and thus promote commitments to the firm (Miller & Le Breton-Miller, 2005). (4) *Emotional attachment* between the family and the firm is vital due to familial intergenerational relationships and the underlying history (Felden et al., 2016). (5) *Family bonds to the firm through dynastic succession* emphasize the goal of passing the business to future generations (Zellweger et al., 2012). This sense of dynasty implies a long-term planning horizon (Berrone et al., 2012; Miller & Le Breton-Miller, 2006).

Another multidimensional model that supports the approach of Berrone et al. (2012) was developed by Vardaman & Gondo (2014). Their model is based on the hypothesis that family firms face conflicts or trade-offs between different SEW dimensions. They cluster SEW into an internal dimension, the desire to retain control and influence, and into an external dimension, the preservation of the firm's image and reputation. The key between those elements is that family principals use internal SEW as the default reference point but switch to external SEW if an event harms the firm's reputation or identity (Vardaman & Gondo, 2014).

In conclusion, our study focuses on the upcoming CSRD imposed by the EC. Translated into a theoretical context, this would correspond to sustainability demands from external stakeholders in an institutional context. The aim is to analyze PFF's potential challenges and opportunities when pushed into this setting. As combinations of SEW dimensions together with specific contexts are responsible for family firms' heterogeneous behavior, (Agostino & Ruberto, 2021) call for empirical evidence, as these heterogeneous behaviors make it ambiguous how family firms would respond to sustainability regulations. Also, Gómez-Mejía et al. (2011) support further research in this area, as references to stakeholders in family business research are often indirect and simplistic. Finally, to provide nuanced considerations, the following chapters refer to the FIBER model (Berrone et al., 2012) and the internal and external SEW perspectives of Vardaman and Gondo (2014).

4.2.2 Family Firms' Heterogenous Sustainability Strategy and Reporting Behavior

4.2.2.1 Family Firms' Proactive and Reactive Sustainability Strategy

A sustainability strategy helps us to determine how family firms behave towards external demands (e.g., sustainability reporting mandate) because a sustainability strategy is a construct in response to external influences, which consists of stakeholders including institutions (Lee, 2011). In the case of family firms, decision makers' interpretation of external influences is guided by salience (Vardaman & Gondo, 2014) or configurations (Hsueh et al., 2023) of SEW dimensions. At this point, it is essential to consider Vardaman and Gondo's (2014) reasoning about the family firm's default script. According to their concept, family firms prioritize preserving SEW dimensions related to external stakeholders. In this vein, the literature refers to the second (*identification of family members with the firm),* third (*binding social ties*), and fifth (*renewal of family bonds to the firm through dynastic succession*) SEW dimension (Cennamo et al., 2012; Hsueh et al., 2023; Vardaman & Gondo, 2014). Nevertheless, Cennamo et al. (2012) add that the rationale for prioritizing external stakeholders is only valid when family firm decision-makers consider at least one of the dimensions mentioned above as their primary reference point. If this is the case, family firms respond to their external stakeholders proactively (Cennamo et al., 2012) and in the context of sustainability with a formalized sustainability strategy (Hsueh et al., 2023). If not, family firms respond reactively to incoming (sustainability) demands (Cennamo et al., 2012). The motivation behind family firms' proactive stakeholder engagement and the underlying prioritization of SEW dimensions are manifold.

First, the strong *(2) identification of family members with the firm,* and stakeholders' perception of the family and the firm as a single entity increases the family's concern about their externally perceived image (Micelotta & Raynard, 2011). Thus, family members' identity with the firm links the family's reputation with the company's survival (Anderson et al., 2002). Consequently, reputational threats to the family are perceived as a risk to the identity and the existence of the family itself (Zellweger et al., 2010). Therefore, a proactive stakeholder approach serves not only as a preservation but also as an improvement of reputation combined with the gain of legitimacy, i.e., seeking social acceptance and credibility (Cennamo et al., 2012; Gómez-Mejia et al., 2011; Hsueh et al., 2023; Suchman, 1995).

Second, family firms with a reference point dominated by (3) *binding social ties* engage proactively with stakeholders to develop social capital (Carney, 2005;

Cennamo et al., 2012). Social capital relates to stakeholder management (Cennamo et al., 2012; Rowley, 1997) and is a source of wealth for the family (Gavana et al., 2017). Hence, family firms seek social capital to enhance their relationship with external stakeholders (Sirmon & Hitt, 2003), to enable partnerships with different sectors (Boehm, 2005), or facilitate the implementation of external norms (J. W. Meyer & Rowan, 1977).

Third, instead of a single salient SEW dimension, the copresence of the (2) *identification of family members with the firm* and the (5) *renewal of family bonds to the firm through dynastic succession* leads to a formalized sustainability strategy (Hsueh et al., 2023). It relates to a proactive sustainability strategy in family business research (Campopiano & Massis, 2015; Déniz, María de la Cruz Déniz & Suárez, 2005; Sharma & Sharma, 2011). Families with a configuration of both dimensions are forward-looking, as they want to transfer their business to the next generations (Berrone et al., 2012) and develop a positive identity in the future (Hsueh et al., 2023). Hence, family firms pursue a proactive sustainability strategy to reduce information asymmetries with external stakeholders by formally communicating sustainability information (Campopiano & Massis, 2015; Terlaak et al., 2018).

As a result, in case of external sustainability demands, family firms either respond with a proactive or reactive sustainability strategy (Campopiano & Massis, 2015; Déniz, María de la Cruz Déniz & Suárez, 2005; Hsueh et al., 2023; Sharma & Sharma, 2011). There is no consensus on which type of strategy is more prevalent (Hsueh et al., 2023). The nomenclature of a proactive or reactive sustainability strategy is not consistent within family business literature, but the definitions of both strategies share common features.

In family business research, a sustainability strategy that is proactive, as Sharma and Sharma (2011) call it, is also defined as formal (Hsueh et al., 2023), philanthropic (Déniz, María de la Cruz Déniz & Suárez, 2005), or explicit (Campopiano & Massis, 2015) (see Fig. 4.1). Independently of its specific name, pursuing such a strategic approach is a voluntary decision by the family. Therefore, it captures the characteristic of going beyond expectations or regulatory requirements (Campopiano & Massis, 2015; Déniz, María de la Cruz Déniz & Suárez, 2005; Hsueh et al., 2023; Sharma & Sharma, 2011). Further common features include the firm's communication of its sustainability activities to stakeholders in addition to intrinsic social values by the family firm's management (Campopiano & Massis, 2015; Déniz, María de la Cruz Déniz & Suárez, 2005; Hsueh et al., 2023; Sharma & Sharma, 2011). Moreover, Déniz María de la Cruz Déniz and Suárez (2005) figured out that a higher number of generational successions characterize family firms in the philanthropic group. This finding is in line

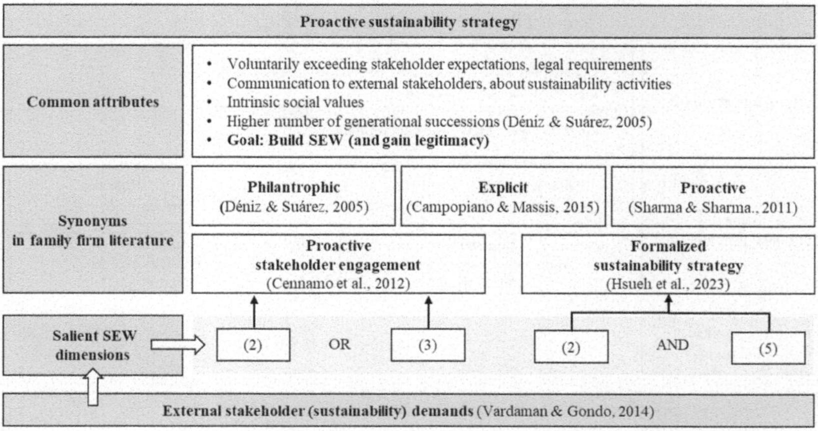

Fig. 4.1 Family firms' proactive sustainability strategy. *Note:* SEW dimensions (2) identification of family members with the firm; (3) binding social ties; (5) renewal of family bonds to the firm through dynastic succession
Source Own figure

with the observation of Hsueh et al. (2023) to follow a proactive sustainability approach.

In contrast, a sustainability strategy that is reactive (Sharma & Sharma, 2011) is described as informal (Hsueh, 2023), socioeconomic (Déniz, María de la Cruz Déniz & Suárez, 2005), or implicit (Campopiano & Massis, 2015) (see Fig. 4.2). The main commonality is to comply with the legal requirements and thus to stay within the "rules of the game" (Déniz, María de la Cruz Déniz & Suárez, 2005; North, 1990). Another shared characteristic of all reactive typologies is the family firm owner's limited sustainability knowledge (Fassin et al., 2011). Beyond that, Déniz María de la Cruz Déniz and Suárez (2005) conclude that family firms in the socioeconomic group have a limited commitment to sustainability due to their smaller size (i.e., turnover and headcount) and resulting limited access to resources. Ultimately, family firms that react reactively to external demands have the central premise of gaining legitimacy and thus preserving their SEW (Berrone et al., 2010; Gómez-Mejia et al., 2011).

As illustrated in Figs. 4.1 and 4.2, family firms' sustainability strategies are heterogeneous due to different priorities (Cennamo et al., 2012; Vardaman & Gondo, 2014) or configurations (Hsueh et al., 2023) of SEW dimensions. The critical differentiator between a proactive and reactive approaches lies in the fact

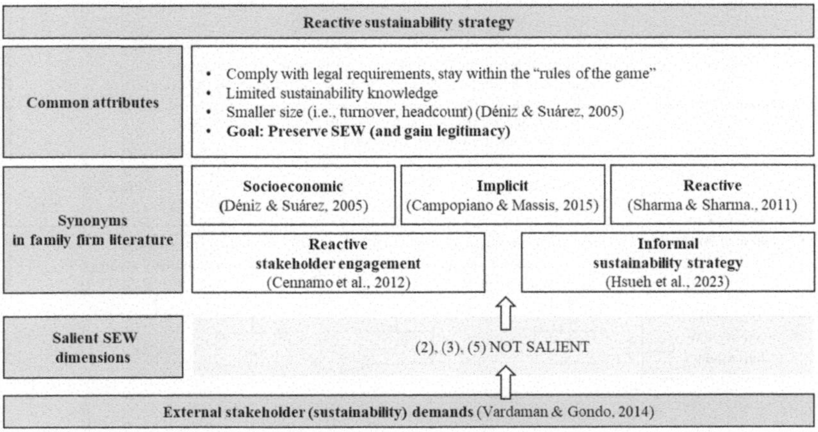

Fig. 4.2 Family firms' reactive sustainability strategy. *Source* Own figure

that family firms with a proactive strategy are more likely to build SEW instead of maintaining it. In contrast, the main commonality lies in the achievement of legitimacy.

4.2.2.2 Family Firms' Sustainability Reporting Behavior

Regardless of whether a family firm is pursuing a reactive or proactive sustainability strategy, external stakeholders should recognize that their sustainability demands have been implemented (Gavana et al., 2017). Therefore, firms go into a dialog with their stakeholders (Gray et al., 1995) and use the governance practice of sustainability reporting (Venturelli et al., 2021) as a tool to communicate their sustainable actions (Campbell, 2004; Venturelli et al., 2021). In this context, communication is the key to recognizing a firm's legitimacy by its stakeholders (Gavana et al., 2017). At this point, it is essential to mention that the current literature on sustainability reporting in family firms refers either to voluntary reporting (Campopiano & Massis, 2015; Venturelli et al., 2021), to publicly listed firms (Aureli et al., 2020; Biswas et al., 2019), or to both (Arena & Michelon, 2018; Gavana et al., 2017; Terlaak et al., 2018). Internationally, the regulations on mandatory sustainability reporting have referred so far to publicly listed companies (Jiang et al., 2023). In the EU, for example, private companies are only affected by a sustainability reporting mandate through the extension of the company scope by the CSRD in 2025 (Lange-Snijders, 2023). Hence, for our research purpose, it is not ideal to derive characteristics of the behavior of voluntary sustainability reporting from publicly listed family firms for three reasons. First, the public status of listed family firms leads to pressure from capital markets, impacting governance practices (Carney et al., 2015). Shareholders' demand for high short-term returns and risk-taking distances public firms from family values such as non-economic goals (Kotlar & Massis, 2013) or long-term orientation, which usually implies sustainable behavior (Miller et al., 2009). Second, according to Jiang et al. (2023), almost all publicly listed firms publish sustainability reports besides their financial reports. In contrast, first-time reporting companies show a lower reporting quality, indicating implementation challenges (Hoffmann et al., 2018). Hence, considering reporting characteristics of more experienced publicly listed companies would not be beneficial either. Third, it is unfavorable to derive best practices from voluntary sustainability reporting due to its specific firm context (Arena & Michelon, 2018). This variability is particularly strong for family firms, as the decision on the reporting content lies at the discretion of family managers (Arena & Michelon, 2018). However, three of the mentioned studies (Aureli et al., 2020; Campopiano & Massis, 2015; Venturelli et al., 2021) overlap with the use case of mandatory sustainability reporting in PFF.

Aureli et al. (2020) indicate that introducing a sustainability reporting mandate encompasses both challenges and opportunities, supporting the necessity to further research both consequences. In their single case study, the authors conclude that the firm perceived the legal obligation of sustainability reporting as a requirement from multiple stakeholders (e.g., employees, local communities, family). However, within a year, the company changed its attitude towards sustainability reporting. Further opportunities were recognized from the initial pressure to comply with regulations and to gain legitimacy. Contrarily, Campopiano and Massis (2015) do not focus on mandatory sustainability reporting but examine the differences in voluntary disclosure of sustainable actions between family and non-family firms but also between private and listed companies. According to their analysis, the listing status and family's influence significantly impact the reporting behavior. For example, private, and listed family firms are less compliant with reporting standards and disclose less information on employee-related topics, but more on environmental issues than their non-family counterparts. Only private family firms tend to report more on their philanthropic activities (e.g., engagement with the local community, donations, sponsorship). Their findings underline the importance of distinguishing between family, and non-family-owned, but also between private and listed companies when analyzing corporate sustainability reporting. Also, Venturelli et al. (2021) indicate the specificity of sustainability reporting within private family firms. They investigated the impact of the first

SEW dimension on voluntary sustainability communication and practices in predominantly private SMEs. According to them, family involvement has a negative impact on voluntary sustainability communication due to the family's fear of disclosing confidential information that could harm their SEW. Thus, the authors support the argument that voluntary sustainability communication is less prevalent in (mainly private) family-run SMEs because of their lower regulatory and stakeholder pressure.

4.2.3 Sustainability Strategy—A Configuration of External Demands

A relevant theory for our research is Lee's (2008) framework, which uses a configurational approach and combines institutional with stakeholder theory. Specifically, family business research supports Lee's approach as a configurational perspective enriching the understanding of family firms' heterogeneous behavior (Hsueh et al., 2023). Lee (2011) states that a firm's sustainability strategy is a construct in response to the intensity and coherence of external influences that consists of institutions and stakeholders (Lee, 2011). The essence of his framework is that only the configuration of the two external influences can explain the intensity and coherence and, thus a firm's chosen sustainability strategy (Lee, 2011). This rationale also applies to family firms, as the absence of regulatory and stakeholder pressure reduces the motivation to communicate sustainability information (Venturelli et al., 2021) or use sustainability standards (Dyer & Whetten, 2006).

On the one hand, institutional theory assumes that institutions exert pressure on organizations to behave in certain ways and to achieve desired outcomes (DiMaggio & Powell, 1983). Hence, institutions are the "rules of the game" comprising formal written rules and informal, unwritten codes of conduct (North, 1990). In particular, formal institutions have the authority to monitor and enforce compliance (Webb et al., 2015), such as the EC with its CSRD. Compliance with rules leads to legitimacy (Suchman, 1995), which enables access to market opportunities (DiMaggio & Powell, 1983). Organizations that fail to comply face penalties (DiMaggio & Powell, 1983) or even lose their license to operate (Gunningham et al., 2003).

On the other hand, the stakeholder theory by Freeman (1984) embeds firms in a broad spectrum of social relations. Freeman (1984) characterizes it as "*groups and individuals who can affect the organization, and is about managerial behavior taken in response to those groups and individuals*" (p. 48). Therefore, firms must balance the interests of different stakeholders and manage their influences (Lee, 2011). Overall, both theories are interdependent and drive companies to respond to social demands (Lee, 2011). Consequently, Lee (2011) justifies his configurational approach with the fact that "*[...] stakeholders can mediate institutional effects by acting as either buffers or amplifiers of institutional influences. Institutions can also mediate stakeholder effects by legitimating or de-legitimating a stakeholder group's claim*" (p. 282). Firms scan their environment and pay attention to the external signal with the most vigorous intensity and coherence, leading to different responses and variable sustainability strategies (Lee, 2011). Lee (2011) differentiates between four strategic responses (see Fig. 4.3).

Obstructionist ("Reactive") sustainability strategy A strategy that results from a configuration of weak external influences. Companies see no incentive to engage in sustainability matters. Moreover, today's markets often force companies to compete on cost, preventing companies from engaging in costly social activities (Lee, 2011).

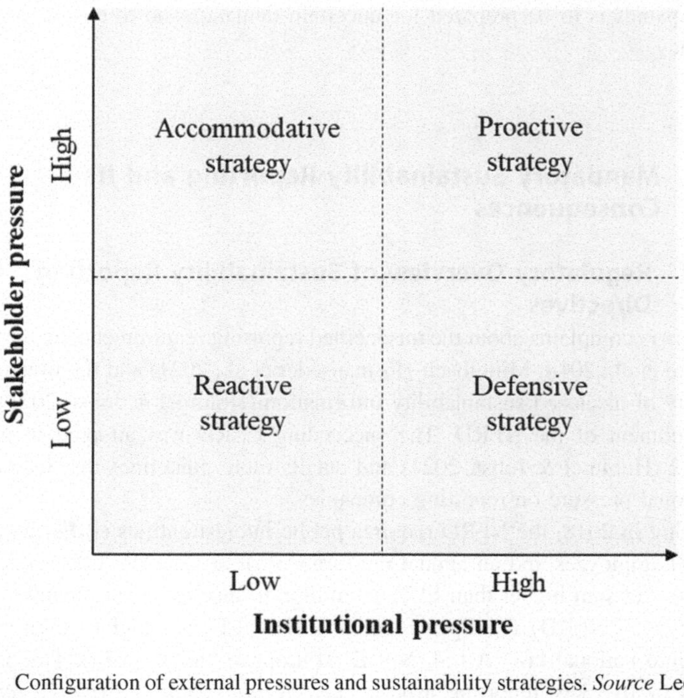

Fig. 4.3 Configuration of external pressures and sustainability strategies. *Source* Lee (2011)

The literature calls this approach also a reactive sustainability strategy (Bini & Bellucci, 2020).

Defensive sustainability strategy Firms follow a defensive approach when facing intense institutional but low stakeholder pressure. They will meet the legal requirements but not go beyond compliance. Hence, firms show no real commitment to sustainability (Lee, 2011).

Accommodative sustainability strategy A combination of weak institutional and high stakeholder pressure leads to an accommodative strategy. Companies are motivated to respond to specific stakeholders' sustainability demands to protect economic interests (Lee, 2011).

Proactive sustainability strategy The joint presence of high institutional and stakeholder pressure results from a proactive strategy (Lee, 2011). Firms surpass the minimum requirements and often integrate sustainability into the value-creation process (Bini & Bellucci, 2020). According to Lee (2011), the main incentive for companies is to be prepared for uncertain demands and to ensure continued legitimacy.

4.2.4 Mandatory Sustainability Reporting and its Consequences

4.2.4.1 Regulatory Overview of Sustainability Reporting Directives

Researchers complains about the unspecified reporting requirements by the NFRD (La Torre et al., 2018; Mittelbach-Hörmanseder et al., 2021) and the limited comparability of disclosed sustainability information (Hummel & Jobst, 2021) led to an amendment of the NFRD. The succeeding CSRD was adopted in November 2022 (Hummel & Jobst, 2021) and entails more guidelines that increase the institutional pressure on reporting companies.

Starting in 2018, the NFRD requires public-interest entities (PIEs) with more than 500 employees and an annual net turnover of at least EUR 40 million or a balance-sheet sum higher than EUR 20 million to disclose a sustainability report (Art. 1, 3, 4; NFRD) (European Union, 2014). EU MS had to transpose the NFRD into national law (Art. 4, NFRD) (European Union, 2014). The directive consists of five key reporting aspects, i.e., *(1) definition of PIE*, *(2) reporting content*, *(3) reporting framework*, *(4) disclosure format*, *(5) external audit*, that each MS can adapt (CSR Europe, Global Reporting Initiative, 2017). Germany almost identically transposed the NFRD by the Corporate Social Responsibility Directive Implementation Act (CSR-RUG) into commercial and corporate law in 2017 (Uwer & Schramm, 2018). The adjustments refer to the *(1) definition of PIE*, which in Germany corresponds to capital market-oriented companies (§ 264d HGB) in addition to insurance and credit institutions, and *(5) the external audit*, which remains voluntary (CSR Europe, Global Reporting Initiative, 2017). Regarding the (2) *reporting content* that aligns with the NFRD, German public firms must disclose general information about their business model and policies, including their outcomes, risks, and key performance indicators (KPIs) in relation to the environment, social and labor issues, human rights, anti-corruption, and bribery matters (Art., 1, NFRD) (European Union, 2014). The information should follow the "double materiality" principle. Thus, the report includes information that is of significance for an understanding of the firm's performance (outside-in) and the impact of its activities on the environment and society (inside-out) (European Parliament, 2021). The directive does not mandate a (3) *reporting framework* but recommends for instance the Global Reporting Initiative (GRI) standards (Recital 9, NFRD) (European Union, 2014). A comparable framework is the Deutscher Nachhaltigkeitskodex (DNK). The (4) *disclosure format* provides for integration into a company's management report or a publication in a separate report (Recital 6, NFRD) (European Union, 2014).

The amendments of the CSRD relate to all five reporting aspects, including a scope expansion of the covered companies. The expansion occurs in several phases, starting in 2024 for companies already subject to the NFRD (Art. 5, CSRD) (European Union, 2022). For research on private firms, it is essential to note that for the financial year 2025, large companies, regardless of their capital-market orientation, must disclose a sustainability report in 2026 (Art. 5, CSRD) (European Union, 2022). On top, the CSRD adjusts the definition of large companies, lowering the employee threshold to 250 (Art. 5, CSRD) (European Union, 2022). In comparison to the NFRD, the (2) *reporting content* (Recitals 30–36; Art. 1, CSRD) (European Union, 2022) must be structured according to the compulsory (3) *reporting framework*, i.e., European Sustainability Reporting Standards (ESRS). The ESRS is based on delegated acts adopted in several sequences (Hummel & Jobst, 2021). The final draft in November 2022 comprises two of three categories, i.e., cross-cutting standards (ESRS 1–2), topical standards regarding the environment (ESRS E1–E5), social (ESRS S1–S4), and governance (ESRS G1-G2), in addition to sector-specific standards, while the third standards are under development (EFRAG, 2022d). A mandatory sustainability report under the CSRD must report on ESRS 2 (general disclosures, strategy, governance, materiality), ESRS E1 (climate change), and ESRS S1 (own workforce). The concretized double materiality principle and the measurement of Scope 3 emissions are noticeable. According to the current ESRS draft, a topic is identified as material if it fulfills one of the two conditions, i.e., outside-in or inside-out (EFRAG, 2022a). Thus, the amount of information classified as material increases. ESRS E1 refers to the classification of greenhouse gas (GHG) emissions by the Greenhouse-Gas-Protocol and demands to disclose emission data on Scope 1 (i.e., direct emissions from firm-owned and controlled resources), Scope 2 (i.e., indirect emissions from the generation of purchased energy) and, Scope 3 (all indirect emissions along firm's value chain and not included in Scope 2 (EFRAG, 2022c). Especially the data collection for scope 3 emissions, which requires the involvement of suppliers, could be challenging (PwC, 2022). CSRD's *(4) disclosure format* requires the inclusion of sustainability information in the management report in an electronic format (Art. 1, CSRD) (European Union, 2022). Lastly, an (5) *external audit* also becomes mandatory (Recital 60, CSRD) (European Union, 2022). The transposition of the CSRD into German law is expected to last until mid-2024 (Ebner Stolz, 2022) (see Table 4.1). Thus, what might be the consequences for German PFF?

4.2.4.2 Twofold Hierarchy on the Consequences of Mandatory Sustainability Reporting

Introducing a sustainability reporting mandate aims to drive change (Christensen et al., 2021). The EC used the disclosure directives to initiate a change process that should result in higher transparency for investors (Ottenstein et al., 2022). In addition to lower firm externalities given the increased importance of double materiality (Christensen et al., 2021; Fiechter et al., 2022). As a result, firms make real changes to their business operations (Christensen et al., 2021). Thus, mandatory sustainability reporting drives organizational change (Garcia-Torea et al., 2023; Ioannou & Serafeim, 2017), which is challenging to manage (Kotter, 1996).

Nevertheless, if challenges are adequately addressed, they can turn into opportunities (Schaltegger et al., 2017). Particularly studies on voluntary sustainability reporting provide insights that companies experience benefits from producing a sustainability report (Gamerschlag et al., 2011; Ryou et al., 2022). However, this dual mission of creating sophisticated accountability mechanisms for sustainability reporting and deriving benefits from it is not straightforward (Nigri & Del Baldo, 2018). It is essential to distinguish between the challenges of integrating

Table 4.1 NFRD and CSRD in comparison

Reporting aspects	**NFRD** (EU directive)	**CSR-RUG** (German transposition)	**CSRD** (EU directive)	**CSR-RUG 2.0** (German transposition)
Definition of PIE / Company scope	Large PIEs with > 500 employees **and** > EUR 40 m net turnover **or** > EUR 20 m balance sheet sum + Credit/insurance institutions	Large public firms, with > 500 employees **and** > EUR 40 m net turnover **or** > EUR 20 m balance sheet sum + Credit/insurance institutions	Applies progressively **Category 2: Large (incl. private) undertakings meeting min. 2 criteria:** > 250 employees > EUR 40 m net turnover > EUR 20 m balance sheet sum	**Pending** (Release mid 2024)
Reporting content	Report on dimensions about matters		Reporting content according to ESRS • ESRS 2 (General disclosures, strategy, governance, (double) materiality • ESRS E1 (Climate change) • ESRS S1 (Own workforce)	
	Dimensions: • Business model • Policies • Outcomes of policy • Risks • KPIs	**Matters:** • Environment • Social & labor issues • Human rights • Anti-corruption & bribery		
Reporting framework	Voluntary choice (e.g., GRI, DNK)		ESRS	
Disclosure format	Annual report or separate report		Annual report in electronic format	

(continued)

Table 4.1 (continued)

Reporting aspects	**NFRD** (EU directive)	**CSR-RUG** (German transposition)	**CSRD** (EU directive)	**CSR-RUG 2.0** (German transposition)
External audit	Member states' decision	Voluntary	Mandatory	
Estimated number of reporting firms	~12,000	~500	~50,000	~15,000

Table 4.2 Case overview

Company	Industry	Founding year	Family generation	Family's role	Turnover[a] [EUR M]	Headcount[a] [#]	Sustainability report
Alpha	Forest products, paper & packaging	1895	5	Executive management	1,050	3,700	Yes
Beta	Forest products, paper & packaging	1807	8	Executive management	950	2,100	Yes
Gamma	Metals	1967	2	Executive management	90	850	No
Delta	Automotive & mobility	1901	6	Supervisory board	3,700	15,700	Yes
Epsilon	Automotive & mobility	1908	4	Executive management	5,300	25,000	Yes
Zeta	Industrial goods	1974	2	Executive management	65	750	In progress
Eta	Transportation & logistics	1946	3	Executive management	1,300	6,400	Yes
Theta	Forest products, paper & packaging	1961	2	Executive management	1,400	7,000	Yes

(continued)

Table 4.2 (continued)

Company	Industry	Founding year	Family generation	Family's role	Turnover[a] [EUR M]	Headcount[a] [#]	Sustainability report
Iota	Machinery & Equipment	1906	4	Supervisory board	2,200	5,400	Yes
Kappa	Software	1988	2	Executive management	101	600	No

[a]Rounded figures
Source. Own table

voluntary or mandatory sustainability reporting. Due to the induced external pressure, these real changes or "real effects" are more likely to result from a reporting mandate than voluntary disclosure (Christensen et al., 2021). After the financial crisis in 2007–09, many countries started to mandate the disclosure of sustainability information (Ioannou & Serafeim, 2017). In Germany, sustainability reporting only became binding ten years later through the CSR-RUG (Gulenko, 2018). Considering the national and institutional context when analyzing a sustainability reporting mandate's challenges and opportunities is crucial for two reasons (Christensen et al., 2021; Ferri, 2017; Gulenko, 2018).

First, institutions' motivation to force companies to publish sustainability reports varies. Thus, Christensen et al. (2021) distinguish between the narrow and broad regulatory approach, while the first aims to meet investors' need for sustainability information. Firms must disclose sustainability information showing the financial impact of sustainability issues on their business and are thus material to investors. In contrast, the broad approach follows the double materiality principle and aims to target the need for sustainability information of society as a whole. Therefore, disclosing a sustainability report based on the double materiality principle is even more challenging due to its diverse target group and varying sustainability knowledge (Christensen et al., 2021). It can be difficult for a company to write a report that is both easy to understand and sufficiently informative.

Second, the disclosure of sustainability information depends on the institution's domestic policy, culture, and religion (Ferri, 2017). Specifically, German society has developed an increased awareness of sustainability, marked by the rise of the Green Party. Besides the external context, the internal context also plays an important role. A few studies addressed Italian companies' challenges in implementing the NFRD but also stressed their high firm-specificity as a limitation (Aureli et al., 2020; Micco et al., 2021).

As a result, it is not ideal to extrapolate the consequences of implementing a sustainability reporting mandate from previous research. Due to the high specificity of our research context (i.e., German PFF), we searched for a context-independent systematization for the consequences of a sustainability reporting mandate. In this vein, we refer to the classification of first- and second-order consequences (Gulenko, 2018; Ioannou & Serafeim, 2017). Gulenko (2018) established a literature review on the consequences of mandatory sustainability reporting and sorted the studies according to the concept of first-and second-order consequences by Ioannou and Serafeim (2017). First-order consequences (FOC) refer to the direct results of a reporting mandate. In contrast, second-order consequences (SOC) include the results of changes in firms' reporting practices (Gulenko, 2018). In our study, these direct results, i.e., FOC, refer to the challenges a PFF must face due to a reporting mandate. Given that SOC are themselves consequences of FOC, we use the term SOC for opportunities that may arise from implementing a sustainability report.

4.2.5 Research Gap and Question

The research stream on the effects of a sustainability reporting mandate for companies in general (Christensen et al., 2021; Ioannou & Serafeim, 2017) and in particular with a focus on the NFRD (Aureli et al., 2020; Fiechter et al., 2022; Micco et al., 2021; Ottenstein et al., 2022), is evolving. In contrast, research on the effects of the new CSRD and its extended target group (i.e., private firms) is relatively scarce. Hence, Ottenstein et al. (2022) and Fiechter et al. (2022) call for research on the effects of the CSRD. Given the relevance of internal and external context combined with the reduced reporting quality in Germany due to the NFRD (Hoffmann et al., 2018), underlines the importance of focusing on the effects and, more specifically, on the challenges (i.e., FOC) and opportunities (i.e., SOC) in German PFFs.

Beyond this, Gulenko (2018) concludes that research on SOC, and especially on the link between FOC and SOC, are missing. She highlights that research on mandatory sustainability reporting could benefit from analyzing a firm's decision to adopt sustainability reporting in response to new regulations due to individuals' decision-making processes, organizational level, and external forces. This call builds the bridge to our second research stream on the organization of PFFs and their socioemotionally influenced decision to report on sustainability.

Current research on sustainability reporting in family firms focuses on voluntary reporting in listed companies (Arena & Michelon, 2018; Gavana et al., 2017; Terlaak et al., 2018). All mentioned studies focus on SEW dimensions that are easily accessible such as family ownership and control. Therefore, Arena and Michelon (2018) or Venturelli et al. (2021) call for research on sustainability reporting in private family firms that consider different SEW dimensions. For this purpose, Gavana et al. (2016) recommend using case studies.

Building on the heterogeneity of sustainability strategies at family firms (Campopiano & Massis, 2015; Déniz, María de la Cruz Déniz & Suárez, 2005; Hsueh et al., 2023; Sharma & Sharma, 2011) and Lee's (2011) model as a theoretical basis, we investigate PFF-specific challenges and opportunities. Our study focuses on the link between the effects of a sustainability reporting mandate and the theories on family firms' sustainability strategy. As a result, we explore the following research question: *What challenges do private family firms face regarding the introduction of a sustainability reporting mandate, and how can a standard framework provide guidance to meet or even exceed the legal requirements and unlock business opportunities?*

4.3 Methodology

4.3.1 Research Design and Sample Selection

We conducted an exploratory, inductive qualitative study with multiple cases to uncover the challenges and opportunities of German PFF caused by the CSRD and thus to answer the research question and build theory (Eisenhardt, 1989; Yin, 2018). The units of analysis (i.e., German PFF) and the observation unit (i.e., the implementation process of a sustainability reporting mandate including its consequences) gave reason for a qualitative research method. Since family firms exhibit SEW configurations that lead to heterogeneous sustainability reporting (Hsueh et al., 2023), experts recommend using qualitative methods for family firm research (Fletcher et al., 2016; Massis & Kammerlander, 2021). In addition, a qualitative approach is suitable for research with changing study conditions (Merriam & Tisdell, 2015), which are also given within the field of sustainability reporting due to the continuous amendments in reporting regulations (Baret & Helfrich, 2019). Another purpose of qualitative research is reflected by its inductive nature and the fact that researchers use qualitative methods for theory-building (Merriam & Tisdell, 2015). Furthermore, the case study format can be justified by context-specific challenges arising from sustainability reporting (Micco et al., 2021) and the type of research question (Yin, 2018). Exploratory case studies are suitable for theory-building and the combination of "what" and "how" questions, which is consistent with the research question of our study (Eisenhardt, 1989; Yin, 2018). Nonetheless, using multiple cases increases the robustness of the developed theory (Eisenhardt & Graebner, 2007).

The population of our study focuses on German PFF due to the extended company scope of the CSRD and several research calls (Arena & Michelon, 2018; Fiechter et al., 2022; Ottenstein et al., 2022). To capture the population of German PFF facing the consequences of the upcoming directive and thus to extend existing theory and replicate previous cases (Eisenhardt, 1989), this study follows the theoretical sampling approach (Glaser & Strauss, 1967). The sample selection within qualitative research is usually purposeful (Merriam & Tisdell, 2015). Hence, Glaser and Strauss (1967) used guided selection criteria in their research.

In our study, the selection of German PFF is guided by an ownership threshold and the firm's market focus. As we choose the definition of a family firm according to Chua et al. (1999), we additionally consider minimum family ownership of 50%. This threshold still justifies a dominant coalition and facilitates an extraction from the population (Chua et al., 1999). Beyond that, all firms must operate in the business-to-business (B2B) market to avoid any distortion due to the market focus. This is because the disclosure behavior regarding sustainability information differs between B2B and business-to-customer (B2C) companies (Johnson et al., 2018). According to the selection criteria, potential companies were randomly selected on the business networking platform LinkedIn. After creating a long list of German PFFs active in the B2B market, we searched for potential interview partners (e.g., sustainability experts) within this pre-selection and contacted them.

The final sample consists of ten family firms with an average founding year of 1926 (see Table 4.1). Hence, every firm was passed on to at least the second or up to the eighth generation, indicating that the sample considers the family firm's typical intergenerational succession within the SEW concept (Gómez-Mejía et al., 2007) and its importance in sustainability (Berrone et al., 2010; García-Sánchez et al., 2021; Labelle et al., 2018). Seven firms have already published a sustainability report, one firm is in the process of creating one at the time of this study, and two firms do not have a sustainability report. The firms have, on average, a headcount of ~ 6,750 employees and a revenue of ~ EUR 1,600 million in 2021 and act in seven different industry clusters.

4.3.2 Data Collection

In case study research for theory building, Eisenhardt (1989) recommends using multiple data collection methods to triangulate and thus substantiate the results, whereas interviews have become the most common primary data source (Eisenhardt & Graebner, 2007). In addition, Yin (2018) proposes maintaining a chain of evidence in case study research. As this explorative multiple case study relies on the research advice of both authors, the database consists of primary and secondary data, according to Eisenhardt (1989), and is supported by Yin's (2018) chain of evidence.

The primary data comprise semi-structured interviews conducted with sustainability experts of all family firms of the sample. Our study followed the rules of the case study protocol, which can be found in the Appendix D (Yin, 2018). To further support qualitative research guidelines, we used mainly open-ended questions (Merriam & Tisdell, 2015) clustered into three thematic fields. The first field contained general questions related to the interviewee's professional position, the family firm structure, and sustainability. The goal was to gain some descriptive firm-specific information and motivational insights into sustainability. The topic of the second cluster was consciously selected concerning the concept of Ioannou et al. (2017) and Gulenko (2018) on FOC and SOC. Therefore, the questions in the second field targeted possible reporting challenges and emerging opportunities or synergies that may result from a sustainability reporting mandate. On the one hand, those thematic fields represented Eisenhardt's suggested predetermined constructs in the interview protocol, which can be adapted over the research process (Eisenhardt, 1989). If these constructs prove essential, they should ground the built theory. On the other hand, this procedure allowed us to create links to the existing literature, which enhanced the internal validity of our study (Eisenhardt, 1989). The third field referred to the outlook regarding introducing a sustainability reporting process. Lastly, the interview questions were overviewed by colleagues to ensure an easy understanding.

The interviews were conducted between February and March 2023 with sustainability representatives, as Eisenhardt and Graebner (2007) recommend interviewing highly experienced informants who can assess the unit of observation from different perspectives. If the firm did not have a sustainability-related job position in place at the time of the study, we instead interviewed board members, as they significantly impact sustainability reporting (Michelon & Parbonetti, 2012). Since the workplaces of the interviewees are spread across Germany, the interviews were conducted via video conferencing platforms. Each interview was prepared in advance by reviewing the company's website to collect additional clarifying questions. At the beginning of each interview, we assured the anonymization of the interview data and asked permission to record the conversation to facilitate the interview guidance (Eisenhardt, 1989). All interviews were subsequently transcribed to increase familiarity with the database and to facilitate data analysis (Merriam & Tisdell, 2015). After the tenth interview, the increase of new insights became smaller as the information began to be repeated. According to Eisenhardt (1989), we stopped adding new cases because theoretical saturation seemed to be reached (Glaser & Strauss, 1967). We recorded 395 min and collected 108 single-spaced pages of transcripts. The Appendix C includes the breakdown of the interview data.

As the unit of observation relates to the disclosure of sustainability information, we intuitively included secondary data from available sustainability reports of the family firms (e.g., applied reporting standard) and supplemented that data

Fig. 4.4 Chain of evidence. *Source* Own figure adapted from Yin (2018)

with information from their websites. Here we included information about accreditations by the International Organization for Standardization (ISO) or EcoVadis (EcoVadis, 2023). The most important standards for sustainability are ISO 14001 (environmental management), ISO 26000 (social responsibility), and ISO 50001 (energy management) (ISO, 2023). We chose these criteria to have nuanced indicators that help us justify the identified reporting challenges and facilitate the archetype classification for users of our framework.

Yin (2018) emphasizes the chain of evidence as it increases the validity of information in the case study. This method allows readers to follow the development of our results by tracing evidence for and backward between the research question and the derived findings (Yin, 2018) (see Fig. 4.4). In our study, the chain of evidence is maintained by covering all five chain elements (i.e., findings, database, interview quotes, case study protocol including interview questions and research question) and by ensuring a clear link through consistent wording between those elements. This rationale is also in line with our coding approach, according to Gioia et al. (2013), where the reader can see data-to-theory connections.

4.3.3 Data Analysis

Eisenhardt (1989) emphasizes that data analysis is at the core of theory building from case studies. Therefore, we looked at comparable case studies in family business research to build on best practices. Strike and Rerup (2016) published a case study on family firms in the renowned Academy of Management Journal using the inductive case analysis method of Gioia et al. (2013) in the context of multiple cases (Eisenhardt, 1989). Our data analysis is based on a similar approach that can be summarized in three phases.

In the first phase, we conducted a within-case analysis (Eisenhardt, 1989) based on case data from several sources (i.e., transcribed interviews, sustainability reports, company websites) to better understand each case as a standalone entity. First, we highlighted the main challenges and opportunities of mandatory sustainability reporting in the transcript of each case. Consequently, we synthesized the highlighted quotes into 57 first-order categories while preserving mostly the terms used by the informants (Gioia et al., 2013). The summarized categories and the corresponding quotes were presented in a table (see Appendix B) to provide evidence regarding the created constructs (Strike & Rerup, 2016). Moreover, we added missing descriptive information (e.g., sustainability norms, founding year, family generation) to the cases from the other data sources.

The second phase focused on the cross-case analysis that builds on the categories and patterns of the previous phase (Eisenhardt, 1989; Yin, 2018). The analysis of similarities and differences between categories (Gioia et al., 2013) and their comparison across cases (Eisenhardt, 1989) enabled us to explore relationships and replicate our findings (Yin, 2018). Thus, we grouped the categories into 23 s-order themes (Gioia et al., 2013). The first 10 themes refer to the reporting challenges and thus to the "what" part of the research question, while the remaining themes refer to the opportunities and thus to the "how" part. Beyond that, based on the synthesis of categories to themes and the descriptive firm information, we were able to group and categorize the cases (Eisenhardt, 1989) into three firm archetypes that will be explained in chapter four.

In the third phase, like Strike and Serup (2016), we analyzed the second-order themes at a higher theoretical level of abstraction and developed aggregate dimensions (Gioia et al., 2013). We built a data structure after creating first-order categories, second-order themes, and aggregated dimensions (see Appendix A). It connects and graphically illustrates these three levels and thus also addresses the previously mentioned data-to-theory link (Gioia et al., 2013). The data structure was the basis for building an inductive framework grounded in data and connecting informants' experiences in theoretical terms (Gioia et al., 2013).

4.4 Results—Mandatory Sustainability Reporting Framework

Based on the within- and cross-case analysis and applying Lee's (2011) theory, we build an inductive framework that illustrates PFF-specific challenges due to a sustainability reporting mandate and provides guidance to unlock business opportunities. The framework consists of three phases (see Fig. 4.5), with phase 1.1 describing the assignment of any PFF to one of the three archetypes, which depend on PFF's individual configuration of external forces (Phase 1.2). Phase 2 depicts which challenges, i.e., FOC, each archetype faces through the implementation of a sustainability reporting mandate. A PFF must face up to four challenge cluster depending on its archetype. Lastly, phase 3 elaborates on

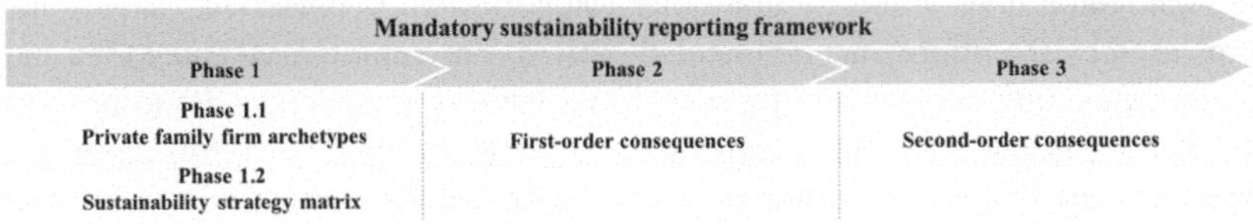

Fig. 4.5 Sequence of phases for the mandatory sustainability reporting framework. *Source* Own figure

how the reporting mandate can be used as an opportunity, i.e., SOC, in different business functions. Accordingly, we recommend that companies applying our framework follow these three phases. Our findings show that the nature and extent of the challenges depend on the archetype, while the direct benefits of the opportunities are archetype independent.

4.4.1 Archetypes and Sustainability Strategy—Know Your Starting Point

Family firm archetypes The first phase of our framework refers to identifying PFF's archetype and its corresponding sustainability strategy. We started by identifying similarities and differences between the cases regarding PFF's market and sustainability characteristics. From this segmentation, we derived three archetypes (i.e., *conservative sustainability denier, cautious first-time reporter, visionary early adopter*). Of our sample, two cases (i.e., *Gamma, Kappa*) belong to the *conservative sustainability denier*, two further falls under the *cautious first-time reporter* (i.e., *Zeta, Iota*), and the remaining (i.e., *Alpha, Beta, Delta, Epsilon, Eta, Theta*) to *the visionary early adopter* (see Fig. 4.6).

The market characteristics consist of macro (i.e., institutional sustainability pressure) and micro factors (i.e., stakeholder sustainability pressure) according to the theoretical framework of Lee (2011). The micro and macro factors are industry-specific and can be either low or high. We determined the level of external pressure based on the interview data. The sustainability characteristics refer to the firm's sustainability mission or vision, its maturity of sustainability reporting, including the use of standards (e.g., GRI, DNK), and accreditations by ISO or EcoVadis. Both accreditations are not mandatory but demonstrate a firm's proactive behavior toward quality, safety, and sustainability.

Fig. 4.6 Private family firm archetypes (Phase 1.1). *Source* Own figure

Family firm archetypes [Company]	Market characteristics		Company specific sustainability characteristics						Strategic approach to sustainability
	Macro and micro factors		Sustainability focus		Sustainability reporting			Sustainability norms/ratings	
	Industry-related institutional sustainability pressure	Industry-related stakeholder sustainability pressure	Sustainability embedded in mission and/or vision	Sustainability department or representative	Sustainability report	Application of reporting standards (e.g., GRI, DNK)	Familiarity with mandatory CSRD regulation	Sustainability ISO norms and/or Ecovadis	
Conservative sustainability denier [Gamma, Kappa]	Low	Low	No	No	No	No	No	No	Reactive strategy
Cautious first-time reporter [Zeta, Iota]	Low	High	Yes	Yes, without direct link to board	Yes, or currently in progress	No	Yes	Yes, only ISO	Accommodative strategy
Visionary early adopter [Alpha, Beta, Delta, Epsilon, Eta, Theta]	High	High	Yes	Yes	Yes	Yes	Yes	Yes, ISO and partly Ecovadis	Proactive strategy

Ultimately, the assigned sustainability strategy per archetype depends on the configuration of the macro and micro factors. The sustainability characteristics are descriptive information of the archetypes and side effects of the respective sustainability strategy. They are not included in the determination of the strategy. In the following, we will describe one representative case study per archetype illustrating the driving factors of the institutional and stakeholder pressure that result in the assigned strategy, but also to give an understanding of the underlying PFF-specific sustainability characteristics.

Conservative sustainability denier *Gamma* is run by the second generation and operates in the metal processing industry. Its firm size (i.e., headcount, turnover) ranks in the lower quartile of the sample. The interviewee was a non-family board member. To date, *Gamma* has not received any request for a sustainability report from its stakeholders. It seems to be an industry-wide phenomenon. "*I have never seen a [sustainability] report from any of our competitors.*" Therefore, *Gamma* shows low external pressure in both categories. Regarding *Gamma's* sustainability focus, it does not embed sustainability in its mission or vision. No information on that could be found in the interview data or on the company's website. It appears that the intrinsic values for sustainability are missing. Accordingly, the firm does not have a sustainability department or representative. Therefore, typical for a *conservative sustainability denier* is its missing sustainability report and thus its lack of experience about reporting standards or the upcoming CSRD. Lastly, *Gamma* has no ISO 14001, 26000, 50001, or EcoVadis accreditation. In summary, *Gamma's* current weak external sustainability pressure and conservative attitude suggest that this archetype would respond to a sustainability reporting mandate with a reactive sustainability strategy. Those firms see no incentive to go beyond legal requirements and want to stay within the "rules of the game" and thus maintain their legitimacy.

Cautious first-time reporter *Iota* is owned by the fourth family generation. The company sells agricultural machinery; its turnover is slightly above the sample's average, and its headcount slightly below. The interview was held with *Iota's* sustainability manager. In contrast to the first archetype, the industry-related stakeholder pressure is high. "*We received requests from customers, especially banks and insurance companies, and they often asked for a sustainability report.*" Also, *Iota's* sustainability focus is more pronounced "*[…] Sustainability is part of every family firm's DNA. This applies to us as well […].*" *Iota* included sustainability in its mission, which indicates a strong identification of the family with the firm. They care about their externally perceived image by sustainability-oriented stakeholders. *Iota* holds close ties to its local community through social investments or school projects, which allows them to build social capital. *Iota* has a sustainability manager but no sustainability department. Furthermore, the sustainability manager is not yet fully integrated into corporate governance. "*There is not a separate sustainability department yet. I spend 100% of my hours on the topic of sustainability in my role as a sustainability manager. Personally, however, I am part of the Construction and Investments department.*" Nevertheless, the topic of sustainability reporting is already evolving. To communicate *Iota's* philanthropic activities, "*[...] in 2019/20, [...] [Iota] published [its] first sustainability report, but it was not based on a reporting standard. [Iota] collected all the sustainability activities [it is] involved and summarized them in the report.*" Thus, PFFs that belong to the archetype of the *cautious first-time reporter* have already published one sustainability report or are in the process of doing so, like *Zeta*, but without considering any reporting standard. Due to their voluntary interest in sustainability reporting, these firms know upcoming mandatory reporting regulations such as the CSRD. Another common feature of this archetype is the accreditation by at least one of the ISO standards for sustainability. *Iota* holds ISO 14001 and 50001 certifications. In conclusion, *Iota's* high stakeholder demands for sustainability led to a proactive sustainability behavior influenced by philanthropy. This archetype wants to be visible in local communities and communicate its activities to specific stakeholder groups (e.g., banks, insurance companies) to increase social capital and reputation. Hence, *cautious first-time reporting* companies pursue an accommodative sustainability strategy.

Visionary early adopter *Theta* was founded in 1961 and is managed and owned by the second generation. Its company size (i.e., turnover, headcount) is close to the average firm size of the sample. The product portfolio includes packaging machinery and packaging materials for fast-moving consumer goods (e.g., food). We interviewed *Theta's* project manager for corporate strategy and sustainability. *Theta* must face high multi-stakeholder (i.e., end customers, direct customers, applicants) and formal institutional sustainability pressure. An increased sustainability awareness among end customers increased the pressure on *Theta's* direct customers. "*[We] noticed that the end consumers of our packages, the people who buy sausage and cheese in the supermarket [...] put pressure on our direct customers, and that, of course, comes back to us.*" Some customers even contact them directly. „*We are busy responding to customer requests [regarding sustainability].*" The human resources department gets sustainability questions from applicants. "*[...] even if we want to hire new staff, young people always ask for [sustainability].*" In contrast to the industries of the first two archetypes, high regulations apply to food packaging, which results in high institutional pressure. "*In the packaging sector in particular, the issue of sustainability, depending on the packaging segment [...] has risen considerably* *in recent years, and we are also quite strongly influenced by regulators, especially when it comes to the food sector.*" *Theta's* sustainability focus includes a sustainability vision, social initiatives (e.g., support of social grocery shops) and a sustainability representative. Its motivational drivers toward sustainability are comparable to the second archetype. The main difference is the integration of sustainability and its representative into the management and governance processes. *Theta* has a formalized sustainability strategy and four strategic fields (i.e., infrastructure, products, governance, social engagement) in which sustainability is anchored, implemented, and tracked. "*[Sustainability] is part of the management process. We have a sustainability steering committee, which consists of the management and me.*" Hence, besides the family's strong identity with the firm, *Theta* cares about its dynastic succession. "*[…] we see it as our responsibility to preserve an environment in which future generations can live.*" The family is forward-looking and wants to develop a positive family identity for future generations. To communicate its social activities and values, *Theta* has voluntarily published a sustainability report for several years. In contrast to the *first-time reporter*, the *visionary early adopter* uses reporting standards. *Theta* used for its sustainability reports the DNK standard. Two additional upgrades in contrast to the last archetype are first, the knowledge about the CSRD and its concrete preparation. Second, all PFF in the sample belonging to the visionary archetype have at least the bronze EcoVadis in addition to sustainability-related ISO certifications. In summary, *Theta's* joint high institutional and stakeholder pressure, including its transgenerational values, led to a formalized strategy and communication. This enables external stakeholders to monitor and evaluate the firm's status quo toward sustainability. Consequently, a PFF within this archetype follows a proactive sustainability strategy beyond minimum requirements.

Sustainability strategy matrix According to our framework, each PFF can be assigned to one of the archetypes and its corresponding sustainability strategy. The mapping between archetype and sustainability strategy can be determined through the sustainability strategy matrix (see left side Fig. 4.7).

Our sample does not include a case with a configuration of low stakeholder and high institutional pressure. One explanation could be the recognized "trickle-down" effect by Ottenstein et al. (2022). This effect states that some non-listed companies might be indirectly affected by a sustainability reporting mandate (e.g., NFRD) of listed companies in the same supply chain. Thus, we assume that due to the trickle-down effect, listed corporate customers in a B2B market will also demand sustainability from their (non-listed) suppliers. Thus, high institutional pressure through norms and regulations in a B2B market would lead to

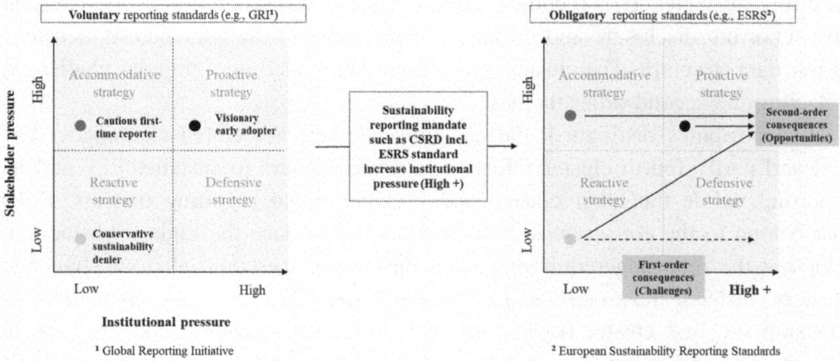

Fig. 4.7 Sustainability strategy matrix (Phase 1.2). *Source* Own figure

increased stakeholder pressure (i.e., sustainability pressure from customers) in its supplier market. A supplier's defensive sustainability strategy that consists of low stakeholder and high institutional pressure would become obsolete.

However, introducing a sustainability reporting mandate leads to FOC and SOC (Gulenko, 2018) for the *conservative sustainability denier* and the *cautious firm-time reporter*. The CSRD regulation will further increase the intensity of formal institutional pressure through additional rules (e.g., ESRS standards), indicated by "high+" (see right side Fig. 4.7). Companies thus have much less flexibility in disclosing their sustainability information than before the CSRD. This is why even the *visionary early adopter* will face FOC and SOC. As we will see in the following chapter, it would be beneficial for the *conservative sustainability denier* not to follow a defensive strategy (see dotted line right side Fig. 4.7) but rather a proactive strategy to benefit from SOC.

4.4.2 Challenges—Be Aware of Obstacles

The second phase of our framework illustrates archetype-specific challenges (i.e., FOC) along the implementation process of a sustainability reporting mandate (see left side Fig. 4.8). Our analysis revealed that the type and degree of challenge a PFF faces depend on its archetype and the corresponding sustainability strategy. Thus, users of our framework can guide through the process according to their assigned archetype. We identified four challenge clusters (i.e., I. Motivational barrier to sustainability (-reporting), II. Organizational sustainability reporting obstacles, III., Technical gaps, efforts, and discontinuities, IV. Hesitant post-reporting disclosure and exchange) that represent the aggregate dimensions of our data structure. The clusters are further subdivided into granular challenges reflecting the second-order themes.

Two attributes distinguish the clusters and their associated challenges. The first and partly fourth cluster refers to intrinsic barriers to sustainability and its reporting, while the other clusters exhibit operational reporting barriers. PFFs that belong to the *conservative sustainability denier* face the highest obstacle in adopting the reporting requirements, as they must overcome all four challenge clusters. Instead, most *cautious first-time reporters* and *visionary early adopters* can skip the first cluster because of their intrinsic motivation and progress in sustainability reporting. Nevertheless, as reporting challenges depend on their context (Gulenko, 2018; Micco et al., 2021), the first challenge cluster might still partially occur for those two archetypes (see dotted boxes in Fig. 4.8). Without considering the status quo of a user of our framework, the *cautious first-time reporter* and *visionary early adopter* show only minor differences in the extent of operational challenges. Continuing the implementation process, given the precise requirements of the new CSRD, the status quo of an archetype becomes irrelevant. Thus, our results show that regardless of the archetype, all PFFs face the same challenges after overcoming the second challenge cluster.

In the following paragraph, we provide illustrative evidence of each challenge cluster and describe how each challenge impedes the implementation process of a sustainability reporting mandate in the related archetype. We also include best practices of the *cautious first-time reporters* and *visionary early adopters* that justify omitting the first and partly the second challenge cluster. Those examples could also be an inspiration for improvement to the *conservative sustainability deniers*. To make use of our rich data, we include representative quotes for each challenge cluster.

I. Motivational barrier to sustainability reporting The first implementation challenge is an intrinsic motivational barrier to sustainability and its reporting. We observed strong evidence for this attitude among the *conservative sustainability denier* and weak to no evidence among the other archetypes. The rejection of reporting is based not only on the reporting itself but also on a fundamental aversion to sustainability. We found two behavioral reasons that need to be overcome in the case of a sustainability reporting mandate.

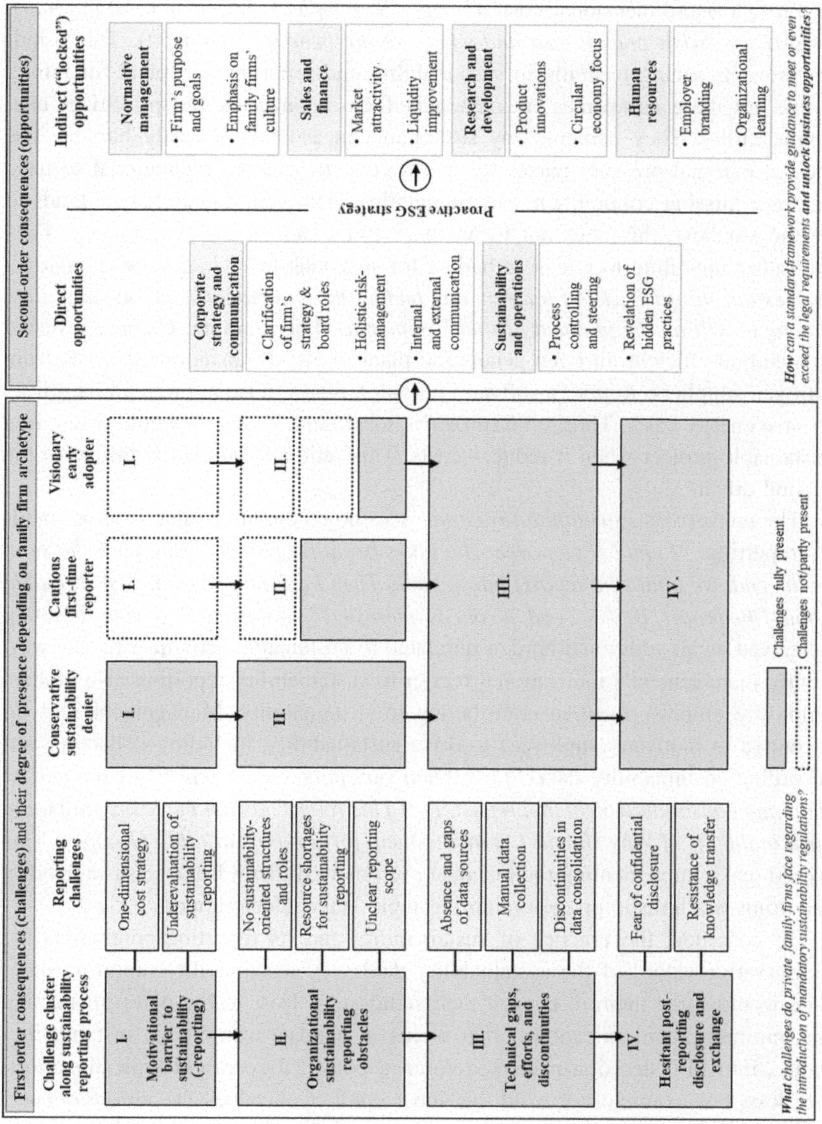

Fig. 4.8 First- and second-order consequences (Phase 2, Phase 3). *Source* Own figure

First, a one-dimensional cost strategy. "*The typical entrepreneurial approach in SMEs is, what does it cost and what are the benefits*" (*Gamma*). This mindset prevents seeing meaning in sustainability and reporting. Atypical for family firms, but these companies' management focuses on costs and prioritizes economic utility. They perceive any sustainable measure as a costly burden. The lack of external pressure makes them less concerned about reputational damage due to a missing commitment to sustainability. Although this archetype tends to be the smallest, this does not mean these PFFs lack financial resources. They are rather unwilling to release a budget for sustainability. "*[…] there is a budget for certain things […]. As long as this budget is not dedicated to sustainability, this topic will not be pursued further*" (*Gamma*). For example, *Gamma* invested in a carbon-efficient nitrogen generation plant to avoid transportation costs from nitrogen suppliers. *Kappa,* a software provider, renewed isolation in all its offices to save energy costs. Thus, a *conservative sustainability denier* would invest in a sustainable project when it reduces costs. This rationale builds the bridge to the second driver.

The *conservative sustainability denier* sees no (economic) value in sustainability reporting. "*I employ someone who takes beautiful photos throughout the year. In the end, we bind [the report] into a book. Then I ask myself what is sustainable about [the report] if, in the end, no one is interested*" (*Gamma*). Reporting is solely perceived as an additional burden unrelated to sustainable activities. In this way, family management's motivational barrier to sustainability reporting also hinders employee empowerment in contributing to sustainability. Management sees no incentive to motivate employees to drive sustainability, including collecting and recording sustainability data. "*[…] When I prepare such a report, I must collect data and consolidate them in a report. […] This report has not made my staff more sustainable. […] Why should I motivate them for a report at all?*" (*Kappa*). This would make implementing the mandate even more difficult because sustainability reporting is a holistic process requiring multi-stakeholder support.

To conclude, the practice of sustainability and its reporting contradicts the conservative values of the sustainability denier. A sustainability reporting mandate would force them to change their mindset, at least to the point of meeting the minimum requirements. In other words, a mandate would push sustainability values into PFF decision-makers' reference points; they would typically prioritize less. For example, to avoid this inner conflict of values the *visionary early adopters Delta*, a sixth-generation automotive supplier, and *Eta*, a third-generation logistics service provider, follow different approaches. *Delta* integrated into its formalized sustainability strategy sustainable KPIs that have the same value as financial KPIs. *Eta's* Head of Sustainability sees the CSRD as an opportunity. "*I like the CSRD because it is so much more than a reporting directive. It is such a huge lever.*"

II. Organizational sustainability reporting obstacles The second challenge cluster starts dealing with the operational reporting process. These obstacles affect all archetypes at this implementation stage but to different degrees. Our analysis showed that the main issue is the organization implementing a sustainability reporting process. The issues start with a lack of organizational structures and roles, followed by resource shortages and an unclear reporting scope. The first two of these second-order themes relate to challenges due to internal firm reasons, and the third due to external political reasons outside the company's control.

The *conservative sustainability denier* has difficulties approaching an incoming sustainability reporting requirement due to missing responsibilities and standardized sustainability management systems (e.g., ISO 14001). For example, the strategic advisor to *Kappa's* CEO seemed overwhelmed. "*What does the CSRD look like? What do I have to do to fulfill it? Who can deal with it? How can relevant fields of action be defined and work packages derived?*" In contrast, for the more advanced archetypes, their clear responsibilities and management systems facilitate the development of project structures for a new reporting requirement. For instance, Case *Delta* created several sustainability reports in the past and thus assigned data owners for each chapter in their sustainability report. The sustainability manager of *Iota* confirmed the benefits of ISO sustainability certificates. "*I have the advantage that our sites have existing certifications, for example, in the energy sector, ISO 50001, and in the environmental sector, ISO 14001, [...] many things that I need for the CSRD are already documented.*"

Following implementation, resource shortages for sustainability reporting are the next identified challenge. The most frequent resource shortages relate to knowledge and time. At this point, the *cautious first-time reporter* starts to experience the full extent of the challenges. The cases belonging to this archetype just began establishing a reporting process. Thus, reporting resources are not yet properly aligned. In terms of knowledge, the first two archetypes have no to little expertise in sustainability reporting. We found that the first point of contact for these PFFs is the quality department, as this business function is already familiar with the requirements of external authorities through audits. "*[...] the topic [of sustainability reporting] was handed over to me because the quality department has no capacity at all [...]*" (*Kappa*). The opinion involving external knowledge between those two archetypes is mixed. *Gamma* and *Iota* are unwilling to work with external consultants, while *Kappa* and *Zeta* are not. "*[...] One of the biggest challenges is knowledge. […] but we need support from external consultants who show us what we need to look at*" (Zeta). *Gamma's* cost focus can explain its hesitation toward external support. Regarding time constraints, the cases of the first two archetypes worry about the missing time capacities for implementing the reporting process rather than maintaining it. This is due to the lengthy familiarization with the reporting obligations, impeded by an oversupply of training materials. "*[…] the very first report under the new standard takes an enormous time to prepare […] I could spend the whole week visiting webinars […] (Iota).* Followed by the subsequent instruction of the employees in the reporting obligations. "*[…] first we have to train the management level, and then transfer it to the whole workforce*" (Zeta). This is confirmed by the cases of the *visionary early adopter* that experienced time savings after the first reporting cycle. "*The initial materiality analysis took the most time*" (*Eta*).

The last obstacle within the second challenge cluster relates to the unclear reporting scope due to constant changes in reporting regulations by policymakers. The transposition of the CSRD into national law has not yet taken place. The new CSR-RUG may deviate from the CSRD. "[…] *it is currently quite difficult to stay up to date with the latest regulatory changes. It feels like there are always new laws and the 50th draft of a law or standard […]*" (*Delta*). In addition, the new ESRS reporting standards and their changing requirements require firms to conduct several gap analyses on their current reporting standard. "*[…] in terms of the CSRD […] we would like to take a closer look what this change from the GRI standard to ESRS means. Thus, we will probably conduct a gap analysis […]*" (*Delta*). This is also an obstacle for the first two archetypes that have never used any standard. "*[…] the first sustainability report is an exercise where we want to approach this ESRS standard to the best of our ability. We will see the results of the first sustainability report at the end of this year and then publish the gap analysis […]*" (*Iota*). Thus, regardless of the archetype, any change in regulations means additional effort to understand the new requirements.

To summarize, archetypes' (i.e., PFFs') heterogeneous sustainability strategy still influences the extent of organizational challenges due to an incoming sustainability reporting mandate. The more advanced archetypes can benefit from their proactive sustainability and reporting behavior (e.g., clear responsibilities, ISO certifications, expert knowledge). However, these benefits seem to diminish based on the specific and changing requirements of the new CSRD. In other words, without considering these external reasons (i.e., unclear reporting scope), the *visionary early adopter* could also have skipped the second challenge cluster.

III. Technical gaps, efforts, and discontinuities The third challenge cluster relates to the second because of its operational attributes. The challenges of the third cluster are independent of the archetype. Implying that any PFF, either with a proactive or a reactive sustainability strategy, will face similar challenges at this stage. All sub-challenges (i.e., second-order themes) involve hurdles in managing the required data. Difficulties in data management include a lack of relevant data sources, followed by a high manual effort for data collection and inconsistencies in data consolidation. The absence and gaps of data sources pose a twofold challenge. First, all archetypes must identify their specific data sources required for the ESRS 2, ESRS E1, and ESRS S1 standards. If business processes along the value chain are not designed to measure these specific sustainability indicators (e.g., GHG emissions), it is almost impossible to find and obtain the required data at all. "*The challenge is to design the processes in such a way that the information needed can be presented transparently and also in a form in which it can be tracked. For example, with the CO_2 calculation, we need to disclose Scope 1, 2, and 3*" (*Theta*). This hurdle is particularly intense for processes beyond a firm's borders, like for the measurement of Scope 3 emissions. "*Data management in the supply chain will be one of the biggest challenges in the coming years*" *(Epsilon)*. "*We are now starting to go deeper into Scope 3. I feel like I'm running into walls" (Eta)*. "*[…] what I find very challenging are the Scope 3 emissions" (Beta)*. All these quotes are from cases belonging to the *visionary early adopter*, although they have the most experience in sustainability reporting. However, once identified, a suitable and measurable process may still have data gaps that need to be filled subsequently. "*[…] trying to get exact figures from your own processes, from the supply chain, to request them […], these are huge challenges*" (*Epsilon*). Most PFFs collect their data manually, which is a timely process. "*For the CO_2 balance, I have 150 waste invoices in my folder, all of which I have to read through manually*" (*Kappa*). "*[…] last year, when we prepared the first carbon footprint […] we had to adapt certain things to get data more quickly. […] to get digital data and not manual evaluations [is a challenge]" (Zeta).*

After data collection, the next step is to merge the sustainability information from the different sources and departments, which is challenging due to system discontinuities. "*The departments have their own measurement systems or digital programs. For example, in HR, some programs that use training information, […] employee structures. In the energy sector, we have an internal digital energy management system, which means that the indicators can also be read out here. And this is how it works in each department, and in the end, we have a [Excel] document, filled out by the respective departments, which we put together with marketing in a sustainability report"* (*Theta*). For companies with international locations, the hurdle of system breaks is even more severe. Here, the technical consolidation is additionally impeded by a cognitive obstacle. Cultures from different countries have diverse sustainability perceptions. Specifically, understanding the social dimension varies across cultures influencing how sustainability is approached, e.g., regarding labor equality or safety. Thus, consolidating inconsistent data collections due to different interpretations of sustainability makes coherent reporting difficult.

Overall, some technical difficulties arise from the specific requirements of the CSRD (e.g., Scope 3 emissions). Thus, even more, experienced firms that have already voluntarily prepared a sustainability report face challenges. This is due to the reason that voluntary reports are often summaries of existing sustainability information. "*Through the voluntary report, we have created transparency and simply written down everything that we are already doing in the area of sustainability*" (*Theta*). Therefore, institutions' requests for sustainability data from processes not yet designed to be reported are challenging for any archetype.

IV. Hesitant post-reporting disclosure and exchange The last challenge cluster reflects a dilemma that affects every archetype. On the one hand, PFFs hesitate to disclose their data to the public after organizing and collecting relevant data. "*Of course, there are certain topics where you consider whether you want to disclose this information. In particular, sensitive data relating to compensation [...]. These topics pose challenges for a family firm, especially if you are locally based*" (*Iota*). This concern is particularly pronounced for the *first-time reporter* due to its accommodative sustainability strategy. These PFFs built strong relationships with external stakeholders, especially to their local communities, where they want to be visible and enjoy a good reputation. Thus, the communication of content that has not been selected by the firm but by a political institution is a concern for those PFFs. On the other hand, PFFs appreciate reading the disclosed reports from industry peers or joining firm associations to learn about best practices. "*[...] we are in regular exchange with other companies that are at the same point as we are. [...] we look what the others are doing, can we copy anything, what can we do better or how are their processes organized*" (*Theta*). Nevertheless, *Theta* only exchanges with public firms or firms outside their industry due to their fear of disclosing confidential data.

4.4.3 Opportunities—Go Beyond Legal Requirements

The third phase of our framework reveals opportunities (i.e., SOC) that result after the introduction of a sustainability reporting process and reports disclosure (see right side Fig. 4.8). We differentiate between direct and indirect or "locked" opportunities along a firm's value chain. Irrespective of the archetype, all PFFs can benefit from the direct opportunities that arise after meeting the minimum reporting requirements. In contrast, a proactive sustainability strategy needs to unlock indirect opportunities. Two business functions, i.e., (1) corporate strategy and communication and (2) sustainability and operations, can benefit from direct opportunities. The other functions, i.e., (3) normative management, (4) sales and finance, (5) research and development, and (6) human resources, can benefit from indirect opportunities.

Direct opportunities Business functions (1) and (2) can benefit from the firm's structured disclosures following the ESRS standards by meeting the minimum reporting requirements without additional effort. Regarding business function (1), using the obligatory ESRS standards provides a strategic structure. "*I derived our sustainability strategy from the ESRS, i.e., E, S, and G, and the chapters […]. And I think you can show this nicely with the chapter structure of the ESRS. […] I perceived it very helpful, the structure, to carry this into the organization*" (*Iota*). More specifically, ESRS 2 standard requires the disclosure of board members' roles and responsibilities (EFRAG, 2022b), which can be helpful for a clear task allocation among family members and corporate governance. In addition, the report provides firms with a holistic overview of their business activities through the double materiality perspective. Thus, improving the firm's risk management. Moreover, the cases experienced improved internal communication through cross-functional collaboration. "*[…] before [the report], each department worked separately, and each department had already done something in the area of sustainability, but it was never really communicated. […] through this report, it has simply become much more structured, and the individual areas could also inform each other*" (*Theta*). But also, external communication as part of the report preparation. "*There are again these synergy effects, such as stakeholder materiality analysis […]. This [stakeholder] exchange is a positive side effect*" (*Iota*). Regarding business function (2), the holistic view also helps to monitor processes through (sustainability) KPIs and thus to identify inefficiencies more quickly. „ *[…] KPI is supposed to provide a target and help us to develop certain processes in a certain direction*" (*Beta*). Lastly, sustainability reporting simultaneously leads to recording sustainable activities and uncovers a hidden potential. "[…] *we already do a lot but in an uncoordinated way.*

That means the different departments, environment in development, in materials, in HR. Things are happening everywhere that you can put into this huge topic of sustainability" (*Epsilon*).

Indirect ("locked") opportunities The information in the sustainability report and the underlying processes can be further leveraged to derive indirect opportunities. Firms that pursue a proactive strategy can benefit from indirect opportunities because of their attitude to exceed stakeholder requirements. They are willing to make extra efforts to turn the report's information into additional value. Therefore, we recommend for PFFs belonging to the *conservative sustainability denier* respond to a sustainability reporting mandate with a proactive rather than a defensive approach to unlocking business opportunities.

A PFF following a proactive approach would recognize the sustainability purpose behind a sustainability reporting process and could develop further motivation and real values for sustainability. Looking at business function (3), a PFF could integrate these new values into its mission, thus sharpening and questioning its purpose. It would provide transparency to stakeholders on what the company stands for and allow for assessing the "future readiness" of a company's business model. "*[...] it is also clearer to everyone what the company is doing. What are the goals? [...] Such a report is, of course, an important component. What is the mission? Where do we want to go? It is simply something that is goal-oriented, a positive side effect of such a report*" (*Theta*). "*[...] And it's not just about how do we make the products more sustainable but how fit is our business model for the future*" (*Eta*). Beyond that, such a sustainability report and its double materiality perspective can also enhance a family's SEW by building enduring ties to multi-stakeholders, improving the firm's reputation, and thus paving the way for future generations.

Another lever of the sustainability report is the facilitated accreditation of sustainability organizations such as EcoVadis. The process transparency and information created by the report can contribute to obtaining other certificates. However, this requires proactive research by firms to identify eligible certifications. In addition, exceeding legal requirements could create a competitive edge if a sustainability report was not an industry standard before the mandate, as for the *conservative sustainability denier*. Thus, even slightly exceeding the requirements can strengthen the brand and increase sales. Reports' resulting process transparency, e.g., through sustainability KPIs, can also reveal waste and resource inefficiencies. Thus, if a report's content is considered correctly, it serves also as a lever to reduce costs. "*[...] especially when I consider the topic of water circuits or energy, then this not only pays off in terms of sustainability but also in terms of profitability [...]*" (*Alpha*). Consequently, those revenue and cost-based arguments represent a lever for business function (4).

A multi-stakeholder view along a firm's value chain, e.g., as a requirement of the reporting standard ESRS E1 to track Scope 3 emissions, also paves the way for product innovation and therefore an opportunity for business function (5) "*[...] if we think in the direction of circular economy, where product development, customers, and also sales sit together, where perhaps from the product development point of view there are ideas that have not been recognized by the customer yet*" (*Iota*).

Lastly, business function (6) can integrate the sustainability report into its workflows to enhance employer branding and organizational learning. *Theta* and *Beta* mentioned that they get unsolicited applications that refer to their sustainability report, especially from young talents that appreciate working for a sustainable employer. However, internally, the report is a learning tool and increases the sustainability awareness of the workforce. "*Of course, we also have high standards for our people. Our employees are also interested, and they also want to understand the term sustainability in the context of the company*" (*Beta*).

In summary, mastering the dual task of integrating sustainability reporting and deriving opportunities from it is not effortless. According to the more experienced archetypes, especially the first reporting cycle is a resource-intensive process in terms of time, expertise, and stakeholder engagement. Especially the updated double materiality concept, due to its outside-in and inside-out assessment, results in a high initial burden. Ultimately, it is necessary first to build on the foundations for the direct before attempting to exploit any indirect opportunities.

4.5 Discussion

4.5.1 Theoretical Implications

The results of our analysis contribute to both the research stream of family firms' heterogeneous sustainability strategy and reporting behavior and the research stream on the effects of a sustainability reporting mandate.

Regarding the first research stream, our findings build on the distinction between a family firm's reactive and proactive strategy toward external demands (Campopiano & Massis, 2015; Cennamo et al., 2012; Déniz, María de la Cruz Déniz & Suárez, 2005; Sharma & Sharma, 2011). We contribute to the literature by deriving three PFF archetypes. Regarding family firms' heterogenous sustainability strategies, the analysis revealed that the attributes of our archetypes and their corresponding sustainability strategy confirm and disconfirm family firm literature in the following aspects.

The PFFs belonging to the *conservative sustainability denier* are cost-driven and subject to low external pressures, leading to a general aversion to sustainability (e.g., no sustainability representative, reporting, vision, ISO accreditation) and a reactive approach. Thus, the cases in our sample showed no motivation to build their SEW, like enhancing reputation or increasing binding social ties with external stakeholders. This is consistent with the findings of Hsueh et al. (2023) and Cennamo et al. (2012), who argue that those family firms place less emphasis on the (2) *family members' identification with the firm*, which is related to reputation, the (3) *binding social ties* and the (5) *renewal of family ties to the firm through dynastic succession* SEW dimension, leading to a reactive approach. Rather untypical for the results of family business research is the *conservative sustainability deniers'* high preference for economic goals (Berrone et al., 2010; Kotlar & Massis, 2013). Moreover, our findings differ from Déniz María de la Cruz Déniz and Suárez (2005), who conclude that family firms that adopt a reactive approach do not have sufficient financial resources to engage in sustainability. According to our findings, the problem lies more in the unwillingness to release a budget for sustainability.

The PFFs belonging to the *cautious first-time reporter* and the *visionary early adopter* developed intrinsic sustainability values and are subject to high external pressures resulting in a proactive sustainability strategy. They employ sustainability managers, have a sustainability vision, engage in, and communicate their social activities, are accredited by sustainability organizations, and prepare for the upcoming CSRD. In line with Hsueh et al. (2023) and Cennamo et al. (2012), those family firms care about their externally perceived image, especially in local communities, are forward-looking, develop a positive family identity for future generations, which in sum indicates a salience of the (2), (3) and (5) SEW dimension. Thus, their goal is to build SEW while gaining legitimacy. Beyond that, our analysis revealed that the PFFs in our sample following a proactive approach are larger (i.e., turnover and headcount) and show a higher number of generational successions, following Déniz María de la Cruz Déniz and Suárez (2005) findings. The difference between the *cautious first-time reporter* and the *visionary early adopter* in their sustainability reporting is the use of standards. PFFs belonging to the *cautious first-time reporter* do not adhere to reporting standards, while the *visionary early adopter* reported for several years according to official standards. This aligns with the findings of Campopiano and Massis (2015). In contrast, both proactive archetypes are hesitant to disclose sustainability information that they have not purposefully selected or to share insights from reporting practices with industry peers. Venturelli et al. (2021) explain this reluctance with the family's involvement in the firm and the fear of losing their SEW.

Regarding the second research stream, we contribute to the literature on family firms' heterogeneous sustainability reporting behavior (Arena & Michelon, 2018; Aureli et al., 2020; Biswas et al., 2019; Campopiano & Massis, 2015; Gavana et al., 2017; Terlaak et al., 2018; Venturelli et al., 2021) via PFF archetypes. Our framework shows that the type (i.e., challenge cluster) and degree (i.e., sub-challenges) of challenge regarding implementing a sustainability reporting mandate depend on the archetype and its corresponding sustainability strategy up to a certain implementation stage. This rationale continues with the opportunities. Each archetype can benefit from direct opportunities after meeting the minimum requirements. Only a proactive approach can unlock indirect opportunities. It seems that a major determinant is the type of sustainability strategy, a construct of external forces. Since the prioritization or configuration of SEW dimensions determines how a family firm reacts to external demands, SEW is a preventive lever to mitigate challenges or gain opportunities. This reasoning applies to implementation stages of sustainability reporting influenced by intrinsic motives such as the first and fourth challenge cluster or the gain of indirect opportunities. Beyond that, following the research call from Arena and Michelon (2018) or Venturelli et al. (2021), we extend family business research on sustainability reporting by focusing on PFF. Under the attributes of a multiple case study, we not only relied on easily accessible SEW dimensions such as family control but also family members' identification with the firm or renewal of family bonds through dynastic succession.

Regarding the second research stream, our framework further extends research on the effects of mandatory sustainability reporting (Fiechter et al., 2022; Ioannou & Serafeim, 2017; Ottenstein et al., 2022) in general and on the challenges and opportunities of the CSRD in particular. Our framework presents four challenge clusters and opportunities in six business functions along a firm's value chain based on the CSRD in German companies. Thus, we are not only contributing to the current scarcity of studies focusing on the upcoming CSRD (Ottenstein et al., 2022) but also on the link between FOC and SOC (Gulenko, 2018).

4.5.2 Managerial Implications

Managing the dual mission of integrating a sustainability reporting mandate and benefitting from this change process is challenging (Garcia-Torea et al., 2023; Nigri & Del Baldo, 2018). Since the dominant coalition, like the family, is the primary agent for successfully managing such an organizational change (Kotter, 1996), our findings are highly relevant for practitioners. The framework serves as a guide and reveals implementation challenges and opportunities. As our analysis shows, the influence of a family firm's typical SEW is especially relevant for the first and fourth challenge cluster as well as for the shift from direct to indirect opportunities. Nonetheless, apart from those socioemotionally influenced consequences, our framework is also relevant for non-family firms that want to prepare for the upcoming CSRD. Therefore, the following managerial implications are twofold.

First, we recommend that PFFs belonging to the cost-driven *conservative sustainability denier* integrate sustainability KPIs into their decisions and link them to financial data. In addition, they should recognize the potential opportunities that may arise from a sustainability reporting mandate through our framework. Both suggestions could facilitate overcoming the inner obstacle of seeing no value in sustainability and its reporting. Since a family's strong identification with the firm, binding social ties and transgenerational values are drivers for following a proactive sustainability strategy (Cennamo et al., 2012; Déniz, María de la Cruz Déniz & Suárez, 2005; Hsueh et al., 2023; Sharma & Sharma, 2011), a *conservative sustainability denier* could put relevance on these SEW dimensions to be motivated going beyond legal requirements and thus benefiting from indirect opportunities. Concerning the fourth challenge cluster and the dilemma between the hesitation to share information with the public and the appreciation of reading the sustainability reports of industry peers to mimic best practices, we advise the following. Regardless of the archetype, families who identify strongly with their firm and fear their image in local communities or sharing confidential report practices with industry peers might participate in firm associations outside their region and industry (see case *Iota*, *Theta*).

Second, for all firms, irrespective of their family or listing status, integrating a sustainability reporting mandate such as the CSRD requires proper organization and data management. Our analysis revealed that firms with standardized sustainability management systems (e.g., ISO 14001) could build on these structures, assigned roles, and data. Therefore, we recommend using any sustainability accreditation as an orientation to facilitate the development of project structures regarding the implementation of a sustainability reporting process. Nevertheless, drawing on the best practices of archetypes with more experience in sustainability reporting, it is evident that the sustainability reporting process becomes much smoother after one reporting cycle, which should serve as a motivation to firms. Lastly, the abundance of regulatory amendments to the reporting requirements is an obstacle outside the company's control. It might be helpful to keep informed via webinars or training material from leading advisory firms.

4.5.3 Limitations and Future Research

Our study is subject to a few limitations that pave the way for future research. The framework shows limits regarding its internal and external context. The challenges and opportunities of the framework suit mainly German PFFs (i.e., internal context) based on the EU's forthcoming CSRD (i.e., external context). Given the strong influence of the internal and external context in analyzing the consequences of mandatory sustainability reporting (Aureli et al., 2020; Christensen et al., 2021; Gulenko, 2018), future research could address both limitations.

In terms of the internal context, developing and testing hypotheses on the identified consequences would further substantiate our findings. However, regardless of the research method, in family business research, it is essential to cautiously generalize the results due to the heterogeneity of family firms (Chua et al., 2012; Evert et al., 2016). Elaborating further on this argument, we must consider that the SEW dimensions influence our framework (Berrone et al., 2012; Gómez-Mejía et al., 2007). Configurations or salient SEW dimensions affect the type and degree of implementation challenges. As indicated in the previous chapter, non-family firms applying our framework must consider this limitation. Thus, it would be interesting to know how a dominant coalition of a non-family firm implements the CSRD and to what extent the consequences differ from our study. Also, a single longitudinal case study could further deepen the consequences and conclude how exactly a family firm manages the path from FOC to SOC. Moreover, we must caution our findings to the industries of our sample. Our framework is susceptible to the influence of industry pressure, which may lead to different assigned sustainability strategies. For example, this limitation is reflected by our sample, not including a case with a defensive sustainability strategy. Although we suspect fewer companies are exposed to low institutional and high stakeholder pressure due to the trickle-down effect, this could also lie in our sample's limited number of industries. Future research could validate the findings in a different industry set up.

Regarding the external context, our study presents early evidence. We identified four challenge clusters based on the forthcoming CSRD and its binding ESRS standards, which are not yet transposed into German law. Although the integration should not deviate as much as in the case of the NFRD, a subsequent check on the conformity between the directive and national law is advisable. Furthermore, it is difficult to extrapolate the identified consequences to firms outside the EU. The motivation of institutions to force companies to produce a sustainability report varies (Christensen et al., 2021), which also indicates different implementation issues. Thus, further research could replicate or extend the findings in different institutional settings.

4.6 Conclusion

By analyzing interview data from multiple cases on the consequences of mandatory sustainability reporting, we created an inductive framework that illustrates which challenges a company faces when implementing sustainability reporting and how the mandate can turn into business opportunities. The sharp scope expansion of the EU's forthcoming CSRD and the associated first-time imposition of a sustainability reporting mandate on most German private family firms gave reason to focus on this specific context. Building on family business research, our findings contribute to the literature by differentiating PFFs based on their current maturity of sustainability reporting and sustainability strategy that is a construct of external forces. This allowed us to derive three PFF archetypes. The identified implementation challenges entail intrinsic and operational barriers. Thus, family firms psychologically anchored SEW dimensions regarding external demands (e.g., binding social ties) influence the PFF archetype's implementation challenges (i.e., intrinsic barriers). Only a SEW configuration that favors proactive behavior towards external demands enables PFF to benefit from indirect business opportunities. From a practitioner's perspective, the operational obstacles are relevant for all company types that want to prepare for the CSRD. Ultimately, our framework serves as a guide to overcoming the obstacles in meeting the sustainability reporting requirements of the EC, a key stakeholder to European companies. Thus, we can preventively assist in maintaining a company's license to operate and realize its full potential.

Appendix

Appendix A. Data Structure

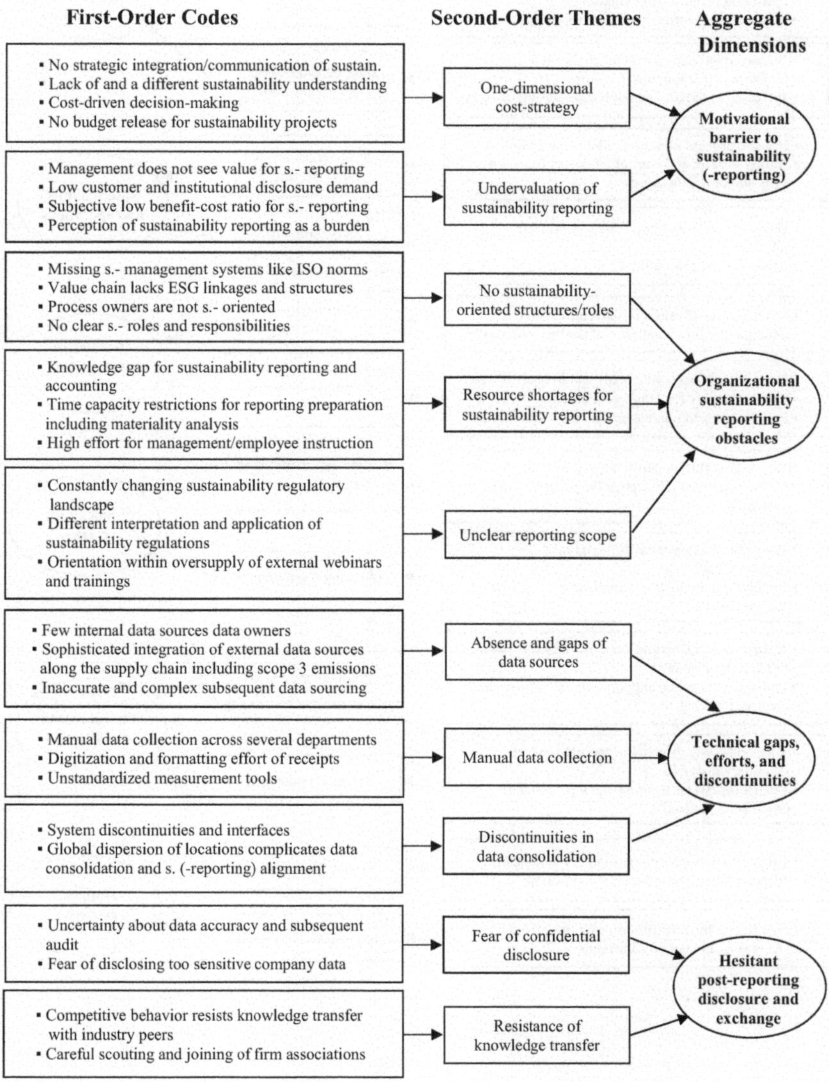

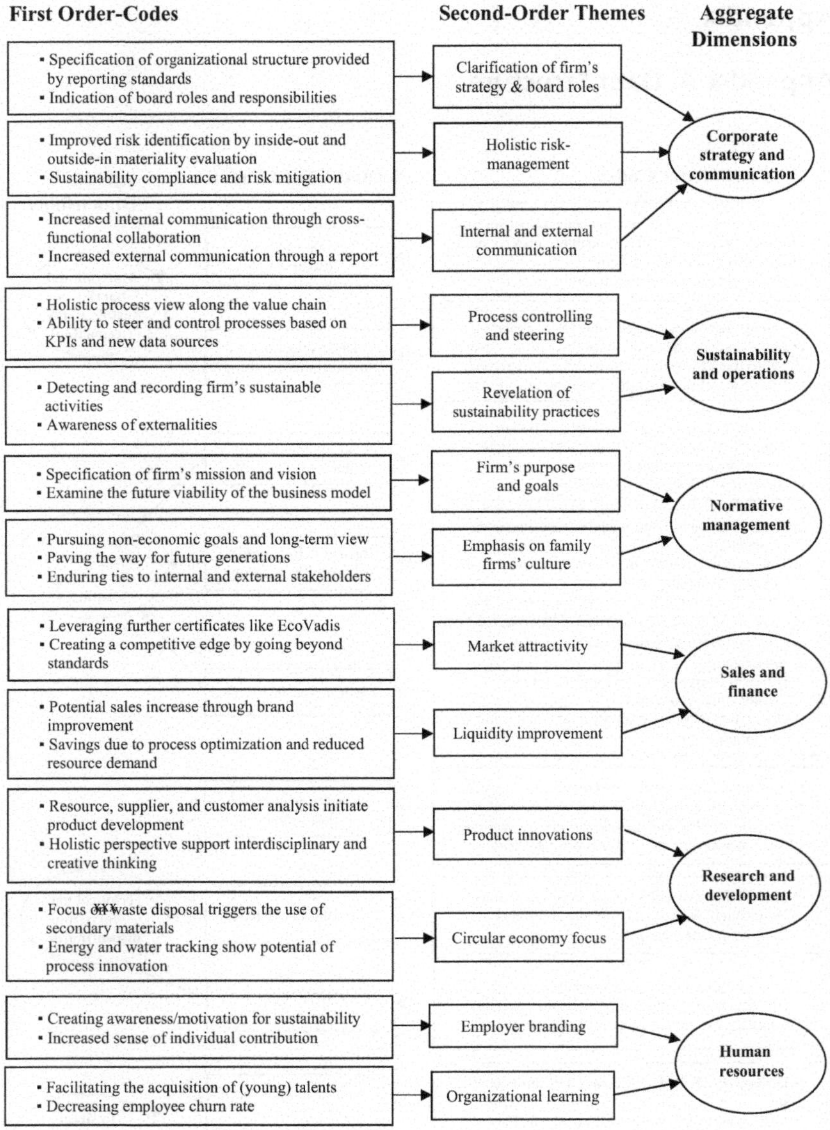
First Order-Codes
Second-Order Themes
Aggregate Dimensions
▪ Specification of organizational structure provided by reporting standards
▪ Indication of board roles and responsibilities
Clarification of firm's strategy & board roles
▪ Improved risk identification by inside-out and outside-in materiality evaluation
▪ Sustainability compliance and risk mitigation
Holistic risk-management
▪ Increased internal communication through cross-functional collaboration
▪ Increased external communication through a report
Internal and external communication
Corporate strategy and communication
▪ Holistic process view along the value chain
▪ Ability to steer and control processes based on KPIs and new data sources
Process controlling and steering
▪ Detecting and recording firm's sustainable activities
▪ Awareness of externalities
Revelation of sustainability practices
Sustainability and operations
▪ Specification of firm's mission and vision
▪ Examine the future viability of the business model
Firm's purpose and goals
▪ Pursuing non-economic goals and long-term view
▪ Paving the way for future generations
▪ Enduring ties to internal and external stakeholders
Emphasis on family firms' culture
Normative management
▪ Leveraging further certificates like EcoVadis
▪ Creating a competitive edge by going beyond standards
Market attractivity
▪ Potential sales increase through brand improvement
▪ Savings due to process optimization and reduced resource demand
Liquidity improvement
Sales and finance
▪ Resource, supplier, and customer analysis initiate product development
▪ Holistic perspective support interdisciplinary and creative thinking
Product innovations
▪ Focus on waste disposal triggers the use of secondary materials
▪ Energy and water tracking show potential of process innovation
Circular economy focus
Research and development
▪ Creating awareness/motivation for sustainability
▪ Increased sense of individual contribution
Employer branding
▪ Facilitating the acquisition of (young) talents
▪ Decreasing employee churn rate
Organizational learning
Human resources

Appendix B. Selected Case-Based Evidence

Aggregate dimension: Motivational barrier to sustainability (-reporting)	
2nd-order codes	Selected evidence on 1st-order codes
One-dimensional cost-strategy	"The typical entrepreneurial approach in SMEs is, what does it cost and what are the benefits." (*Gamma*) "[…] there is a budget for certain things […]. As long as this budget is not dedicated to sustainability, this topic will not be pursued further" (*Gamma*) "Yes, and would you also say that because of a cost–benefit issue, there might not be an advantage here either? Kappa: Yes, that is quite a big issue for us." (*Kappa*)
Undervaluation of sustainability reporting	"I employ someone who takes beautiful photos throughout the year. In the end, we bind [the report] into a book. Then I ask myself what is sustainable about [the report] if, in the end, no one is interested." (*Gamma*) "[…] When I prepare such a report, I must collect data and consolidate them in a report. […] This report has not made my staff more sustainable. […] Why should I motivate them for a report at all?" (*Kappa*)
Aggregate dimension: Organizational sustainability reporting obstacles	
2nd-order codes	Selected evidence on 1st-order codes

(continued)

(continued)

Aggregate dimension: Motivational barrier to sustainability (-reporting)	
No sustainability-oriented structures/ roles	"What does the CSRD look like? What do I have to do to fulfill it? Who can deal with it? How can relevant fields of action be defined and work packages derived?" (*Kappa*) "I have the advantage that our sites have existing certifications, for example, in the energy sector, ISO 50001, and in the environmental sector, ISO 14001, […] many things that I need for the CSRD are already documented." (*Iota*) (Best practice) "This means that we have templates and data to collect, which are usually Word or Excel documents, and we have clearly defined data owners for all areas or for all thematic areas in the sustainability report, who sit in the individual departments and who then receive these templates at the start of the data collection phase and fill them in." (*Delta*) (Best practice)
Resource shortages for sustainability reporting	"[…] the topic [of sustainability reporting] was handed over to me because the quality depart ment has no capacity at all […]." (*Kappa*) "[…] One of the biggest challenges is knowledge. […] but we need support from external consultants who show us what we need to look at." (*Zeta*) "[…] the very first report under the new standard takes an enormous time to prepare […] I could spend the whole week visiting webinars […]." (*Iota*) "The initial materiality analysis took the most time." (*Eta*) "[…] on the one hand, the competence has to be built up somewhere, of course, which means that just as there are specialists for financial reporting, there need to be specialists for sustainability reporting." (*Delta*)

(continued)

(continued)

Aggregate dimension: Motivational barrier to sustainability (-reporting)	
Unclear reporting scope	"[…] it is currently quite difficult to stay up to date with the latest regulatory changes It feels like there are always new laws and the 50th draft of a law or standard […]." (*Delta*) "[…] in terms of the CSRD […] we would like to take a closer look what this change from the GRI standard to ESRS means. Thus, we will probably conduct a gap analysis […]." (*Delta*) "[…] the first sustainability report is an exercise where we want to approach this ESRS standard to the best of our ability. We will see the results of the first sustainability report at the end of this year and then publish the gap analysis […]." (*Iota*) "The knowledge of it at all. It is a new topic. To be comprehensively informed, what does it mean now, how can it be interpreted. What do I have to do now or not? We quickly came to the point, when does it start, are we really affected or not […]." (*Eta*)
Aggregate dimension: Technical gaps, efforts, and discontinuities	
2nd-order codes	Selected evidence on 1st-order codes
Absence and gaps of data sources	"The challenge is to design the processes in such a way that the information needed can be presented transparently and also in a form in which it can be tracked. For example, with the CO_2 calculation, we need to disclose Scope 1, 2, and 3." (*Theta*) "Data management in the supply chain will be one of the biggest challenges in the coming years." (Epsilon) "We are now starting to go deeper into Scope 3. I feel like I'm running into walls." (*Eta*) "[…] what I find very challenging are the Scope 3 emissions." (*Beta*) "[…] trying to get exact figures from your own processes, from the supply chain, to request them […], these are huge challenges." (*Epsilon*)

(continued)

(continued)

Aggregate dimension: Motivational barrier to sustainability (-reporting)	
Manual data collection	"For the CO_2 balance, I have 150 waste invoices in my folder, all of which I have to read through manually." (*Kappa*) "[…] last year, when we prepared the first carbon footprint […] we had to adapt certain things to get data more quickly. […] to get digital data and not manual evaluations [is a challenge]." (*Zeta*) "At the moment, the whole thing [report preparation] is quite a manual process." (*Delta*) "Some [sustainability] numbers have to be recorded manually […]." (*Eta*)
Discontinuities in data consolidation	"The departments have their own measurement systems or digital programs. For example, in HR, some programs that use training information, […] employee structures. In the energy sector, we have an internal digital energy management system, which means that the indicators can also be read out here. And this is how it works in each department, and in the end, we have a [Excel] document, filled out by the respective departments, which we put together with marketing in a sustainability report." (*Theta*) "In a company like ours, the challenge is that we have about 60 subsidiaries in a group. That means, how do I build something like that for the group or do I have to do it for each individual company and then consolidate it again for the group? So you can't talk about man-days, we are talking about man-years, which are really wasted, I would say, in order to create really compliant reports." (*Epsilon*)
Aggregate dimension: *Hesitant post-reporting disclosure and exchange*	
2nd-order codes	Selected evidence on 1st-order codes

(continued)

(continued)

Aggregate dimension: Motivational barrier to sustainability (-reporting)	
Fear of confidential disclosure	"Of course, there are certain topics where you consider whether you want to disclose this information. In particular, sensitive data relating to compensation […]. These topics pose challenges for a family firm, especially if you are locally based." (*Iota*) "[…] on the one hand, what do I want to say and release as a company, of course, you don't want to completely disclose everything you do in the company." (*Epsilon*)
Resistance of knowledge transfer	"[…] we are in regular exchange with other companies that are at the same point as we are. […] we look what the others are doing, can we copy anything, what can we do better or how are their processes organized." "So primarily engineering companies, but packaging-wise rather not, no." (*Theta*) "[…] to possibly also network and exchange with other companies." (*Eta*)
Aggregate dimension: *Corporate strategy and communication*	
2nd-order codes	Selected evidence on 1st-order codes
Clarification of firm's strategy & board roles	"I derived our sustainability strategy from the ESRS, i.e., E, S, and G, and the chapters […]. And I think you can show this nicely with the chapter structure of the ESRS. […] I perceived it very helpful, the structure, to carry this into the organization." (*Iota*) "[…] Sustainability is increasingly becoming a lighthouse project in our company. […] and now we are a lighthouse project where other departments should orient themselves. That can really have a big impact and have a positive effect." (*Eta*) "Yes, and we take that into the corporate structure and corporate objectives, into the KPIs and give them concrete figures. Put concrete numbers behind it." (*Beta*)

(continued)

(continued)

Aggregate dimension: Motivational barrier to sustainability (-reporting)	
Holistic risk management	"I looked at what requirements are there for us? What does a global compact have? What does the food retailer say? What do consumers want? What have we already committed to? What is already there and then I screened the documents, what are the topics? I then clustered these topics, which resulted in fields of action with individual topics. And this was then simplified again in a questionnaire. We also discussed whether we should hold a workshop […]. Then we prepared the topics and fields of action in an Excel questionnaire. Afterwards, I held an information event with internal stakeholders, such as representatives from specialist departments, who evaluated the topics. So from an inside-out and outside-in perspective with numbers from 0 to 4, but also for the possibility of a qualitative assessment. But I also involved external stakeholders, but not as many as internal […]. And then I evaluated the whole thing quantitatively, but I also took something from the qualitative. In the end, I came up with a matrix. This shows which topics are particularly relevant and which are not. I then discussed the results again with the management and asked them whether they agreed or not." (*Eta*) Yes, we would probably like to work with a questionnaire, so we have discussed it for a long time, different possibilities. The tendency is to work with a questionnaire using Microsoft Forms, so that we can contact the department as a whole and also our stakeholders, customers and others. In addition, we would like to use platforms such as our supplier day to address specific topics. And possibly conduct personal surveys of internal departments, really the board of directors and so on. But for the most part, a questionnaire will be digital." (*Iota*)

(continued)

(continued)

Aggregate dimension: Motivational barrier to sustainability (-reporting)	
Internal and external communication	[…] before [the report], each department worked separately, and each department had already done something in the area of sustainability, but it was never really communicated. […] through this report, it has simply become much more structured, and the individual areas could also inform each other." (*Theta*) "There are again these synergy effects, such as stakeholder materiality analysis […]. This [stakeholder] exchange is a positive side effect." (*Iota*)
Aggregate dimension: *Sustainability and operations*	
2nd-order codes	Selected evidence on 1st-order codes
Process controlling and steering	" […] KPI is supposed to provide a target and help us to develop certain processes in a certain direction." (Beta) "So there's a lot of process optimization right behind it too […]." (*Theta*) "Each department has of course worked a little bit in its own area, but that certain topics are now being looked at more holistically along the value chain of the products, i.e., quite consciously at times." (*Iota*)
Revelation of sustainability practices	"[…] we already do a lot but in an uncoordinated way. That means the different departments, environment in development, in materials, in HR. Things are happening everywhere that you can put into this huge topic of sustainability." (*Epsilon*) "[…] rather, we have compiled a list of topics that are already underway but have never been communicated in terms of sustainability." (*Iota*) "You might not even be aware that every energy saving and so on is also a contribution to this. This is already decisively bundled and presented, and I assume that a report like this will make the whole thing a bit more detailed." (*Alpha*)
Aggregate dimension: *Normative management*	

(continued)

(continued)

Aggregate dimension: Motivational barrier to sustainability (-reporting)	
2nd-order codes	Selected evidence on 1st-order codes
Firm's purpose and goals	"[…] it is also clearer to everyone what the company is doing. What are the goals? […] Such a report is, of course, an important component. What is the mission? Where do we want to go? It is simply something that is goal-oriented, a positive side effect of such a report." (*Theta*) "[…] And it's not just about how do we make the products more sustainable but how fit is our business model for the future." (*Eta*)
Emphasis on family firms' culture	[…] is part of every DNA in a family business. That's how it is with us, you can see that the topic of sustainability is not only being addressed here for the report, for the reporting, but rather in such a way that many topics of the past have already been fundamentally implemented and sustainability has always been taken into consideration." (*Iota*) "We are talking about a family business that has been successful on the market for over 200 years, and this is a generational contract, so the generations have done this very, very consciously and very responsibly, always with a view to the future generation. Yes, well, that's the great thing, that as a family business, they can have a bit more long-term vision than perhaps some capital market-oriented companies have." (*Kappa*)
Aggregate dimension: *Sales and finance*	
2nd-order codes	Selected evidence on 1st-order codes

(continued)

(continued)

Aggregate dimension: Motivational barrier to sustainability (-reporting)	
Market attractivity	"I think so. Yes, yes exactly. If you get a good rating, then the customers also decide accordingly. They all want to have a positive image. I think that also plays a big role." (*Zeta*) "The compulsory reporting definitely makes it easier to answer the questionnaires for EcoVadis […]." (*Iota*) "A report is also incredibly helpful for the EcoVadis rating. The rating, I can probably refer to the report on page so and so for 80% of the questions. Once you have done the work, a rating is much easier." (*Eta*) "We are in the process of consulting EcoVadis for the first time. The connection is that the large amount of information we had to collect for EcoVadis can be used well for reporting." (*Theta*)
Liquidity improvement	"[…] especially when I consider the topic of water circuits or energy, then this not only pays off in terms of sustainability but also in terms of profitability […]." (Alpha) "But especially if I include the topic of water cycles or even energy, then that not only pays off in terms of sustainability, but also in terms of profitability and thus future security." (Alpha) "Yes, when we talk about opportunities, we think first and foremost about the cost issue. I say, is this a sustainable solution? And then the question is, what does it cost me or? Maybe it will even save me money." (Epsilon)
Aggregate dimension: *Research and development*	
2nd-order codes	Selected evidence on 1st-order codes

(continued)

(continued)

Aggregate dimension: Motivational barrier to sustainability (-reporting)	
Product innovations	"[…] sustainability is an opportunity, quite clearly, because it means that new machines are being produced that are much more energy-efficient, which of course also becomes a competitive factor." (*Theta*) "Innovations, because you have to be constantly creative and think, what can we do better?" (*Zeta*) "[…] where you can also see such opportunities and where you can perhaps build up new business models, evaluate them, validate them, so that you can really create something new." (*Epsilon*)
Circular economy focus	"[…] if we think in the direction of circular economy, where product development, customers, and also sales sit together, where perhaps from the product development point of view there are ideas that have not been recognized by the customer yet" (*Iota*) "New products, yes. If we now look at the topic of waste disposal and the Closed Substance Cycle Waste Management Act or closed substance cycle waste management in exactly this direction. That we are now trying to work with secondary raw materials or with, let's say, green carbide." (*Zeta*)
Aggregate dimension: Human resources	
2nd-order codes	Selected evidence on 1st-order codes
Employer branding	"Yes, also with the unsolicited applications. We receive unsolicited applications, and the topic of sustainability is mentioned immediately." (*Theta*) "Where we have received very positive feedback is actually with new talents. We have a lot of interest, even from trainees, from academics to industrial workers, who like to use it as a reference to understand what kind of company this actually is? So what do you deal with?" (*Beta*)

(continued)

(continued)

Aggregate dimension: Motivational barrier to sustainability (-reporting)	
Organizational learning	"Of course, we also have high standards for our people. Our employees are also interested, and they also want to understand the term sustainability in the context of the company." (*Beta*) "First we have to train the staff, let's say the management level, and only then transfer it to the whole workforce." (*Zeta*) "Yes, you notice with young employees or trainees that I am now increasingly being invited to give lectures. People are also interested in the topic. Last year we also had the training for energy and resource scouts for the first time, so there's already a lot going on." (*Theta*)

Appendix C. Breakdown of interview data

Company	Interview partner's job title	Interview length [min]	No. of transcript pages [#]
Alpha	Senior Vice President Sustainability & Innovation	28	6
Beta	Sustainability Manager	40	9
Gamma	Member of the Board	31	6
Delta	Strategy Specialist Sustainability	38	8
Epsilon	Chief Corporate Responsibility Officer	45	10
Zeta	Environmental Management Representative	47	10
Eta	Head of Sustainability & Communication	41	9
Theta	Project Manager Corporate Strategy & Sustainability	40	10
Iota	Sustainability Manager	42	11

(continued)

(continued)

Company	Interview partner's job title	Interview length [min]	No. of transcript pages [#]
Kappa	Strategic Advisor to CEO	43	10

Appendix D. Case Study Protocol

The following structure is based on the recommendations of Yin (2018).

Section A: Overview of the Case Study
Goal: The goals of this case study is twofold. Firstly, the study aims to uncover possible challenges in private German family firms due to the upcoming regulations on sustainability reporting (e.g., CSRD). Secondly, this study will identify potential opportunities that may arise from such a reporting mandate and show how family firms can benefit from them.

Research question:
What challenges do private family firms face regarding the introduction of a sustainability reporting mandate, and how can a standard framework provide guidance to meet or even exceed the legal requirements and unlock business opportunities?

Research unit:

- **Unit of analysis:** Private German family firms
- **Observation unit:** Implementation process of a sustainability reporting mandate and associated challenges and opportunities

Relevant literature and research stream:

- **Research stream 1:** Family firms' heterogeneous sustainability strategy and reporting behavior
- **Relevant literature:** (Cennamo et al., 2012; Hsueh et al., 2023; Sharma & Sharma, 2011; Vardaman & Gondo, 2014)
- **Research stream 2:** Effects of a sustainability reporting mandate
- **Relevant literature:** (Christensen et al., 2021; Fiechter et al., 2022; Ottenstein et al., 2022)

Section B: Data Collection Procedures
Multiple data collection methods to triangulate results:

- Primary data source: Semi-structured interviews with sustainability representatives of private German family firms
- Secondary data source: Firms' sustainability reports, company websites
- Chain of evidence as a tool for following the development of results through data collection and analysis

Section C: Interview Questions
Part 1: Background information of interviewee, family firm's structure and motivation to sustainability

1.1 **Interviewee's role**

- Could you please give me a brief introduction about your position and your tasks, touchpoints to the topic of sustainability?

1.2 **Company structure**

- How is the ownership and leadership structure of your employer as a family firm?
- Does your company have a separate board committee/department for sustainability matters?

1.3 **Motivation for sustainability**

- Which role does sustainability play within your company and how has it changed over time?
- What is your firm's motivation or intention for [company specific sustainability initiative, program, product etc.]?

Part 2: Sustainability reporting, challenges, and opportunities

2.1 **Motivation for sustainability reporting**

- Does your company create a sustainability report?
  ☐ If yes, left column. Otherwise, right column

Sustainability reporting in practice	Sustainability reporting not in practice
• What is your firm's motivation to report on sustainability topics voluntarily?	• Why does your company not report on sustainability topics?
2.2 Current reporting process	

(continued)

(continued)

Sustainability reporting in practice	Sustainability reporting not in practice
Report integration: • Is the sustainability report a standalone report or integrated into financial reporting? If, yes or no, why? **Reporting:** • How is the current reporting process? *Further question if sustainability reporting process is already well established* *Responsibilities:* • Which departments/persons are responsible for sustainability reporting? • Is external assurance used? If yes, why? *Scope:* • On what topics do you report on? • Why and how did you choose them? *Standardization:* • Do you have a standardized reporting process, or do you use any reporting standards, e.g., GRI? If yes or no, why? *Measurement:* • How do you collect/measure data? • How do you consolidate data? *Communication:* • Where do you disclose your sustainability report?	
2.3 Reporting challenges (First-order consequences)	
• Are you already familiar with mandatory sustainability regulations (e.g., CSRD)? If yes, what kind of measures has your company already taken? • What is (would be) the biggest current (potential) direct challenge regarding the implementation of the beforementioned mandatory directives and regulations? • If we split the topic of sustainability into its clusters, E = Environment, S = Social, G = Government. Do (you think) these challenges differ within those clusters? If yes, why?	
2.4 Synergies and opportunities (Second-order consequences)	
• Do you see any positive synergies or opportunities apart from the direct effects due to a mandatory sustainability reporting process?	

Part 3: Outlook and additional remarks

3.1 **Outlook**

- Do you have a roadmap or plan to deal with the introduction of those mandatory reporting regulations?
- Have you considered using external consultancy or take advice from industry peers?

3.2 **Additional remarks**

- Do you have any other ideas or thoughts on the topic that were not asked or that are currently on your agenda?

Assessment of Financial Performance of Decarbonization

5

The Influence of Family Ownership—Does it Pay for Family Firms to Decarbonize?

Johanna C. Schulze-Berge

This chapter assesses the linkage between corporate environmental performance (CEP) and corporate financial performance (CFP) in family firms via econometric techniques. I add to the question, "When does it pay to be green?" by investigating the condition of being a family firm. Existing research on the linkage between CEP and CFP for family firms is scarce, yields inconclusive findings, and lacks studies that express CEP via corporate carbon performance. Based on firm panel data from 74 private German family firms, I demonstrate a positive relationship between CEP expressed as carbon intensity and CFP expressed as Return on Assets (ROA) and Return on Equity (ROE). Moreover, I provide evidence for a moderating effect within the family firm dataset: the disclosure of a firm's CEP. My findings inform practitioners and regulators that decarbonization is financially incentivized in the absence of regulation, while widespread disclosure of corporate carbon footprints yields additional financial benefits.

This chapter has been accepted, presented, and published in the proceedings at the 45th EAA Annual Congress in Helsinki in 2023 and at IFERA23 "Back to the Core" in Krakow in 2023. A full paper version was published in the Academy of Management Proceedings (2023; Issue 1).

J. C. Schulze-Berge (✉)
TUM School of Management, Technical University of Munich, Munich, Germany
e-mail: Johanna.Schulze-Berge@whu.edu

G. Friedl (ed.), *Decarbonizing German Family Firms*, Familienunternehmen und KMU, https://doi.org/10.1007/978-3-658-47801-8_5

5.1 Introduction

Although it is unimaginable to exclude decarbonization from any economic, political, or societal agenda, decarbonization progress is lacking. On the 27th Conference of the Parties to the United Nations Framework Convention on Climate Change (COP27), United Nations' (UN) Secretary-General Antonio Guterres highlighted the urgency of successful decarbonization yet again: "Greenhouse gas emissions keep growing. Global temperatures keep rising. And our planet is fast approaching tipping points that will make climate chaos irreversible" (United Nations, 2022c). On top of this, French President Macron recognized that changes in the conditions under which firms decarbonize must not impede decarbonization progress: "We won't sacrifice our commitments under Russia's threat" (French Embassy India, 2022). UK Prime Minister Rishi Sunak agrees and even suggests decarbonization activities should be even more prioritized, as "diversifying our energy supplies by investing in renewables is precisely the way to insure ourselves against the risks of energy dependency" (UK Government, 2022).

Since one-fourth of all greenhouse gas emissions in Germany were incurred by manufacturing firms (German Environmental Agency, 2023), firms feel addressed by the above statements, highlighting that decarbonization is a necessity irrespective of arising challenges (Åhman et al., 2017). Yet, despite the high relevance of decarbonization for the industrial sector, firms might feel torn between their decarbonization and economic goals in the short term, for instance, via high initial investments (T. Hahn et al., 2010; Haque, 2017; van der Byl & Slawinski, 2015). Evidence for a win-win relationship, in which decarbonization improves financial performance, could aid in reconciling decarbonization and economic goals (Song et al., 2017; van der Byl & Slawinski, 2015). Therefore, the question "Does it pay to be green?" has emerged as a relevant question, which has also been manifested by empirical research in this field since the 1970s (Bragdon & Marlin, 1972; Busch et al., 2020; King & Lenox, 2002). Due to at times diverging results, the question has further evolved to "When does it pay to be green?" (Busch & Lewandowski, 2017; Lewandowski, 2017; Trumpp & Günther, 2017) to make more targeted statements about the conditions that enable companies to benefit financially from environmental initiatives (Endrikat et al., 2014; Garcés-Ayerbe et al., 2022; Grewatsch & Kleindienst, 2017).

One condition that has rarely been investigated thus far is the condition of being a family firm (Garcés-Ayerbe et al., 2022; Grewatsch & Kleindienst, 2017), although "ownership is among the most powerful forces that affect a firm's strategy and performance" (Grewatsch & Kleindienst, 2017, p. 26). Hence, family firms are substantially different from non-family firms and therefore, findings from the study of non-family firms cannot necessarily be applied (Blumentritt, 2006; Carney et al., 2015; Chrisman, Chua & Steier, 2005). In line with this, a family firm's motivation to decarbonize is distinct, as family firms strive to protect their socioemotional wealth (SEW) (Berrone et al., 2010; Block & Wagner, 2014; Garcés-Ayerbe et al., 2022; P. Sharma & Sharma, 2011). In addition, two relevant theories for the CEP-CFP relationship find a particular application for family firms. First, family firms are equipped with unique characteristics and capabilities to be assessed within the natural resource-based view (Garcés-Ayerbe et al., 2022; Neubaum et al., 2012). Second, also the stakeholder theory varies in its application due to the family as an additional stakeholder group (López-Pérez et al., 2018; Zellweger & Nason, 2008).

While there is abundant literature on the linkage between corporate environmental performance (CEP) and corporate financial performance (CFP) for non-family firms, predominantly pointing towards a positive relationship (e.g., Fuji et al. 2013; Gallego-Álvarez et al. 2015, van Emous et al. 2021), the research on family firms is not only rare but has also yielded diverging results (Craig & Dibrell, 2006; Garcés-Ayerbe et al., 2022; Huang et al., 2014; Neuman, 2013). These could be rooted in the usage of different measurement approaches for CEP (Busch & Lewandowski, 2017; E. M. Günther & Hoppe, 2014; Song et al., 2017; Trumpp & Günther, 2017) since a commonly recognized measurement framework is missing (E. M. Günther & Hoppe, 2014; Trumpp et al., 2015). Corporate carbon performance is a good exception, as the measurement of carbon dioxide (CO_2) emissions is clearly defined through globally accepted standards such as the Global Reporting Initiative or the Greenhouse Gas Protocol (Downar et al., 2021; Iwata & Okada, 2011). It has evolved to be the commonly recognized CEP measure used within non-family firm literature (Busch et al., 2020; Delmas et al., 2015; Fujii et al., 2013; Gallego-Álvarez et al., 2015; Lewandowski, 2017; Trumpp & Günther, 2017). A lack of analysis of the CEP-CFP relationship, where CEP is measured accordingly, leaves a crucial gap in the family firm research.

Furthermore, 90% of all German firms are family firms, which makes them the central backbone of successful German decarbonization (Stiftung Familienunternehmen, 2019a). It is, therefore, essential to explore whether family firms, as a special organizational form, can achieve a win-win situation between CEP and CFP. Hence, the following research question emerges: *"Does it pay for family firms to decarbonize?"*

To address this research question, I build a new, unbalanced dataset encompassing 74 private family firms for the timeframe of nine years (2013–2021). CEP is defined as corporate carbon performance, which is depicted as the inverse value of a firm's carbon intensity in this study. CFP considers a firm's profitability, expressed via the performance indicators Return on Assets (ROA) and Return on Equity (ROE). In addition, I introduce two moderating variables: the dirtiness of an *Industry* (Iwata & Okada, 2011; Mani & Wheeler, 1998) and the *Disclosure* of a firm's carbon performance (Delmas et al., 2015).

The panel regression's results on the relation between CEP and CFP show a positive, linear relationship between CEP and CFP for family firms. More precisely, the linear relationship is between CEP, thus the inverse of the logarithm of carbon intensity, and CFP. Consequently, it pays off more for firms to decarbonize once a moderate carbon intensity has been reached. Concerning the two moderating effects, I do not find evidence for a significant impact of *Industry* on the CEP-CFP relationship, while *Disclosure* has a significant, positive effect on the CEP-CFP relationship.

Compared with previous literature, I contribute in three distinct ways. First, I comply with the call for analyses assessing the impact of family ownership on the CEP-CFP relationship, aiming to reconcile conflicting results from the past and draw more refined conclusions about when to expect positive future returns (Garcés-Ayerbe et al., 2022; Grewatsch & Kleindienst, 2017).

Second, I show a moderating effect through voluntary public disclosure of carbon performance, which has rarely been investigated in the literature before (Delmas et al., 2015). Through consideration of this moderating variable, contradictory empirical evidence from the past might be reconciled. While disclosure of CEP has already gained importance (Methven O'Brien & Dhanarajan, 2016), I postulate its importance will even increase through its function as a competitive advantage and differentiator of firms. Subsequently, the reasons for this effect should be further explored, covering topics such as target performance measurement (Young & O'Byrne, 2001), external assurance provision (Ioannou & Serafeim, 2019), or proactivity of decarbonization strategies (Endrikat et al., 2014).

Third, to the best of my knowledge, I am the first to utilize corporate carbon performance to measure CEP for family firms. Corporate carbon performance data is rare, as family firms are not yet obliged by law to report it, and there exists no official directory that bundles the voluntarily shared data. Carbon performance has many advantages over other CEP measures, such as unambiguity through international reporting standards. Its' usage further enables me to bridge two previously distinct literature streams on the CEP-CFP relationship and family firms and perform initial comparisons between family and non-family firms regarding their ability "to be paid to be green."

For practitioners in family firms, I show that decarbonization, on average, pays off with increasing financial returns along the decarbonization journey. The relationship between CEP and CFP further improves with carbon performance disclosure. Consequently, firms can deploy a win-win mindset, increasing their decarbonization activities and reporting while benefitting financially.

My findings can further inform future climate laws and regulations. I show that family firms are financially incentivized to decarbonize even in the absence of regulation. While future regulation should not primarily focus on differentiation between industries, more firms should be informed, incentivized, or even obligated to disclose their environmental performance publicly.

5.2 Literature Review

5.2.1 Theoretical Foundation

A considerable amount of theorizing has been done regarding the relationship between CEP and CFP. While some scholars claim that firms are financially rewarded for engaging in environmental performance, others claim the opposite. Fig. 5.1 visualizes the different perspectives and the underlying theories on the CEP-CFP relationship.

Supporters of a win-win relationship (Porter & van der Linde, 1995) stress that environmental performance leads to an enhancement of financial performance, as firms correct for inefficiencies and invest in innovations, which leads to increased competitiveness of their offerings and consequently to higher profits. In light of this viewpoint, two complementary theoretical frameworks have manifested: the natural resource-based view (NRBV) and the instrumental stakeholder theory. First, the NRBV developed by Hart in 1995 stresses that "a firm can obtain sustainable competitive advantages from strategic resources and capacities for the environmental sustainability of its economic activity" (Garcés-Ayerbe et al., 2022, p. 4). At the core of this theory are strategic resources and capacities that are rare and inimitable, thus leading to a sustained competitive advantage (Hart, 1995; Hart & Dowell, 2011; Menguc & Ozanne, 2005; Russo & Fouts, 1997; Sharma & Vredenburg, 1998). Second, the instrumental stakeholder theory (Donaldson & Preston, 1995; Jones, 1995) also advises a positive relationship between CEP and CFP, as meeting the environmental expectations of various stakeholders leads to an improved financial performance by unlocking competitive advantages such as enhanced reputation and management attention or faster adaptation to external demands (Orlitzky et al., 2003).

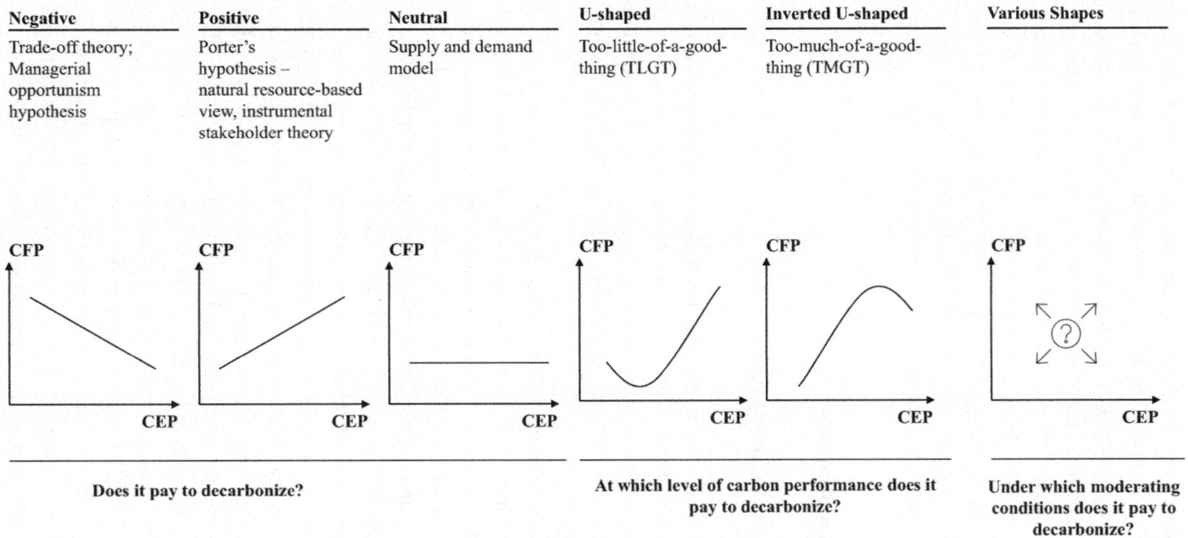

Fig. 5.1 CEP-CFP relationships. *Source* Own figure developed from Tumpp and Günther (2017), López-Pérez et al. (2018), Fuji et al. (2013)

Another group of researchers argues that the relationship between CEP and CFP follows a classical supply and demand model, in which a cost-benefit analysis reveals the optimal level of environmental investment that maximizes a firm's profits (McWilliams & Siegel, 2001). Last, proponents of a trade-off theory claim that environmental investments generate costs that negatively reduce firm profits (Andersson et al., 2018; Friedman, 1970; Levitt, 1958). Accordingly, the managerial opportunism theory explains that managers adjust their environmental investments depending on the firm's financial performance (Preston & O'Bannon, 1997). While managers tend to maximize profits by reducing environmental investments in times of good financial firm performance, managers invest heavily in environmental investments in times of bad financial firm performance to justify the lack of profits (Hang et al., 2018).

To reconcile these contrasting theories regarding the impact of CEP on CFP, the research focus has shifted from "Does it pay to be green?" to "When does it pay to be green?". Two theories, "Too-much-of a-good-thing" (TMGT) in the form of a U-shape and "Too-little-of-a-good-thing" (TLGT) in the form of an inverted U-shape are the prevalent theories in this field (Lewandowski, 2017; Trumpp & Günther, 2017). Both of these theoretical concepts include inflection points where the relationship between CEP and CFP switches as an optimal or minimum level of CEP has been reached so that more differentiated statements are made based on a firm's environmental performance level (Lewandowski, 2017; Trumpp & Günther, 2017). Also, analyzing internal and external moderating conditions helps to further differentiate the question of "When does it pay to be green?" (Endrikat et al., 2014; Grewatsch & Kleindienst, 2017). One condition that has rarely been investigated thus far is the condition of being a family firm (Garcés-Ayerbe et al., 2022; Grewatsch & Kleindienst, 2017), although "ownership is among the most powerful forces that affect a firm's strategy and performance" (Grewatsch & Kleindienst, 2017, p. 26).

5.2.2 Empirical Evidence

There is an abundance of literature focusing on the CEP-CFP relationship, usually covering accounting-based and market-based financial performance (Busch & Lewandowski, 2017; Endrikat et al., 2014). As private family firms are not listed on any stock market, market-based financial performance in terms of Tobin's q and Total Shareholder Return (TSR) is not available. Therefore, this chapter will only consider accounting-based financial performance, with a particular interest in

ROA and ROE as commonly accepted and prevalent metrics investigated (Busch et al., 2020; Gallego-Álvarez et al., 2015; Lewandowski, 2017).

Meta-studies in the field of CEP and CFP (Dixon-Fowler et al., 2013; Hang et al., 2018; Orlitzky et al., 2003) find a positive linkage between CEP and CFP. The same holds for meta-analyses specifically focusing on CEP, defined as corporate carbon performance (Busch & Lewandowski, 2017; Galama & Scholtens, 2021). Also, in the course of single empirical studies, the opinion of a positive linear relationship (Fujii et al., 2013; Gallego-Álvarez et al., 2015; van Emous et al., 2021) or a positive relationship in a U-shaped setting (Lewandowski, 2017; Trumpp & Günther, 2017) seem to prevail. The only study in this field focusing on Germany by Velte in 2017 also shows a positive relationship between CEP, expressed as environmental, social, governance (ESG) performance, and CFP.

Outliers constitute the studies of Delmas et al. in (2015) and Busch et al. in (2020), where the latter is a replication and extension of the study of Delmas et al. in terms of the temporal and geographical scope. Both show a negative relationship between CEP and CFP. The different findings could be rooted in the usage of partially extrapolated data instead of real values (Busch et al., 2020). Both authors use *Trucost* as the database, of which around 50% of the data are *Trucost's* estimations (Busch et al., 2020). Moreover, Delmas et al. (2015) recognize that the effect on the financial accounting performance might be hindered by the utilized data between 2004–2008 when there was still significant insecurity regarding upcoming GHG regulation. From a market-based perspective, Delmas et al. (2015) find a positive relationship, showing that investors expected changes in external conditions such as regulation but that no passed regulation has impacted firms' accounting performance yet.

Meanwhile, there is also an additional, smaller research stream that specifically targets family firms. Various definitions of a family firm exist (O'Boyle et al., 2012; Posch & Speckbacher, 2012). A key feature of family firms is the dominant influence of the family (Chua et al., 1999; König et al., 2013), which I define as 50% of the ownership rights to be in possession of one or a small number of families. The 50% threshold contrasts the 20% ownership rights rule, which is commonly applied for publicly listed family firms (La Porta et al., 1999). Interests of the family are more evident in private family firms, as ownership is less scattered (Cruz et al., 2015). In addition, only 10% of firms on the German benchmark index DAX are considered family firms according to the 20% ownership rights definition (Stiftung Familienunternehmen, 2019a). Thus, the findings of generic CEP-CFP work cannot be applied to private family firms.

The CEP-CFP literature with a specific focus on the condition of being a family firm is not only scarce but also shows diverse results (Adomako et al.,

2019; Craig & Dibrell, 2006; Garcés-Ayerbe et al., 2022; Huang et al., 2014; López-Pérez et al., 2018; Neubaum et al., 2012), stemming most likely from different measures of CEP. CEP is adequately described as a multidimensional construct, where the results cannot be transferred or compared between different dimensions and definitions of CEP (Busch & Lewandowski, 2017; Trumpp et al., 2015). For instance, different environmental challenges affect firms' operations differently (Fujii et al., 2013) and stakeholder reactions vary depending on the type of environmental problem (Iwata & Okada, 2011). Among the literature on the relationship between CEP and CFP, each author uses a different definition of CEP. While several authors apply self-defined constructs for firms' corporate social responsibility, environmental orientation, or management (Adomako et al., 2019; Craig & Dibrell, 2006; López-Pérez et al., 2018; Neubaum et al., 2012), Garcés-Ayerbe et al. (2022) are the first to use a clearly defined, quantifiable term for environmental performance: the annual amount of environmental investment. In this manner, they find a positive relationship between CEP and CFP, which matches the results of Craig and Dibrell (2006) and López-Pérez et al. (2018). Meanwhile, Neubaum et al. (2012) and Adomako et al. (2019) obtain no significant relationship between CEP and CFP for family firms. No study has considered the impact of corporate carbon performance on CFP for family firms.

5.2.3 Hypotheses Development

Family firms' motivation to engage in CEP is rooted in the phenomenon called socioemotional wealth (SEW), which can be described as "the non-financial aspects of the firm that meet a family's affective needs such as identity, the ability to exercise family influence, and the perpetuation of the family dynasty" (Gómez-Mejía et al., 2007, p. 106). Family firms engage in environmental activities to protect their SEW (Berrone et al., 2010; Block & Wagner, 2014), e.g., expressed via an excellent corporate reputation, transgenerational value, or close relationships with their employees, because of the imbrication of the family and the business (Berrone et al., 2012; Brundin et al., 2014; Habbershon et al., 2003).

Linking the SEW with the NRBV is a new pathway, which was introduced by Garcés-Ayerbe et al. in 2022 in the course of discussions about the financial performance implications of environmental investments. In family firms, decisions are made with a long-term, transgenerational mindset (Brundin et al., 2014; Le Breton-Miller & Miller, 2006). Through the family's interest in the firm's long-term strategic development, family firms may be willing to pursue investments that go beyond standard payoff calculations (Brundin et al., 2014). This fits longer payback cycles of environmental initiatives that often require significant investments in the short term (van der Byl & Slawinski, 2015). Moreover, family firms are known for establishing social capital and long-term relationships (Carney, 2005; Kammerlander & Prügl, 2016). This leads to reduced costs for managing diverse and sometimes complex alliances for environmental initiatives (Mohr & Puck, 2013) and faster credibility gains for environmental initiatives in the public (Debicki et al., 2017). Family firms are further notable for carefully selecting their strategic investments (Craig & Dibrell, 2006; Kammerlander & Prügl, 2016), as their wealth is directly linked to the family firm (Carney, 2005; Cruz et al., 2010). A more careful selection of environmental projects can enable a superior CFP in the long run (Craig & Dibrell, 2006). Furthermore, family firms often establish close ties with their employees and practice a culture built on shared values (Schulze et al., 2001) so that employees feel more involved and committed to the firm's activities (Craig & Dibrell, 2006; Huang et al., 2014; Kammerlander & Prügl, 2016). Once a family firm has decided to decarbonize, corporate environmental performance activities are therefore expected to be executed more effectively and generate more innovations (Craig & Dibrell, 2006; Huang et al., 2014). High independence and flexibility in decision-making processes (Brundin et al., 2014; von Stietencron, 2013), in contrast to hierarchical decision-making structures, also serve as a facilitator of environmental innovations (Craig & Dibrell, 2006). In conclusion, family firms possess intangible resources that help them select and pursue environmental activities, which can enable better financial performance as postulated by the NRBV (Garcés-Ayerbe et al., 2022).

Moreover, applying the SEW to the stakeholder theory is also a promising pathway. Stakeholder theory in the context of family firms is different due to the existence of an additional stakeholder group: the family (Zellweger & Nason, 2008). Family firms have a special incentive to satisfy a growing number of stakeholders (Berrone et al., 2010; Sharma, 2001, 2004; Zellweger & Nason, 2008) due to the overlap between the business and the family systems (López-Pérez et al., 2018). Family firms integrate "stakeholders' expectations into their strategic choices to protect their family identification and image" (García-Sánchez et al., 2021, p. 1016). Therefore, meeting the environmental claims of stakeholders is strongly relevant for family firms (Habbershon et al., 2003; López-Pérez et al., 2018). In 2018, López-Pérez et al. show that the positive effect of environmental activities on the financial firm value is more pronounced for family firms than non-family firms. This holds for the direct impact of environmental activities as well as the indirect impact of environmental activities via corporate reputation (López-Pérez et al., 2018). Therefore, the SEW theory, in conjunction with the

NRBV and the instrumental stakeholder theory, respectively, form the foundation to hypothesize the following:

> ***Hypothesis 1 (H1):*** *The CEP-CFP relationship for family firms is positive, i.e., the lower a family firm's CO_2 intensity, the higher its CFP.*

Past literature in the field of CEP and CFP has shown that it is reasonable to further divide a sample of firms depending on their industry affiliation. Kim and Bae postulate in 2022 that firms follow diverse production processes so that they will also react differently to climate regulations. In 2011, Delmas et al. also find that industries that vary in their carbon intensity will face different regulations and deploy different strategies against pollution. Iwata and Okada (2011) provide empirical evidence for the link between the dirtiness of industries based on emissions per unit of output (see Appendix B) and their environmental performance. It seems that firms from carbon-intensive, so-called "dirty industries" face higher costs until they meet regulations and achieve a reasonably good environmental performance. Consequently, it takes longer for them to generate additional revenues through the recognition of environmentally friendly products and corporate image. For this reason, I hypothesize:

> ***Hypothesis 2 (H2):*** *The positive effect of CEP on CFP will be weaker for family firms from dirty industries than for family firms from clean industries.*

Albeit German family firms are not included in mandatory carbon disclosure agreements such as the Non-Financial Reporting Directive (NFRD) (European Parliament, 2014), many family firms disclose their carbon emission information publicly on their website or in sustainability reports. In 2021, Downar et al. found that firms that disclose their carbon performance publicly are more strongly incentivized to improve their emissions than their counterparts that report emissions only in the inner firm context. They base this on the so-called targeted disclosure cycle theory by Fung in 2007, which states that disclosure triggers the real effects of the disclosed variables. The underlying reason is that disclosure influences stakeholders' behavior (Fung, 2007). Firms forecast these changes in behavior and pursue initiatives to improve the disclosed results (Fung, 2007). Next to more dedicated management of the disclosed variables, public disclosure leads firms to include the variable of interest in their performance evaluation and incentive system (Kaplan & Anderson, 2007; Young & O'Byrne, 2001), enabling the dual pursual, tracking, and achievement of carbon and financial performance goals. In addition, firms that report their CO_2 emissions publicly are more likely to pay for external insurance provisions and follow accepted reporting guidelines, which improves the quality of the CO_2 information (Ioannou & Serafeim, 2019), making a positive linkage between CEP and CFP more feasible. Last, firms that voluntarily report their CO_2 information to the public can further be regarded as proactive in their strategic approach toward carbon performance. Proactive approaches to CEP lead to a better CFP (Endrikat et al., 2014; King & Lenox, 2002; Sharma & Vredenburg, 1998) through process restructuring, material savings, and more process innovation (Russo & Fouts, 1997). In conclusion, I state the following hypothesis:

Hypothesis 3 (H3): *The positive effect of CEP on CFP will be stronger for family firms that publicly disclose their CEP than for family firms without public disclosure.*

5.3 Empirical Analysis

5.3.1 Sample Description

To test my hypotheses, I have built an unbalanced panel dataset for German family firms from the manufacturing sector. Since there is no official registry for family firms in Germany, several publicly available lists[1] and databases[2] were used to find German family firms. Identified firms were analyzed along the sampling process depicted in Fig. 5.2.

Publicly listed firms are ruled by different governance mechanisms (Cruz et al., 2015) and are often defined by a threshold of only 20% family ownership (La Porta et al., 1999). Service firms are structurally different from manufacturing firms (Trumpp & Günther, 2017) and not as heavily impacted by environmental issues (Iwata & Okada, 2011). Therefore, all publicly listed firms and private family firms with less than 50% ownership rights by the family, as well as service firms, were excluded before environmental data availability was investigated.

In this study, environmental data is defined by corporate carbon performance. I purposefully use CO_2 emissions, as they are directly linked to climate change (Trumpp & Günther, 2017), crucial for ~ 50,000 European firms to comply with

[1] "Lexikon der Deutschen Familienunternehmen" (Venohr and Langenscheidt, 2015); "Top 500 German Family Businesses - the economy most dependent on family enterprises" by Family Capital (2022).

[2] Carbon Disclosure Project (CDP) and Science-Based Target initiative (SBTi).

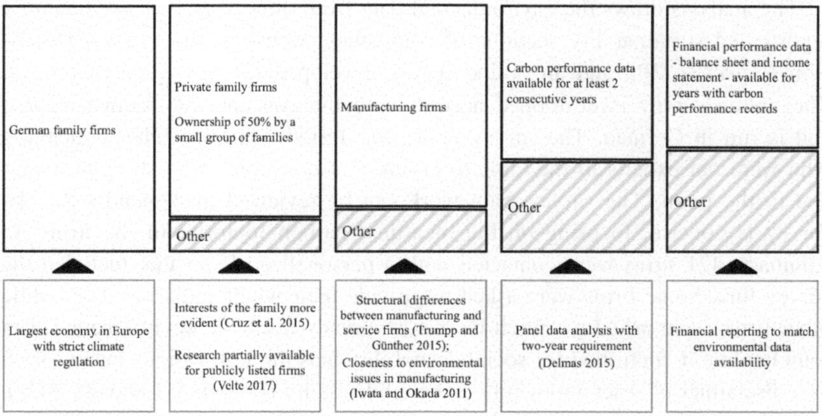

Fig. 5.2 Sampling process. *Source* Own figure

the Corporate Sustainability Reporting Directive (CSRD) (European Commission, 2023) and clearly defined and quantifiable through global reporting standards like the Global Reporting Initiative or the Greenhouse Gas Protocol instead of any arbitrarily defined environmental scores (Iwata & Okada, 2011). More specifically, I collect the annual sum of Scope 1 and 2 CO_2- (equivalents) per year and firm, excluding Scope 3 emissions. Scope 1 and 2 are sufficient to incorporate relevant "investments, innovations and operational changes" (Misani & Pogutz, 2015, p. 153) and the emission scope does not impact the empirical outcome (Busch et al., 2020). While carbon performance can be expressed in relative or absolute terms, I use a relative measure by dividing total carbon emissions by sales, similar to many other studies in this field (Busch et al., 2020; Busch & Lewandowski, 2017; Downar et al., 2021; Trumpp & Günther, 2017). In this manner, extraordinary growth and size-related events, such as acquisitions or process outsourcing, are incorporated (Busch et al., 2020; Busch & Lewandowski, 2017; Downar et al., 2021; Trumpp & Günther, 2017). I utilize the inverse of carbon intensity to signal that a low value indicates good corporate carbon performance (Busch et al., 2020; Trumpp & Günther, 2017). To avoid inconsistencies in the definition of CEP with previous studies for non-family firms (Busch et al., 2020; Delmas et al., 2015; Iwata & Okada, 2011), I use annual reported emissions in contrast to rarely used measure of year-on-year changes in carbon performance.

The analysis draws the environmental data from three sources—sustainability reports and sustainability sections of companies' websites, the *Carbon Disclosure Project (CDP)*, and an online survey developed for this research project. The online survey is developed according to the concepts of Neuman (2013) and is run in German. The survey guide was tested with researcher colleagues who were not experts in the topic to ensure that questions were straightforward and to the point. The survey framework can be reviewed in Appendix A. The survey is concise, focusing on the measured carbon footprint of the firms. In summary, 421 firms were contacted with a personalized letter that included the survey link. Some firms were asked to provide their whole emission data, while other firms were asked to enrich the set of already available environmental data found online. I controlled for social desirability bias through various means, such as a disclaimer of strict anonymity and confidentiality (Bergen & Labonté, 2020), self-administration of questionnaires, and the neutral formulation of items (Nederhof, 1985). The response rate is 11%, similar to other survey-based family firm studies, such as Kammerlander et al. (2020: 12%) and Cruz et al. (2010: 11%). In terms of controlling for a nonresponse bias (Armstrong & Overton, 1977), I ensured that there were no significant differences between respondents and non-respondents in terms of size, age, and industry mix. Ultimately, 5% of the firms that provided survey data form part of the final sample since many firms filled in CO_2 emission data for only one year, were adversely impacted by company restructuring, or did not publish all needed financial performance figures.

The list of firms with emission data for at least two consecutive years, which is a criterion also applied by other authors (Delmas et al., 2015), was complemented with financial data for the independent and control variables. CFP can cover four aspects: liquidity, profitability, growth, and stock market performance (Hamann et al., 2013). In this work, I focus on CFP expressed as profitability via financial ratios, namely ROA and ROE, which are generally accepted measures of a firm's financial performance and in line with previous studies (Busch et al., 2020; Gallego-Álvarez et al., 2015; Lewandowski, 2017). Data is retrieved from *Dafne*, a database provided by *Bureau van Dijk* that contains comprehensive information on private companies in Germany. Potential data lags were filled up with the Federal Gazette (Bundesanzeiger), which is Germany's central platform for pronouncements, announcements, and legally relevant company news. Through this separate financial data collection, I controlled for common-method bias (Podsakoff et al., 2003).

Table 5.1 illustrates the distribution of the sample observations. The final sample comprises an unbalanced panel dataset of 74 German manufacturing firms containing historical CO_2- (equivalent) and financial data from 2013 to 2021, yielding 242 observations in a time-lagged scenario and 296 observations in a non-time-lagged scenario. The panel is unbalanced because the number of firm-year observations varies between two to nine years. Since family firms are not regulated by any mandatory environmental reporting yet, firms can deliberately decide whether they measure their carbon performance in CO_2 or CO_2 equivalents (CO_2e), also encompassing other greenhouse gases next to carbon dioxide. As firms do not share the input factors for their CO_2e calculations, the translation back to pure CO_2 emissions is not feasible. However, in Germany in 2021, CO_2 accounted for 87% of all greenhouse gases, so the impact of the additional greenhouse gases is rather small (German Environmental Agency, 2021). Therefore, 50 firms in my sample report their carbon performance in CO_2e, while 24 firms report their carbon performance in CO_2. In addition, I ensure that there are no significant differences between the subgroups in terms of their industry affiliation, size expressed as revenues or employees, and probability for public disclosure, so it is not necessary to differentiate the sample accordingly. In chapter three, I also control whether the descriptive statistics are similar (see Appendix C).

I tested the representativeness of my sample in terms of firm size, age, and industry. The firms in my sample earned an average of ~ 2,800 million euros in revenue in 2020, while they employed an average of ~ 15,000 employees. Consequently, they are significantly larger than a typical German family firm, which consists of up to 49 employees (Gottschalk & Lubczyk, 2019) and one million euros in revenue (Gottschalk & Lubczyk, 2019). Yet, I purposefully intended a larger firm size, as the financial data availability is very limited for small and medium-sized firms without public reporting requirements of a detailed balance sheet and profit and loss statement as defined by German law (German Federal Office of Justice, 2022). In terms of age, most firms were founded between 1900 and 1950, with an average age of 112 years in 2022, when the research was administered. This figure matches the average age of German family firms described in other analyses (Family Capital, 2022; Gottschalk & Lubczyk, 2019). Moreover, the sample represents the split between clean and dirty firms (see Appendix B) in Germany well, with 69% of firms from clean industries in this sample, compared to 61% of clean industries observed by the German Federal Statistical Office (German Federal Statistical Office, 2019). The distribution of the single industries within the German manufacturing sector is also adequately represented. Minor differences can be observed regarding the glass and ceramics industry, which is underrepresented by 5%, while the pharmaceutical industry is overrepresented by 3% (German Federal Statistical Office, 2019). In sum, the characteristics of my sample indicate the results may not be generalizable for

Table 5.1 Distribution of the sample

		Sample distribution	
		N	%
Environmental data availability	2–3 years	39	52.7
	4–5 years	16	21.6
	>5 years	19	25.7
Unit of measurement	CO_2	24	32.4
	CO_2e	50	67.6
Environmental data disclosure	Public disclosure	48	64.9
	No public disclosure	26	35.1
Founding year	1800–1900	26	35.1
	1901–1950	36	48.6
	1951–2000	12	16.2
Employees	**Average, in 2020**		
	<500	9	12.2
	500–2,000	22	29.7
	>2,000	43	58.1
Revenues	**Yearly, in 2020**		
	<500 m €	33	44.6
	500–1,000 m €	14	18.9
	>1,000 m €	27	36.5
Industry	**"Clean" industries**		
	Transportation equipment	13	17.6
	Machinery	11	14.9
	Electric appliances	9	12.2
	Other manufacturing	9	12.2
	Foods	8	10.8
	Glass and ceramics products	1	1.4
	"Dirty" industries		
	Metal products	10	13.5
	Rubber and plastic products	6	8.1
	Pharmaceutical	3	4.1

(continued)

Table 5.1 (continued)

		Sample distribution	
		N	%
	Chemicals	2	2.7
	Paper and pulp	2	2.7
Total		**74**	**100**

Source. Own table

smaller family firms, while otherwise, a good representation of a German family firm is given.

5.3.2 Methodology

I utilize an ordinary least square regression analysis to measure the effect of CEP on CFP in family firms. While *i* denotes the firm, *j* describes the industry, and *t* represents time.

First, I set up Model 1 as a linear baseline model, which I apply to the whole firm sample to test hypothesis 1 (H1). I will further apply Model 1 to four subsamples. Thus, I investigate whether the estimation results differ for the subgroups that I mention in the course of hypothesis two (H2), namely clean and dirty firms, and three (H3), firms with public disclosure and firms without public disclosure. Other researchers proceed similarly (Iwata & Okada, 2011; Kim & Bae, 2022; Trumpp & Günther, 2017). Subsequently, I assess whether any differences between these subsamples are significant through the introduction of interaction terms. Model 2 tests whether the effect of industry affiliation is significant by introducing the interaction term between *CEP* and *Industry*. Model 3 tests separately whether public disclosure has a significant impact by assessing the interaction term of *CEP* and *Disclosure*. This procedure resembles the approaches by authors like Leonidou et al. in 2013 and Iwata and Okada in 2011. *Industry* is a dummy variable stating whether firms are from clean industries (see Appendix B). The variable *Disclosure* depicts whether firms share their environmental data publicly.

Model 1: Baseline model

$$CFP' = ß_0 + ß_1 * CEP_{i,t-1} + ß_2 * Leverage_{i,t} + ß_3 * Size_{i,t} + ß_4 * Growth_{i,t} + ß_5 * Capital\ Intensity_{i,t} + u_{j,t} + \epsilon_{i,t}$$

Model 2: Industry model

$$
\begin{aligned}
CFP' = {} & ß_0 + ß_1 * CEP_{i,t-1} + ß_3 * Size_{i,t} + ß_4 * Growth_{i,t} \\
& + ß_5 * Capital\ Intensity_{i,t} + ß_6 * Industry_{i,t} \\
& + ß_7 * CEP_{i,t-1} * Industry_{i,t} + u_{j,t} + \epsilon_{i,t}
\end{aligned}
$$

Model 3: Disclosure model

$$
\begin{aligned}
CFP' = {} & ß_0 + ß_1 * CEP_{i,t-1} + ß_2 * Leverage_{i,t} + ß_3 * Size_{i,t} \\
& + ß_4 * Growth_{i,t} + ß_5 * Capital\ Intensity_{i,t} \\
& + ß_6 * Disclosure_{i,t} + ß_7 * CEP_{i,t-1} * Disclosure_{i,t} + u_{j,t} + \epsilon_{i,t}
\end{aligned}
$$

with $CFP' = \{ROE\}$

The multivariate framework includes several control variables that are likely to determine the dependent variable. I include a variable to control for *Size* measured as a firm's number of employees (Garcés-Ayerbe et al., 2022; Kim & Bae, 2022; Trumpp & Günther, 2017). While some authors claim that the firm's size has a positive impact on the profitability due to the higher availability of assets and resources (Trumpp & Günther, 2017) and the increased visibility of these firms (Bansal & Roth, 2000), other authors claim that a large size may hinder profitability via a more hierarchical, inflexible structure (King & Lenox, 2002). I further control for a firm's *Leverage* measured as a firm's total debt divided by a firm's total assets (Delmas et al., 2015; Trumpp & Günther, 2017; Velte, 2017). As high leverage is associated with high financial risk or worsened supplier conditions, leverage is expected to harm CFP (Busch et al., 2020; Iwata & Okada, 2011). Furthermore, I consider *Capital Intensity* calculated as capital expenditures divided by total assets (Trumpp & Günther, 2017; van Emous et al., 2021). Capital intensity could yield growth opportunities via additional assets and investments (Busch et al., 2020; Busch & Lewandowski, 2017), while some authors also demonstrate its' negative impact (King & Lenox, 2002). Last, I control for *Growth* expressed as a firm's annual sales ratio, which also potentially impacts a firm's profitability positively (Delmas et al., 2015; Trumpp & Günther, 2017) or negatively (Gallego-Álvarez et al., 2015; Iwata & Okada, 2011).

In line with existing research (Busch et al., 2020; Trumpp & Günther, 2017), I seek to address the presence of endogeneity between *CEP* and *CFP* by using a one-year time-lagged (*t−1*) measure of CEP. To correct for skewed distributions, *CEP* and *Size* are transformed using logarithms. A Hausman test shows no systematic differences between the random and fixed effects model (Prob >

chi2 > 0.05). Therefore, I choose the random effects model for efficiency reasons, similar to Gallego-Álvarez et al. in 2015 and Fujii et al. in 2013. In addition, to control for the unobserved industry- and time-specific effects (Baird et al., 2012; Iwata & Okada, 2011; van Emous et al., 2021), I introduce u in addition to ϵ, the remainder stochastic disturbance term. Since the time horizon for the average firm in my sample is relatively short, this study controls for the industry instead of the firm-specific effects (Iwata & Okada, 2011).

5.4 Results

5.4.1 Econometric Analyses

Table 5.2 illustrates the descriptive statistics after winsorizing all continuous variables at the fifth and 95th percentiles. The sample means of the profitability ratios *ROA* and *ROE* are positive, which shows that the firms in the sample have been operating profitably between the years 2013–2021. Furthermore, Appendix C compares the descriptive statistics of firms using CO_2 and firms using CO_2e as the unit of measurement. Due to similar reported statistics, I will proceed with the regression analysis for the joint sample of firms.

Table 5.3 shows the bivariate correlation coefficients for the variables in the empirical analysis. There is a positive association between *CEP* and profitability expressed as *ROA* and *ROE*. The comparably high correlation between *ROA* and *ROE* is uncritical, as both are dependent variables that are used in separate analyses. As the variance inflation factors (VIFs) of all explanatory variables are below 2 (mean VIF = 1.04), multicollinearity does not impact the analysis.

5.4.2 Examination Results

I present the results of panel regression analysis on the relation between CEP and CFP for the whole sample in Table 5.4. According to Model 1, if CO_2 intensity is decreased by 1%, *ROA* increases by 0.005% or 0.00005 units ($p < 0.01$) and *ROE* by 0.01% or 0.0001 units ($p < 0.05$). More precisely, the functional form describing the CEP-CFP relationship is a linear relationship between *CEP*, so the inverse of the logarithm of carbon intensity and CFP expressed as *ROA*. The graph decreases more slowly with increasing carbon intensity. Therefore, it pays off more for firms to decarbonize once a moderate carbon intensity has been reached. Firms will experience relatively smaller gains in *ROA* at the beginning

Table 5.2 Descriptive statistics

Variable	Description	Mean	Median	SD	Minimum	Maximum
ROA	Net income divided by total assets	0.042	0.042	0.036	−0.027	0.112
ROE	Net income divided by equity	0.097	0.091	0.092	−0.077	0.309
CEP	Log of the inverse of carbon intensity (Scope 1 and 2 CO_2(e) / sales)	10.480	10.425	1.174	8.475	12.701
Size	Log of number of employees (yearly average)	8.040	7.956	1.569	5.382	11.070
Leverage	Total debt / total assets	0.374	0.389	0.161	0.118	0.638
Capital Intensity	Total capital expenditures / total assets	0.069	0.061	0.040	0.006	0.155
Growth	Annual change in sales ratio	0.018	0.018	0.085	−0.152	0.176
Industry	Indication whether a firm belongs to a clean industry	0.682	1.000	0.467	0	1
Disclosure	Indication whether a firm publicly disclosed its' carbon performance	0.599	1.000	0.491	0	1

Note. Descriptive statistics for the entire sample, covering 242 observations with a one-year time lag. The sample covers observations over the period 2013–2021. All continuous variables are winsorized at the 5 and 95 percentiles. ROA = return on assets; ROE = return on equity; CEP = corporate environmental performance; Growth = sales growth; Size = firm size; Industry = dirtiness defined as carbon intensity (see Appendix B), dichotomous variable is equal to unity if industry is clean, zero if dirty; Disclosure = dichotomous variable is equal to unity for a firm with external CEP disclosure, zero otherwise
Source. Own table

Table 5.3 Summary of bivariate correlation coefficients

	1	2	3	4	5	6	7	8	9
1. ROA	1.000								
2. ROE	0.758	1.000							
3. CEP	0.001	0.006	1.000						
4. Size	−0.090	−0.043	−0.049	1.000					
5. Leverage	−0.270	0.126	0.002	0.022	1.000				
6. Capital Intensity	0.026	0.024	0.030	0.100	0.186	1.000			
7. Growth	0.262	0.104	0.014	−0.017	0.026	0.139	1.000		
8. Industry	−0.055	0.028	−0.244	0.090	0.191	−0.019	−0.030	1.000	
9. Disclosure	0.027	−0.003	0.141	0.046	−0.048	0.040	0.019	0.002	1.000

Note. The coefficients are based on the full sample of 242 observations. The variables are defined in Table 5.2
Source. Own table

Table 5.4 Regression analysis on the CEP-CFP relationship

Model 1—Full sample		
Dependent variable	ROA	ROE
CEP	0.005 (0.002)***	0.010 (0.005)**
Size	−0.003 (0.001)**	−0.009 (0.004)**
Leverage	−0.060 (0.014)***	0.058 (0.038)
Capital Intensity	0.033 (0.051)	−0.078 (0.142)
Growth	0.144 (0.024)***	0.366 (0.065)***
R^2	0.247	0.178
Adjusted R^2	0.231	0.160

Note. Standard errors are in parentheses. The variables are defined in Table 5.2
* $p < 0.1$; ** $p < 0.05$; *** $p < 0.01$
Source. Own table

of their decarbonization journey compared with the gains in *ROA* after they have already partially reduced their carbon intensity. For *ROA*, the coefficients of the control variables *Size, Leverage,* and *Growth* are all statistically significant, while *Capital Intensity* shows no significant effect. *Size* and *Leverage* have a negative impact on ROA, whereas *Growth* exerts a positive influence. Overall, *ROE* yields very similar results to *ROA*. However, only *Growth* and *Size* are significant. The explanatory power of the model inferred from the adjusted R-squares is ~23% for *ROA* and ~16% for *ROE*, which is higher than the findings from comparable studies by Busch et al. in 2020 as well as Lewandowski in 2017 and slightly lower than the work by Gallego-Álvarez et al. in 2015. In conclusion, I accept hypothesis 1, stating a positive relationship between CEP and CFP.

I show the estimation results of the panel regression analysis on the relation between CEP and CFP for the clean and dirty firm samples separately in Table 5.5. On the one hand, the findings for ROA from the main regression analysis do still apply for the firms from clean industries with a coefficient of 0.05 ($p < 0.05$) and an adjusted R-squares of 20%, while I do not obtain any significant results in terms of ROA for firms from dirty industries. On the other hand, findings for ROE are significant for firms from dirty industries ($p < 0.1$) and not for firms from clean industries. Despite these differences between the subsamples, neither the dummy variable *Industry* nor the interaction term *CEP* × *Industry* is significant in Model 2. Therefore, I can't find evidence for a significant moderating effect of *Industry* on the CEP-CFP relationship. Hence, I reject hypothesis 2.

Table 5.5 Regression analysis on the CEP-CFP relationship moderated by industry

	Model 1—"Clean" Firms		Model 1—"Dirty" Firms		Model 2—Interaction Industry × CEP	
Dependent variable	ROA	ROE	ROA	ROE	ROA	ROE
CEP	0.005 (0.002)**	0.007 (0.007)	0.005 (0.003)	0.012 (0.007)*	0.004 (0.003)	0.014 (0.009)
Size	−0.003 (0.002)*	−0.005 (0.005)	−0.006 (0.002)***	−0.018 (0.006)***	−0.004 (0.001)**	−0.009 (0.004)**
Leverage	−0.029 (0.018)	0.108 (0.052)**	−0.129 (0.022)***	−0.062 (0.053)	−0.060 (0.014)***	0.054 (0.041)
Capital Intensity	−0.007 (0.062)	−0.128 (0.180)	0.143 (0.088)	0.045 (0.216)	0.034 (0.052)	0.034 (0.052)
Growth	0.139 (0.028)***	0.358 (0.082)***	0.187 (0.042)***	0.445 (0.102)***	0.144 (0.024)***	0.107 (0.145)***
Industry					−0.010 (0.041)	−0.0112 (0.119)
CEP × Industry					0.001 (0.004)	−0.009 (0.011)
R^2	0.221	0.171	0.430	0.325	0.247	0.170
Adjusted R^2	0.196	0.145	0.390	0.277	0.225	0.145

Note. Standard errors are in parentheses. The variables are defined in Table 5.2. The definition of industries into "clean" and "dirty" is depicted in Appendix B
* $p < 0.1$; ** $p < 0.05$; *** $p < 0.01$
Source. Own table

I review hypothesis 3 by running model 1 for a subset of firms that disclose their CO_2 information publicly as well as for a subset of firms without publication of this information. The results can be reviewed in Table 5.6. The subsample of firms with public disclosure shows a positive, strongly significant effect of *CEP* on *ROA*. If CO_2 intensity is decreased by 1%, *ROA* increases by 0.009% or 0.00009 units ($p < 0.01$) and *ROE* by 0.014% or 0.00014 units ($p < 0.05$), respectively. The coefficient increased in size, while the significance level also improved compared with the baseline estimations of the full model. Also, the explanatory power in the form of adjusted R-squares increases to 39% for *ROA* and 24% for *ROE*. Meanwhile, the results of the firms without public disclosure do not show significant results for the variable *CEP*, irrespective of whether *ROA* or *ROE* is used as the financial performance variable. In addition, the interaction term *CEP* × *Disclosure* is positive and significant for *ROA* ($p < 0.05$) and *ROE* ($p < 0.1$). Although the coefficient of *CEP* is not significant in this model specification, the null hypothesis that both coefficients *CEP* and *CEP* × *Disclosure* are simultaneously zero can be rejected via an F-test ($p < 0.01$). Consequently, these findings stress that disclosure positively moderates the relationship between CEP and CFP and I accept hypothesis 3.

Finally, I performed several robustness analyses to see if the results for ROA in Model 1 would change through model specifications. Within my robustness checks, my findings are largely identical, which can be reviewed in Table 5.7. Irrespective of whether the control variable *Size* is expressed as total assets instead of the number of employees, a two-year time lag is applied instead of a one-year

Table 5.6 Regression analysis on the CEP-CFP relationship moderated by disclosure

	Model 1 – "Disclosure" Firms		Model 1 – "No Disclosure" Firms		Model 3—Interaction CEP × Disclosure	
Dependent variable	ROA	ROE	ROA	ROE	ROA	ROE
CEP	0.009 (0.002)***	0.014 (0.006)**	0.006 (0.005)	0.016 (0.013)	−0.001 (0.003)	−0.003 (0.009)
Size	−0.010 (0.002)***	−0.021 (0.005)***	−0.002 (0.003)	−0.006 (0.009)	−0.003 (0.001)	−0.008 (0.004)
Leverage	−0.061 (0.016)***	0.057 (0.046)	−0.115 (0.030)***	−0.075 (0.083)	−0.063 (0.014)	0.053 (0.039)
Capital Intensity	0.064 (0.057)	−0.030 (0.168)	0.068 (0.083)	0.038 (0.226)	0.044 (0.051)	−0.054 (0.142)
Growth	0.114 (0.025)***	0.296 (0.075)***	0.144 (0.036)***	0.381 (0.100)***	0.140 (0.023)*	0.355 (0.065)***
Disclosure		−0.092 (0.042)				−0.195 (0.116)
CEP × Disclosure		0.009 (0.004)*				0.019 (0.011)
R^2	0.409	0.262	0.312	0.174	0.264	0.190
Adjusted R^2	0.387	0.235	0.274	0.129	0.242	0.165

Note. Standard errors are in parentheses. The variables are defined in Table 5.2
* $p < 0.1$; ** $p < 0.05$; *** $p < 0.01$.
Source. Own table

Table 5.7 Robustness checks

Dependent variable	Model 1—Total assets as firm size	Model 1—Two-year time lag	Model 1—Winsorization 1st percentiles	Model 1—U-shaped Model (curvilinear)
	ROA	ROA	ROA	ROA
CEP	0.004 (0.002)**	0.004 (0.002)*	0.005 (0.002)**	−0.241 (0.127)*
CEP^2				0.708 (0.624)
Size	−0.004 (0.002)**	−0.003 (0.002)	−0.005 (0.002)***	−0.004 (0.001)**
Leverage	−0.062 (0.014)***	−0.049 (0.016)***	−0.069 (0.016)***	−0.058 (0.014)***
Capital Intensity	0.035 (0.051)	−0.058 (0.060)	0.035 (0.052)	0.031 (0.051)
Growth	0.143 (0.024)***	0.169 (0.028)***	0.140 (0.025)***	0.144 (0.024)***
R^2	0.244	0.241	0.227	0.249
Adjusted R^2	0.228	0.219	0.210	0.230

Note. Standard errors are in parentheses. The variables are defined in Table 5.2.
* $p < 0.1$; ** $p < 0.05$; *** $p < 0.01$
Source. Own table

time lag, or the winsorization is changed to 1% and 99% percentiles instead of 5% and 95% percentiles, the coefficients do not seem to be impacted by the selection of the estimation methodology and the significance prevails ($p < 0.05$ / $p < 0.1$). I further demonstrate that the linear relationship is the most suitable model specification, as the quadratic term of CEP is not statistically significant. Consequently, there is no evidence for a curvilinear relationship.

5.5 Discussion

5.5.1 Contribution

This study makes not only a relevant contribution to the pronounced research stream on the relationship between CEP, defined as corporate carbon performance, and CFP, expressed as profitability (Busch et al., 2020; Busch &

Lewandowski, 2017; Delmas et al., 2015; Fujii et al., 2013; Galama & Scholtens, 2021; Gallego-Álvarez et al., 2015; Lewandowski, 2017; Trumpp & Günther, 2017; van Emous et al., 2021), but adds also to the rare literature concerning the impact of CEP, as a multi-dimensional construct, on family firms (Craig & Dibrell, 2006; Garcés-Ayerbe et al., 2022; Huang et al., 2014; López-Pérez et al., 2018). Last, my findings entail management implications for practitioners in family firms and policy implications for regulators.

Theoretical Implications

I follow the call for papers to assess the conditions underlying the relationship between CEP and CFP to reconcile conflicting results from the past and draw more refined conclusions about when to expect positive financial performance from CEP in the future (Busch & Lewandowski, 2017; Endrikat et al., 2014; Galama & Scholtens, 2021; Grewatsch & Kleindienst, 2017). My results show a positive, linear relationship between CEP and CFP for the group of family firms, which is also robust to various changes in the model specifications (see Table 5.7). Thus, I support the findings by Garcés-Ayerbe et al. in 2022 that the improvement of CEP, if measured through clearly defined, quantifiable metrics, such as the amount of environmental investment or carbon emission, has a positive impact on the profitability of family firms.

Although corporate carbon performance data of family firms is rare and needs to be collected individually, to the best of my knowledge, I am the first to establish a database for family firms that measures CEP as carbon intensity. This measurement technique encompasses many advantages, such as clearly defined measurement standards and a direct linkage to climate change (Trumpp & Günther, 2017) as well as a direct relevance for 50,000 firms in meeting the requirements of the CSRD (European Commission, 2023). In addition, since I am the first to use the measure of carbon performance for family firms, it allows me to perform a novel comparison between family and non-family firms in this field. The predominant opinion of a positive relationship between CEP and CFP seems to apply to the organizational firm type "family firm" as well. While some authors in the non-family firm literature also contend a positive, linear relationship (Fujii et al., 2013; Garcés-Ayerbe et al., 2022; van Emous et al., 2021), other authors show a positive, curvilinear relationship (Lewandowski, 2017; Trumpp & Günther, 2017), for which I did not find evidence. I will purposefully not assess the effect size of CEP on CFP between family firms and non-family firms, as these analyses are highly sensitive to model specifications (Busch & Lewandowski, 2017; Endrikat et al., 2014; Galama & Scholtens, 2021) and, therefore, a comparison between separate projects in this detail is not reasonable. Nonetheless, my study serves as an initial bridge between two previously distinct research streams: the CEP-CFP relationship and family firms.

Making these findings more refined, I reveal via an insignificant interaction term that the dummy variable *Industry*, stating whether a firm belongs to a clean or dirty industry, does not moderate the relationship between CEP and CFP. Yet, the calculations in the clean subsample show significant results for a positive relationship between CEP and CFP for ROA, while the dirty subsample yields no significant results, which matches the findings by Iwata and Okada in 2011 and Galama and Scholtens in 2021. In the past, literature covering the CEP-CFP relationship rarely evaluated the significance of the interaction term in addition to the calculations in subsamples. I show that performing this extra step of the analysis leads to a new assessment of the results, relativizing industry differences in this context.

Moreover, to the best of my knowledge, I am the first, in the context of the CEP-CFP relationship, to show that *Disclosure* of carbon performance positively moderates the relationship between CEP and CFP. The majority of literature only tested whether the carbon measurement was voluntary or mandatory, often even yielding insignificant results (Busch & Lewandowski, 2017; Galama & Scholtens, 2021). The only study to test the significance of disclosure before is the study by Delmas et al. from 2015, which observes all environmental firm data and not only carbon performance. However, their study dates back to the years 2004–2008 and was adversely impacted by regulatory uncertainty. In addition, the authors were surprised that the *Disclosure* variable was insignificant in their analysis (Delmas et al., 2015). Via reconsidering this moderating variable, contradictory empirical evidence from the past might be reconciled. While disclosure of CEP has already gained importance (Methven O'Brien & Dhanarajan, 2016), I further postulate that its importance will further increase as diligent tracking and reporting of carbon performance are increasingly perceived as a competitive advantage and differentiator among firms. As a next step, the reasons and their weighting for this effect should be further explored, covering topics such as enhanced target performance measurement and integration into management systems (Downar et al., 2021; Kaplan & Anderson, 2007; Young & O'Byrne, 2001), external assurance provision (Ioannou & Serafeim, 2019), or proactivity of decarbonization strategies (Endrikat et al., 2014; King & Lenox, 2002; Russo & Fouts, 1997; Sharma & Vredenburg, 1998).

Regarding the theoretical framework underlying my findings, my results provide evidence for the applicability of the NRBV and the instrumental stakeholder theory in the context of family firms. I confirm the linkage of the SEW theory with the NRBV (Hart, 1995) as recently introduced by Garcés-Ayerbe et al. (2022), while extending it by linking the SEW theory also with the instrumental stakeholder theory

(Donaldson & Preston, 1995; Jones, 1995). Due to the imbrication of the family and the business (Habbershon et al., 2003), meeting stakeholder expectations concerning CEP strongly influences CFP in family firms (López-Pérez et al., 2018).

Managerial and Regulatory Implications
For practitioners in family firms, I show that decarbonization can pay off and hope to incentivize an increase in decarbonization activities, especially before regulation for large family firms becomes active with the CSRD in 2024, obligating family firms to report their carbon performance in 2026 for the first time (European Commission, 2023). In addition, these findings might help practitioners to reconcile environmental and financial goals in firms' strategic decision-making, which has also been the target of previous studies (Diaz-Moriana et al., 2022; Epstein et al., 2015; Smith & Lewis, 2011). Through my findings, firms are encouraged to deploy a win-win mindset, increasing their decarbonization activities and benefitting from proactively sharing their carbon performance with the public.

My policy implications for regulators include that firms are financially incentivized to decarbonize in the absence of regulation, while the effect size is larger once a moderate level of carbon performance has already been reached. This knowledge should be reflected upon to optimize the number and timing of newly introduced regulations. While future regulation should not primarily target the differentiation between industries, more initiatives for public disclosure should be launched, incentivizing more firms to share their carbon performance publicly.

5.5.2 Limitations and Future Research

Despite the abovementioned contributions, my study has a few limitations, which should also be regarded as an inspiration for future research. First, data collection in this field of research is very challenging since private family firms do not have to disclose environmental data and are also often excluded from financial disclosure obligations. Therefore, there is a limitation to my sample, which contains 74 manufacturing firms that simultaneously provide carbon and financial data. In 2013, Fujii et al. were similarly challenged to find consolidated firm data. Moreover, in my sample, not all of the 74 manufacturing firms report CO_2 already since 2013. While some firms have data available for nine years, the average only reports CO_2 emissions for four years. Hence, performing the same study with an enlarged panel data set would be a promising future investigation. With the introduction of the CSRD in 2024, the number of firms with CO_2 tracking and reporting will drastically increase, so collecting a larger sample is more feasible.

Second, all firms in my sample are headquartered in Germany and are defined as large based on their number of employees. Investigating family firms in non-European countries might be interesting, as European firms are all impacted by somewhat similar climate regulations and consumer sentiments characterized by high decarbonization ambitions. Furthermore, it should be tested whether small firms also reap financial benefits from decarbonization, given potential resource constraints.

Third, all firms in the database currently voluntarily track their carbon performance without legal obligation. The positive moderating effect of proactive environmental strategies on the CEP-CFP relationship is undisputed (Endrikat et al., 2014; King & Lenox, 2002; Klassen & Whybark, 1999; Sharma & Vredenburg, 1998). Yet, I would argue in this sample, only those firms can be defined as proactive that share their carbon footprint publicly.

Fourth, just like other studies in this field, my study is subject to endogeneity and CEP and CFP could reinforce each other (Busch et al., 2020). However, I addressed this by lagging CEP by one year in the main analysis and two years in the robustness check (Busch et al., 2020; Trumpp & Günther, 2017) as well as introducing multiple control variables (van Emous et al., 2021). I further reduce the risk of endogeneity by controlling for unobserved industry and time heterogeneity (Iwata & Okada, 2011).

Fifth, our study only covers accounting-based financial performance and does not consider market-based financial performance, as Tobin's q or TSR do not exist for private family firms. Therefore, I might not capture the long-term value of decarbonization to a full extent because market-based measures are regarded as more long-term oriented than accounting-based measures (Busch et al., 2020; Delmas et al., 2015).

5.6 Conclusion

The implications of this research regarding the question "When does it pay to decarbonize?" are twofold. First, I show that it pays to decarbonize under the condition of being a private family firm, which matches the prevailing opinion in extant non-family firm literature. The theoretical framework is the SEW theory in conjunction with the NRBV and the instrumental stakeholder theory, respectively. Second, public disclosure of carbon performance positively moderates the CEP-CFP relationship. While practitioners in family firms are encouraged to further decarbonize, both practitioners and regulators should strive for more transparency in corporate carbon performance.

Appendix

Appendix A. Abbreviated Survey Outline

1. Company Identification
2. GHG emission measuring technique & recorded values
2.1.Used Standard (Global Reporting Initiative / Greenhouse Gas Protocol)
2.2.Unit of Measurement (CO_2 / CO_2e)
2.3.Emissions for the years 2013–2021
2.4.Special occurrences explaining discontinuities in the emission figures
3. Anonymity Disclaimer

Source. Own figure

Appendix B. Classification of Industries Based on Emissions Per Unit of Output

Clean	Dirty
Foods	Paper and pulp
Textiles and Apparels	Chemicals
Textiles and Apparels	Pharmaceutical
Machinery	Rubber and plastic products
Glass and ceramics products	Iron and steel
Electric appliances	Nonferrous metals
Transportation equipment	Nonferrous metals
Precision instruments	
Other products	

Note. Classification according to Mani and Wheeler (1998); similar representation by Iwata and Okada (2011)
Source. Own figure

Appendix C. Supplementary Descriptive Statistics

	Sample with CO_2 as unit of measurement			Sample with CO_2e as unit o		
Variable	Mean	Median	SD	Mean	Median	SD
ROA	0.041	0.048	0.038	0.042	0.400	0.034
ROE	0.093	0.082	0.101	0.100	0.098	0.084
CEP	10.537	10.522	1.037	10.440	10.17	1.262
Size	7.720	7.612	1.559	8.261	8.040	1.542
Leverage	0.353	0.358	0.156	0.389	0.400	0.164
Capital Intensity	0.064	0.061	0.035	0.072	0.062	0.043
Growth	0.014	0.014	0.085	0.021	0.019	0.085
Industry	0.768	1.000	0.486	0.622	1.000	0.486
Disclosure	0.626	1.000	0.495	0.580	1.000	0.495

Note. Descriptive statistics for 99 observations with CO_2 as unit of measurement and 143 observations for CO_2e as unit of measurement. The sample covers observations over the period 2013–2021. All continuous variables are winsorized at the 5 and 95 percentiles. The variables are defined in Table 5.2
Source. Own table

Conclusion

6

Gunther Friedl

6.1 Summary of the Research Findings

Given the UN Secretary General's emphasis at COP 27 on the urgency of meeting the ambitious climate targets of the Paris Agreement to prevent further GHG-related consequences, it is necessary to target major emitters. Within the EU, Germany is releasing the highest amount of CO_2 emissions, the main component of GHG. Due to the strong macroeconomic presence of German family firms, focusing on this specific target group is inevitable to accelerate and ensure the EU's decarbonization path. Thus, the four chapters in this research consortium deal with the holistic management process of decarbonization in German family firms, starting with the quantification of GHG emissions (Chap. 2) through the implementation of the collected data (Chaps. 3 and 4) to the financial impact analysis of decarbonization (Chap. 5).

Chap. 2 addresses why and how family firms account for GHG emissions along their value chain, enriched with an analysis of their challenges within this measurement process. In contrast to Chap. 4, the findings on the challenges of Chapter I refer to the time before any reporting mandate. Given this research setting, the first study elaborates on the stakeholder theory by Freeman (1984), the legitimacy theory by Cotter and Najah (2012) and the principal-agent theory by Jensen and Meckling (1976). The qualitative analysis of 13 cases reveals intrinsic factors such as family firms' typical long-term generational thinking and the willingness to contribute to society, but also customer demand as an extrinsic

G. Friedl (✉)
TUM School of Management, Technical University of Munich, Munich, Germany
e-mail: gunther.friedl@tum.de

G. Friedl (ed.), *Decarbonizing German Family Firms*, Familienunternehmen und KMU, https://doi.org/10.1007/978-3-658-47801-8_6

motivational factor that motivates family firms to account for their GHG emissions. These intrinsic and extrinsic stimuli are not equally present across family firms leading to varying degrees of measuring and accounting for emissions. Thus, we identify four archetypes (i.e., sustainability frontrunners, intrinsically driven reporters, extrinsically driven reporters, and sustainability laggards) that condense and metaphorically illustrate the differences in the GHG emission accounting process and its underlying motivation between the cases. Family-owned companies face fundamental (i.e., missing sense of urgency and limited personnel availability) and processual challenges (i.e., lack of standardized emission data and formats, complex collection of Scope 3 emissions, unprecise company steering due to assumption-based data) when measuring and accounting for their GHG emissions. Lastly, the practical implications of this study show that an increased sense of urgency towards emission accounting within the firm and especially among top-level management can facilitate managing emission data in combination with a further data format standardization.

After measuring and accounting emission data, it is vital to create value from this information and key performance indicator (KPI) by integrating it into a firm's decision-making to manage goal tensions between economic and environmental goals.

Thus, Chap. 3 deals with the questions of why and how family firms manage economic and environmental goals in their strategic decision-making process. Due to high initial investments into decarbonization with long payback cycles, economic and environmental goals might contradict each other in the short-term. Goal tensions can be specifically severe in the family firm context due to the overlap between the family and the business. Based on the attention-based view by Ocasio (1997) and the cross-case analysis of the interview data from eleven family firms, ten expert interviews, and archival data, we developed a framework on balancing economic and environmental goals in family firms. Besides its theoretical contributions, the model offers practical implications for family firms as it creates a link between a firm's motivation to decarbonize and one of the four identified strategies (i.e., presence of environmental information (incl. innovation), designated capital expenditures (CapEx), artificial CO_2 price, and no integration) for balancing economic and environmental goals. Beyond that, we found that a family firm's motivation for environmental activities stems not only from intrinsic (e.g., transgenerational value, family reputation) but also from extrinsic (e.g., client demand, competitive advantage) goals.

To inform stakeholders about a firm's decarbonization strategy and progress, sustainability directives have become a standard tool for communicating a firm's sustainability efforts.

For this reason, we explore in Chap. 4 the consequences of the upcoming CSRD on family firms. As the new directive targets private organizations, the multiple case study refers to ten private family firms. Our result is a framework that illustrates sustainability reporting implementation challenges due to the CSRD and provides guidance to overcome these challenges and instead unlock business opportunities. Hence, the findings have theoretical and practical relevance. This chapter draws on Lee's (2011) theoretical framework, which combines institutional and stakeholder theory. Both theories occur to varying degrees and force companies to meet social demands. This leads firms to respond with different sustainability strategies. Therefore, looking at the composition of institutional and stakeholder forces helps to understand a firm's strategic choice. This allowed us to derive three archetypes of private family firms that face varying degrees of the four sustainability reporting implementation challenge clusters. Thus, we contribute to the literature by differentiating private family firms based on their sustainability strategy and maturity of sustainability reporting. Moreover, we identified direct and indirect opportunities along a firm's value chain. Irrespective of the archetype, all companies can benefit from direct opportunities, e.g., increase of internal and external communication, that arise after introducing a reporting process. In contrast, the indirect opportunities, e.g., product innovation and improvement, must be unlocked through a proactive sustainability strategy.

Although companies increasingly report on their decarbonization progress and activities, their economic performance, e.g., expressed in profitability, still remains a priority. This also holds for family firms that want to guide their business into the next generation. Therefore, a complex question arises: "Does it pay for family firms to decarbonize?".

Chap. 5 consists of a panel regression based on data from 74 private German family firms from 2013 to 2021 and answers the above question by analyzing the relationship between Corporate Environmental Performance (CEP) and Corporate Financial Performance (CFP), using a firm's carbon intensity as a measure for CEP, and ROA, as well ROE as corresponding proxies for CFP. In addition, an *industry's dirtiness* and a *firm's carbon performance disclosure* served as moderating variables. The econometric analysis shows a clear positive, linear relationship between CEP and CFP for family firms. Beyond this, the moderator *industry dirtiness* does not impact the CEP-CFP relationship, while the *firm's carbon performance disclosure* has a significant positive effect. Consequently, family firms can financially benefit from their decarbonization efforts, especially when they disclose their carbon performance figures and activities. Hence, regulators should incentivize carbon performance disclosure instead of differentiating carbon regulation between industries.

Considering all the findings, the measurement, management, reporting, and assessment of GHG emissions and successful decarbonization can positively impact family firms' competitiveness. Due to the great heterogeneity of family firms, there is no "one-size-fits-all" approach, but our findings and developed models consider different archetypes, applied strategies, or SEW dimensions.

6.2 Avenues for Future Research

As mentioned in the individual chapters, each chapter is subject to its own limitations, which pave the way for future research. Looking holistically at the limitations, we can distinguish between methodological and content-related limitations.

Methodologically, adjustments can be made concerning the selected sample, data collection, and analysis. First, the sample mainly refers to large German family firms with high visibility in the market. Due to stakeholders' rising sustainability expectations, these companies may already be more sensitive to decarbonization and, therefore, already proactively engage in this area, which could impact the findings. In addition, German regulations, such as the transposed NFRD, differ across EU member states, which could also indicate alternative challenges. Hence, future research could purposefully select different family firm sizes from different institutional contexts. Second, three chapters are based on qualitative data from interviews since most private firms are not yet obliged to produce a sustainability report or disclose any emission data. However, we expect an increase in data availability and quality due to the future introduction of the CSRD. In 2025, companies must disclose a sustainability report for the financial year 2024 under a standardized framework (i.e., ESRS). We, therefore, motivate future researchers to assess our findings deductively through a survey or a regression analysis based on data from the upcoming sustainability reports. Finally, all of our chapters refer to multiple cases, which is necessary to increase the robustness of our developed theories. However, in contrast to multiple cases, a single longitudinal case study can provide more nuanced insights, which is particularly helpful in family business research due to family firms' high heterogeneity. Future studies could, therefore, focus on the influence of different SEW dimensions as well as on the influence of one specific industry or country.

Regarding content constraints, our decarbonization analysis refers to the environmental segment within the sustainability acronym ESG (i.e., Environment, Social, Governance). Appropriately, the CSRD's mandatory reporting standard (i.e., ESRS) includes three parts based on ESG segmentation. Thus, the new directive not only increases the quantity and quality of the mentioned environmental data but also the data on the social and governance elements. Thus, sustainability and family business research could, for example, further investigate the achievement of the 17 UN Sustainable Development Goals also with regard to the “S” and “G” segments more precisely.

6.3 Concluding Remarks

Considering the findings of the four chapters, we conclude that research on family firms is an interesting context to study sustainability, including the most debated topic of decarbonization. Our findings aim to equip family firms to successfully decarbonize, because family firms represent one of the most critical levers to achieve the transition to a low-carbon economy in the EU and, thus, also in Germany. This is not only justified by their dominant economic presence and their share of carbon emissions over the last decades but also by their specific behavior. The intrinsic motivation of family firms to protect their SEW serves as the foundation to proactively engage in decarbonization activities. Thus, family firms’ typical characteristics, e.g., desire for transgenerational value or enduring ties with their stakeholder, can create additional momentum for the EU’s and Germany’s path toward net zero CO_2 emissions. Our findings should therefore motivate researchers, regulators, and politicians to collaborate with this particular company type and its specific needs, not only to ensure and accelerate the implementation of the UN Sustainable Development Goals, but also to preserve an organizational form that is instrumental for value creation and innovation since centuries. After family firms have formed the backbone of the German economic success, they should now form the backbone of the German decarbonization.

References

Adams, C. A., & Frost, G. R. (2008). Integrating sustainability reporting into management practices. *Accounting Forum, 32*(4), 288–302. https://doi.org/10.1016/j.accfor.2008.05.002

Adomako, S., Amankwah-Amoah, J., Danso, A., Konadu, R., & Owusu-Agyei, S. (2019). Environmental sustainability orientation and performance of family and nonfamily firms. *Business Strategy and the Environment, 28*(6), 1250–1259. https://doi.org/10.1002/bse.2314

Adu, D. A., Flynn, A., & Grey, C. (2022). Executive compensation and sustainable business practices: The moderating role of sustainability-based compensation. *Business Strategy and the Environment, 31*(3), 698–736. https://doi.org/10.1002/bse.2913

Aerts, W., & Cormier, D. (2009). Media legitimacy and corporate environmental communication. *Accounting, Organizations and Society, 34*(1), 1–27. https://doi.org/10.1016/j.aos.2008.02.005

Agostino, M., & Ruberto, S. (2021). Environment-friendly practices: Family versus nonfamily firms. *Journal of Cleaner Production, 329*, 129689. https://doi.org/10.1016/j.jclepro.2021.129689

Åhman, M., Nilsson, L. J., & Johansson, B. (2017). Global climate policy and deep decarbonization of energy-intensive industries. *Climate Policy, 17*(5), 634–649. https://doi.org/10.1080/14693062.2016.1167009

Ahn, Y. (2022). A socio-cognitive model of sustainability performance: Linking CEO career experience, social ties, and attention breadth. *Journal of Business Ethics, 175*(2), 303–321. https://doi.org/10.1007/s10551-020-04651-w

Albertini, E. (2013). Does environmental management improve financial performance? A Meta-Analytical Review. *Organization & Environment, 26*(4), 431–457. https://doi.org/10.1177/1086026613510301

Altenburger, R., & Bachner, C. (2020). Integrierte nachhaltige Unternehmensführung von Familienunternehmen. In K. Butzer-Strothmann & F. Ahlers (Eds.), *Integrierte nachhaltige Unternehmensführung* (pp. 107–124). Springer. https://doi.org/10.1007/978-3-662-61168-5_7

Altenburger, R. & Schmidpeter, R. (Eds.). (2018). *Management-Reihe Corporate Social Responsibility. CSR und Familienunternehmen: Gesellschaftliche Verantwortung im Spannungsfeld von Tradition und Innovation* (1st ed.). Springer Gabler.

G. Friedl (ed.), *Decarbonizing German Family Firms*, Familienunternehmen und KMU, https://doi.org/10.1007/978-3-658-47801-8

Anderson, R. C., Mansi, S. A., & Reeb, D. M. (2002). *Founding family ownership and the agency cost of debt*. Vorab-Onlinepublikation. https://doi.org/10.2139/ssrn.303864

Andersson, F. W., Johansson, D., Karlsson, J., Lodefalk, M., & Poldahl, A. (2018). The characteristics of family firms: Exploiting information on ownership, kinship, and governance using total population data. *Small Business Economics, 51*(3), 539–556. https://doi.org/10.1007/s11187-017-9947-6

Aparicio, G., Basco, R., Iturralde, T., & Maseda, A. (2017). An exploratory study of firm goals in the context of family firms: An institutional logics perspective. *Journal of Family Business Strategy, 8*(3), 157–169. https://doi.org/10.1016/j.jfbs.2017.08.002

Arena, C., & Michelon, G. (2018). A matter of control or identity? Family firms' environmental reporting decisions along the corporate life cycle. *Business Strategy and the Environment, 27*(8), 1596–1608. https://doi.org/10.1002/bse.2225

Argote, L., & Greve, H. R. (2007). A behavioral theory of the firm —40 years and counting: Introduction and impact. *Organization Science, 18*(3), 337–349. https://doi.org/10.1287/orsc.1070.0280

Armstrong, J. S., & Overton, T. S. (1977). Estimating nonresponse bias in mail surveys. *Journal of Marketing Research, 14*(3), 396. https://doi.org/10.2307/3150783

Astley, W. G., Axelsson, R., Butler, R. J., Hickson, D. J., & Wilson, D. C. (1982). Complexity and cleavage: Dual explanations of strategic decision-making [I]. *Journal of Management Studies, 19*(4), 357–375. https://doi.org/10.1111/j.1467-6486.1982.tb00114.x

Aureli, S., Del Baldo, M., Lombardi, R., & Nappo, F. (2020). Nonfinancial reporting regulation and challenges in sustainability disclosure and corporate governance practices. *Business Strategy and the Environment, 29*(6), 2392–2403. https://doi.org/10.1002/bse.2509

Baird, P. L., Geylani, P. C., & Roberts, J. A. (2012). Corporate social and financial performance Re-examined: Industry effects in a linear mixed model analysis. *Journal of Business Ethics, 109*(3), 367–388. https://doi.org/10.1007/s10551-011-1135-z

Bansal, P., & Roth, K. (2000). Why companies go green: A model of ecological responsiveness. *Academy of Management Journal, 43*(4), 717–736. https://doi.org/10.2307/1556363

Baret, P., & Helfrich, V. (2019). The "trilemma" of non-financial reporting and its pitfalls. *Journal of Management and Governance, 23*(2), 485–511. https://doi.org/10.1007/s10997-018-9430-z

Baron, J. N., Hannan, M. T., & Burton, M. D. (1999). Building the iron cage: Determinants of managerial intensity in the early years of organizations. *American Sociological Review, 64*(4), 527. https://doi.org/10.2307/2657254

Bauer, S., Marie-Jeanne Kurdziel, Gabriela Iacobuta, Clara Brandi, Jean Carlo Rodríguez, Delphine Deryng, Jonas Hanshom, Niklas Höhne, Sybrig Smit & Srinivasa Srigiri. (2021). *Working together to achieve the Paris climate goals and sustainable development - 2021*. https://doi.org/10.23661/r1.2021

Baumüller, J., & Grbenic, S. O. (2021). Moving from non-financial to sustainability reporting: Analyzing the EU commission's proposal for a Corporate Sustainability Reporting Directive (CSRD). *Facta Universitatis, Series: Economics and Organization, 18*(4), 369–381. https://doi.org/10.22190/FUEO210817026B

Bergen, N., & Labonté, R. (2020). Everything Is perfect, and we have no problems": Detecting and limiting social desirability bias in qualitative research. *Qualitative Health Research, 30*(5), 783–792. https://doi.org/10.1177/1049732319889354

Bernard-Rau, B., & Schnerring, G. (2022). Gabler Kompakt-Lexikon Corporate Social Responsibility: Schlüsselbegriffe einer nachhaltigen Wirtschaft in Deutsch und Englisch. *Springer Gabler*. https://doi.org/10.1007/978-3-658-34940-0

Berrone, P., Cruz, C., & Gomez-Mejia, L. R. (2012). Socioemotional wealth in family firms. *Family Business Review, 25*(3), 258–279. https://doi.org/10.1177/0894486511435355

Berrone, P., Cruz, C., Gomez-Mejia, L. R., & Larraza-Kintana, M. (2010). Socioemotional wealth and corporate responses to institutional pressures: Do Family-controlled firms pollute less? *Administrative Science Quarterly, 55*(1), 82–113. https://doi.org/10.2189/asqu.2010.55.1.82

Bini, L., & Bellucci, M. (2020). Integrated sustainability reporting: Linking environmental and social information to value creation processes. *Springer*. https://doi.org/10.1007/978-3-030-24954-0

Biswas, P. K., Roberts, H., & Whiting, R. H. (2019). The impact of family vs non-family governance contingencies on CSR reporting in Bangladesh. *Management Decision, 57*(10), 2758–2781. https://doi.org/10.1108/MD-11-2017-1072

Blanco, C., Caro, F., & Corbett, C. J. (2017). An inside perspective on carbon disclosure. *Business Horizons, 60*(5), 635–646. https://doi.org/10.1016/j.bushor.2017.05.007

Block, J. H., & Wagner, M. (2014). The effect of family ownership on different dimensions of corporate social responsibility: Evidence from large US firms. *Business Strategy and the Environment, 23*(7), 475–492. https://doi.org/10.1002/bse.1798

Blumentritt, T. (2006). The relationship between boards and planning in family businesses. *Family Business Review, 19*(1), 65–72. https://doi.org/10.1111/j.1741-6248.2006.00062.x

Boehm, A. (2005). The participation of businesses in community decision making. *Business & Society, 44*(2), 144–177. https://doi.org/10.1177/0007650305275770

Böttcher, C. F., & Müller, M. (2015). Drivers, practices and outcomes of Low-carbon operations: Approaches of German automotive suppliers to cutting carbon emissions. *Business Strategy and the Environment, 24*(6), 477–498. https://doi.org/10.1002/bse.1832

Boukherroub, T., Bouchery, Y., Corbett, C. J., Fransoo, J. C., & Tan, T. (2017). Carbon footprinting in supply chains. In Y. Bouchery, C. J. Corbett, J. C. Fransoo, & T. Tan (Eds.), *Springer series in supply chain management. Sustainable supply chains* (Vol. 4, pp. 43–64). Springer. https://doi.org/10.1007/978-3-319-29791-0_3

Bragdon, J. B., & Marlin, J. (1972). Is pollution profitable? *Risk Management, 19*(4), 9–18.

Broadbent, J., Laughlin, R., & Willig-Atherton, H. (1994). Financial controls and schools: Accounting in 'Public' and 'private' spheres. *The British Accounting Review, 26*(3), 255–279. https://doi.org/10.1006/bare.1994.1017

Brockhaus, R. H. (2004). Family business succession: Suggestions for future research. *Family Business Review, 17*(2), 165–177. https://doi.org/10.1111/j.1741-6248.2004.00011.x

Brundin, E., Samuelsson, E. F., & Melin, L. (2014). Family ownership logic: Framing the core characteristics of family businesses. *Journal of Management & Organization, 20*(1), 6–37. https://doi.org/10.1017/jmo.2014.15

Busch, T., Bassen, A., Lewandowski, S., & Sump, F. (2020). Corporate carbon and financial performance revisited. *Organization & Environment, 35*(1), 154–171. https://doi.org/10.1177/1086026620935638

Busch, T., & Lewandowski, S. (2017). Corporate carbon and financial performance: A meta-analysis: Corporate carbon and financial performance. *Journal of Industrial Ecology, 22*,. https://doi.org/10.1111/jiec.12591

Campbell, D. (2004). A longitudinal and cross-sectional analysis of environmental disclosure in UK companies—a research note. *The British Accounting Review, 36*(1), 107–117. https://doi.org/10.1016/j.bar.2003.09.001

Campopiano, G., & de Massis, A. (2015). Corporate social responsibility reporting: A content Aanalysis in family and Non-family firms. *Journal of Business Ethics, 129*(3), 511–534. https://doi.org/10.1007/s10551-014-2174-z

Carney, M. (2005). Corporate governance and competitive advantage in Family-controlled firms. *Entrepreneurship Theory and Practice, 29*(3), 249–265. https://doi.org/10.1111/j.1540-6520.2005.00081.x

Carney, M., van Essen, M., Gedajlovic, E. R., & Heugens, P. P. (2015). What do we know about private family firms? A Meta-analytical review. *Entrepreneurship Theory and Practice, 39*(3), 513–544. https://doi.org/10.1111/etap.12054

Carrera, N. (2017). What do we know about accounting in family firms? *Journal of Evolutionary Studies in Business, 2*(2), 97–159. https://doi.org/10.1344/jesb2017.2.j032

Carroll, A. B. (1979). A Three-dimensional conceptual model of corporate performance. *Academy of Management Review, 4*(4), 497–505. https://doi.org/10.2307/257850

Cennamo, C., Berrone, P., Cruz, C., & Gomez-Mejia, L. R. (2012). Socioemotional wealth and proactive stakeholder engagement: Why Family-controlled firms care more about their stakeholders. *Entrepreneurship Theory and Practice, 36*(6), 1153–1173. https://doi.org/10.1111/j.1540-6520.2012.00543.x

Cespa, G., & Cestone, G. (2007). *Corporate social responsibility and managerial entrenchment.* Vorab-Onlinepublikation. https://doi.org/10.2139/ssrn.993685

Chen, S., Chen, X., & Chengf, Q. (2008). Do family firms provide more or less voluntary disclosure? *Journal of Accounting Research, 46*(3), 499–536. https://doi.org/10.1111/j.1475-679X.2008.00288.x

Chrisman, J. J., Chua, J. H., Pearson, A. W., & Barnett, T. (2012). Family involvement, family influence, and family-centered Non–economic goals in small firms. *Entrepreneurship Theory and Practice, 36*(2), 267–293. https://doi.org/10.1111/j.1540-6520.2010.00407.x

Chrisman, J. J., Chua, J. H., & Sharma, P. (2005). Trends and directions in the development of a strategic management theory of the family firm. *Entrepreneurship Theory and Practice, 29*(5), 555–575. https://doi.org/10.1111/j.1540-6520.2005.00098.x

Chrisman, J. J., Chua, J. H., & Steier, L. (2005). Sources and consequences of distinctive familiness: An introduction. *Entrepreneurship Theory and Practice, 29*(3), 237–247. https://doi.org/10.1111/j.1540-6520.2005.00080.x

Chrisman, J. J., Memili, E., & Misra, K. (2014). Nonfamily managers, family firms, and the winner's curse: The influence of noneconomic goals and bounded rationality. *Entrepreneurship Theory and Practice, 38*(5), 1–25. https://doi.org/10.1111/etap.12014

Christensen, H. B., Hail, L., & Leuz, C. (2021). Mandatory CSR and sustainability reporting: Economic analysis and literature review. *Review of Accounting Studies, 26*(3), 1176–1248. https://doi.org/10.1007/s11142-021-09609-5

Chua, J. H., Chrisman, J. J., De Massis, A., & Wang, H. (2018). Reflections on family firm goals and the assessment of performance. *Journal of Family Business Strategy, 9*(2), 107–113. https://doi.org/10.1016/j.jfbs.2018.02.001

Chua, J. H., Chrisman, J. J., & Sharma, P. (1999). Defining the family business by behavior. *Entrepreneurship Theory and Practice, 23*(4), 19–39. https://doi.org/10.1177/104225879902300402

Chua, J. H., Chrisman, J. J., Steier, L. P., & Rau, S. B. (2012). Sources of heterogeneity in family firms: An introduction. *Entrepreneurship Theory and Practice, 36*(6), 1103–1113. https://doi.org/10.1111/j.1540-6520.2012.00540.x

Clarkson, P. M., Li, Y., & [Yue], Richardson, G. D. & Vasvari, F. P. (2008). Revisiting the relation between environmental performance and environmental disclosure: An empirical analysis. *Accounting, Organizations and Society, 33*(4–5), 303–327. https://doi.org/10.1016/j.aos.2007.05.003

Connelly, B. L., Certo, S. T., Ireland, R. D., & Reutzel, C. R. (2011). Signaling theory: A review and assessment. *Journal of Management, 37*(1), 39–67. https://doi.org/10.1177/0149206310388419

Corley, K. G., & Gioia, D. A. (2004). Identity ambiguity and change in the wake of a corporate spin-off. *Administrative Science Quarterly, 49*(2), 173–208. https://doi.org/10.2307/4131471

Cormier, D., & Magnan, M. (1999). Corporate environmental disclosure strategies: Determinants, costs and benefits. *Journal of Accounting, Auditing & Finance, 14*(4), 429–451. https://doi.org/10.1177/0148558X9901400403

Cosma, S., Leopizzi, R., Nobile, L., & Schwizer, P. (2022). Revising the Non-financial reporting directive and the role of board of directors: A lost opportunity? *Journal of Applied Accounting Research, 23*(1), 207–226. https://doi.org/10.1108/JAAR-04-2021-0102

Cotter, J., & Najah, M. M. (2012). Institutional investor influence on global climate change disclosure practices. *Australian Journal of Management, 37*(2), 169–187. https://doi.org/10.1177/0312896211423945

Craig, J., & Dibrell, C. (2006). The natural environment, innovation, and firm performance: A comparative study. *Family Business Review, 19*(4), 275–288. https://doi.org/10.1111/j.1741-6248.2006.00075.x

Cruz, C., Galdeano & Garces, L. (2015). Corporate governance in publicly traded family firms. *III Banca March - IE Report*, Artikel 978-84-606-9756-5. https://www.ie.edu/business/centros/Proyectos/Informe%20Gobierno%20Corporativo_EN_ultimo.pdf. Accessed: 26. June 2024.

Cruz, C., Gómez-Mejia, L. R., & Becerra, M. (2010). Perceptions of benevolence and the design of agency contracts: CEO-TMT relationships in family firms. *Academy of Management Journal, 53*(1), 69–89. https://doi.org/10.5465/amj.2010.48036975

CSR Europe & GRI (2017). *Member state implementation of directive 2014/95/EU: Comprehensive overview of how Member States are implementing A comprehensive overview of how Member States are implementing the EU Directive on Non-financial and Diversity Information.* https://www.accountancyeurope.eu/wp-content/uploads/1711-NFRpublication-GRI-CSR-Europe.pdf. Accessed: 18. August 2022.

Cyert, R. M. & March, J. G. (1992). *A behavioral theory of the firm* (2nd ed.). Wiley-Blackwell.

Dangelico, R. M., Nastasi, A., & Pisa, S. (2019). A comparison of family and nonfamily small firms in their approach to green innovation: A study of Italian companies in the agri-food industry. *Business Strategy and the Environment, 28*(7), 1434–1448. https://doi.org/10.1002/bse.2324

De Massis, A. & Kammerlander, N. (2021). *Handbook of qualitative research methods for family business*. Handbooks of Research Methods in Management. Elgar. https://doi.org/10.4337/9781788116459

De Massis, A., & Kotlar, J. (2014). The case study method in family business research: Guidelines for qualitative scholarship. *Journal of Family Business Strategy, 5*(1), 15–29. https://doi.org/10.1016/j.jfbs.2014.01.007

De Massis, A., Pramodita, S., Chua, J. H., & Chrisman, J. J. (2012). Family business studies: An annotated bibliography. *Edward Elgar*. https://doi.org/10.4337/9781781002988

Debicki, B. J., van de Graaff Randolph, R. & Sobczak, M. (2017). Socioemotional wealth and family firm performance: A stakeholder approach. *Journal of Managerial Issues, 24*, 82–111. https://www.jstor.org/stable/45176535. Accessed: 26. June 2024.

Deegan, C. (2002). Introduction. *Accounting, auditing & accountability journal, 15*(3), 282–311. https://doi.org/10.1108/09513570210435852

Delmas, M., & Toffel, M. W. (2004). Stakeholders and environmental management practices: An institutional framework. *Business Strategy and the Environment, 13*(4), 209–222. https://doi.org/10.1002/bse.409

Delmas, M. A., Nairn-Birch, N., & Lim, J. (2015). Dynamics of environmental and financial performance. *Organization & Environment, 28*(4), 374–393. https://doi.org/10.1177/1086026615620238

Dénizde la Cruz Déniz & Suárez, M. K. C., M. (2005). Corporate social responsibility and family business in Spain. *Journal of Business Ethics, 56*(1), 27–41. https://doi.org/10.1007/s10551-004-3237-3

Depoers, F., Jeanjean, T., & Jérôme, T. (2016). Voluntary disclosure of greenhouse gas emissions: Contrasting the carbon disclosure project and corporate reports. *Journal of Business Ethics, 134*(3), 445–461. https://doi.org/10.1007/s10551-014-2432-0

Diaz-Moriana, V., Clinton, E. & Kammerlander, N. (2022). Untangling goal tensions in family firms: A sensemaking approach. *Journal of Management Studies*, Artikel joms.12845. Vorab-Onlinepublikation. https://doi.org/10.1111/joms.12845

Dibrell, C., & Memili, E. (2019). The Palgrave handbook of heterogeneity among family firms. *Springer International Publishing*. https://doi.org/10.1007/978-3-319-77676-7

Die Bundesregierung. (2022). *Generationenvertrag für das Klima: Klimaschutzgesetz 2021*. https://www.bundesregierung.de/breg-de/themen/klimaschutz/klimaschutzgesetz-2021-1913672#:~:text=Mit%20der%20%C3%84nderung%20des%20Klimaschutzgesetzes,August%202021%20in%20Kraft%20getreten. Accessed 26. June 2024.

DIHK. (2023, 16. April). *CSRD: Viele Unternehmen betroffen von neuer Nachhaltigkeitsberichterstattung*. https://www.ihk.de/hagen/innovation/csrd-im-ueberblick/csrd-im-ueberblick2-5674688. Accessed: 26. June 2024.

DiMaggio, P. J., & Powell, W. W. (1983). The iron cage revisited: Institutional isomorphism and collective rationality in organizational fields. *American Sociological Review, 48*(2), 147. https://doi.org/10.2307/2095101

Dixon-Fowler, H. R., Slater, D. J., Johnson, J. L., Ellstrand, A. E., & Romi, A. M. (2013). Beyond "does it pay to be green?" A meta-analysis of moderators of the CEP–CFP relationship. *Journal of Business Ethics, 112*(2), 353–366. https://doi.org/10.1007/s10551-012-1268-8

Donaldson, T., & Preston, L. E. (1995). The stakeholder theory of the corporation: Concepts, evidence, and implications. *The Academy of Management Review, 20*(1), 65. https://doi.org/10.2307/258887

Downar, B., Ernstberger, J., Reichelstein, S., Schwenen, S., & Zaklan, A. (2021). The impact of carbon disclosure mandates on emissions and financial operating performance. *Review of Accounting Studies, 26*(3), 1137–1175. https://doi.org/10.1007/s11142-021-09611-x

Drucker, P. F. (1954). *The practice of management* [Nachdr.]. HarperCollins.

Duran, P., Kammerlander, N., van Essen, M., & Zellweger, T. (2016). Doing more with less: Innovation input and output in family firms. *Academy of Management Journal, 59*(4), 1224–1264. https://doi.org/10.5465/amj.2014.0424

Dyer, W. G., & Whetten, D. A. (2006). Family firms and social responsibility: Preliminary evidence from the S&P 500. *Entrepreneurship Theory and Practice, 30*(6), 785–802. https://doi.org/10.1111/j.1540-6520.2006.00151.x

Ebner Stolz. (2022). *CSRD: Umsetzung in deutsches Recht bis Anfang Juli 2024 - Ebner Stolz.* https://www.ebnerstolz.de/de/csrd-umsetzung-in-deutsches-recht-bis-anfang-juli-2024-431221.html. Accessed: 26. June 2024.

EcoVadis. (2023). *Über Ecovadis.* https://ecovadis.com/de/about-us/. Accessed: 26. June 2024.

Edmans, A. (2020). Company purpose and profit need not be in conflict if we 'grow the pie.' *Economic Affairs, 40*(2), 287–294. https://doi.org/10.1111/ecaf.12395

EFRAG (2022a). *Double Materiality Guidelines.* https://www.efrag.org/Assets/Download?assetUrl=/sites/webpublishing/SiteAssets/Appendix%202.6%20-%20WP%20on%20draft%20ESRG%201.pdf. Accessed: 26. June 2024.

EFRAG (2022b). *Draft ESRS 2 General disclosure November 2022.* https://www.efrag.org/Assets/Download?assetUrl=%2Fsites%2Fwebpublishing%2FSiteAssets%2F07.%2520Draft%2520ESRS%25202%2520General%2520disclsoures%2520November%25202022.pdf. Accessed: 26. June 2024.

EFRAG (2022c). *Draft European Sustainability Reporting Standards - ESRS E1 Climate Change.* https://www.efrag.org/Assets/Download?assetUrl=%2Fsites%2Fwebpublishing%2FSiteAssets%2F08%2520Draft%2520ESRS%2520E1%2520Climate%2520Change%2520November%25202022.pdf. Accessed: 26. June 2024.

EFRAG (2022d). *Draft European Sustainability Reporting Standards. Appendix I—Disclosure Requirements index.* https://www.efrag.org/Lab2. Accessed: 26. June 2024.

Eggert, J., & Hartmann, J. (2021). Purchasing's contribution to supply chain emission reduction. *Journal of Purchasing and Supply Management, 27*(2), 100685. https://doi.org/10.1016/j.pursup.2021.100685

Eisenhardt, K. M. (1989). Building theories from case study research. *The Academy of Management Review, 14*(4), 532. https://doi.org/10.2307/258557

Eisenhardt, K. M., & Graebner, M. E. (2007). Theory building from cases: Opportunities and challenges. *Academy of Management Journal, 50*(1), 25–32. https://doi.org/10.5465/amj.2007.24160888

Eisenhardt, K. M., & Zbaracki, M. J. (1992). Strategic decision making. *Strategic Management Journal, 13*(S2), 17–37. https://doi.org/10.1002/smj.4250130904

Elkington, J. (1998). Accounting for the triple bottom line. *Measuring Business Excellence, 2*(3), 18–22. https://doi.org/10.1108/eb025539

Endrikat[Jan], Guenther, E [Edeltraud] & Hoppe, H., J. (2014). Making sense of conflicting empirical findings: A meta-analytic review of the relationship between corporate environmental and financial performance. *European Management Journal, 32*(5), 735–751. https://doi.org/10.1016/j.emj.2013.12.004

Engert, S., & Baumgartner, R. J. (2016). Corporate sustainability strategy – bridging the gap between formulation and implementation. *Journal of Cleaner Production, 113*, 822–834. https://doi.org/10.1016/j.jclepro.2015.11.094

Epstein, M. J., Buhovac, A. R., & Yuthas, K. (2015). Managing social, environmental and financial performance simultaneously. *Long Range Planning, 48*(1), 35–45. https://doi.org/10.1016/j.lrp.2012.11.001

Ethiraj, S. K., & Levinthal, D. (2009). Hoping for A to Z while rewarding only A: Complex organizations and multiple goals. *Organization Science, 20*(1), 4–21. https://doi.org/10.1287/orsc.1080.0358

European Commission (2018). *Communication from the Commission to the European Parliament, the European Council, the Council, the European central bank, the European Economic and Social Committee and the Committee of the regions action plan: Financing sustainable growth.* https://eur-lex.europa.eu/legal-content/EN/TXT/?uri=CELEX%3A52018DC0097. Accessed: 26. June 2024.

European Commission. (2019). *The European Green Deal.* https://eur-lex.europa.eu/resource.html?uri=cellar:b828d165-1c22-11ea-8c1f-01aa75ed71a1.0002.02/DOC_1&format=PDF. Accessed: 26. June 2024.

European Commission. (2020). *Renewed sustainable finance strategy and implementation of the action plan on financing sustainable growth.* https://finance.ec.europa.eu/publications/renewed-sustainable-finance-strategy-and-implementation-action-plan-financing-sustainable-growth_en. Accessed: 26. June 2024.

European Commission. (2022a). *Corporate sustainability reporting.* https://finance.ec.europa.eu/capital-markets-union-and-financial-markets/company-reporting-and-auditing/company-reporting/corporate-sustainability-reporting_en. Accessed: 26. June 2024.

European Commission. (2022b). *A European Green Deal: Striving to be the first climate-neutral continent.* https://ec.europa.eu/info/strategy/priorities-2019-2024/european-green-deal_en. Accessed: 26. June 2024.

European Commission. (2023). *Corporate sustainability reporting.* https://finance.ec.europa.eu/capital-markets-union-and-financial-markets/company-reporting-and-auditing/company-reporting/corporate-sustainability-reporting_en#legislation. Accessed: 26. June 2024.

European Environment Agency. (2023). *EEA Greenhouse Gases - Data Viewer: Data Viewer on Greenhouse Gas Emissions and Removals.* https://www.eea.europa.eu/data-and-maps/data/data-viewers/greenhouse-gases-viewer. Accessed: 22. June 2023.

European Parliament. (2014). *DIRECTIVE 2014/95 - Official Journal of the European Union: Amending directive 2013/34/eu as regards disclosure of non-financial and diversity information by certain large undertakings and groups.* https://eur-lex.europa.eu/legal-content/EN/TXT/?uri=CELEX%3A32014L0095. Accessed: 26. June 2024.

European Parliament (2021). *BRIEFING Implementaion Appraisal - Non-financial Reporting Directive.* https://www.europarl.europa.eu/RegData/etudes/BRIE/2021/654213/EPRS_BRI(2021)654213_EN.pdf. Accessed: 26. June 2024.

European Parliament, & European Council (2014). Directive 2014/95/EU Amending Directive 2013/34/EU as Regards Disclosure of Non-Financial and Diversity Information by Certain Large Undertakings and Groups. *Official Journal of the European Union, 330*, 1–9. https://eur-lex.europa.eu/eli/dir/2014/95/oj. Accessed: 26. June 2024.

European Parliament, & European Council (2022). Directive (EU) 2022/2464 Amending Regulation (EU) No 537/2014, Directive 2004/109/EC, Directive 2006/43/EC and Directive 2013/34/EU, as Regards Corporate Sustainability Reporting. *Official Journal of the European Union, 322*, 15–80. http://data.europa.eu/eli/dir/2022/2464/oj. Accessed: 26. June 2024.

European Union. (2014). *Directive 2014/95/EU of the European Parliament and of the Council of 22 October 2014 amending Directive 2013/34/EU as regards disclosure of non-financial and diversity information by certain large undertakings and groups Text with EEA relevance*. https://eur-lex.europa.eu/legal-content/EN/TXT/PDF/?uri=CELEX:32014L0095. Accessed 26.06.2024.

European Union. (2022). *Directive (EU) 2022/2464 of the European Parliament and of the Council of 14 December 2022 amending Regulation (EU) No 537/2014, Directive 2004/109/EC, Directive 2006/43/EC and Directive 2013/34/EU, as regards corporate sustainability reporting (Text with EEA relevance)*. https://eur-lex.europa.eu/legal-content/EN/TXT/?uri=CELEX%3A32022L2464. Accessed: 26. June 2024.

Evert, R. E., Martin, J. A., McLeod, M. S., & Payne, G. T. (2016). Empirics in family business research. *Family Business Review, 29*(1), 17–43. https://doi.org/10.1177/0894486515593869

EY. (2022). *How the EU's New Sustainability Directive ("CSRD") is Becoming a Game Changer*. https://www.ey.com/en_ro/news/2022/11/how-the-eus-new-sustainability-directive-is-becoming-a-game-chan. Accessed: 29. January 2023.

Familienunternehmen im Fokus. (2022). *Kärcher gewinnt den Deutschen Nachhaltigkeitspreis*. https://familienunternehmen.eu/familienunternehmen-karcher-deutscher-nachhaltigkeitspreis/. Accessed: 26. June 2024.

Family Capital. (2022). *Top 500 German Family Businesses - the economy most dependent on family enterprises*. https://www.famcap.com/top-500-german-family-businesses-the-economy-most-dependent-on-family-enterprises/. Accessed: 26. June 2024.

Fassin, Y., van Rossem, A., & Buelens, M. (2011). Small-business owner-managers' perceptions of business ethics and CSR-related concepts. *Journal of Business Ethics, 98*(3), 425–453. https://doi.org/10.1007/s10551-010-0586-y

Felden, B., Fischer, P., Graffius, M. & Marwede, L. (2016). Illustrating complexity in the brand management of family firms. In E. S. Berger & A. Kuckertz (Eds.), *FGF Studies in Small Business and Entrepreneurship. Complexity in Entrepreneurship, Innovation and Technology Research: Applications of Emergent and Neglected Methods* (1st ed., pp. 219–244). Springer. https://doi.org/10.1007/978-3-319-27108-8_11

Fereday, K. (2019). *200 Quotes on Climate Change: Perfect for school assignments or work presentations*. Independently published.

Ferri, L. M. (2017). The influence of the institutional context on sustainability reporting. *A Cross-National Analysis. Social Responsibility Journal, 13*(1), 24–47. https://doi.org/10.1108/SRJ-11-2015-0172

Fiechter, P., Hitz, J.-M., & Lehmann, N. (2022). Real effects of a widespread CSR reporting mandate: Evidence from the European Union's CSR Directive. *Journal of Accounting Research, 60*(4), 1499–1549. https://doi.org/10.1111/1475-679X.12424

Fletcher, D., de Massis, A., & Nordqvist, M. (2016). Qualitative research practices and family business scholarship: A review and future research agenda. *Journal of Family Business Strategy, 7*(1), 8–25. https://doi.org/10.1016/j.jfbs.2015.08.001

Forbes (16. Januar 2018). *BlackRock CEO Tells Companies To Contribute To Society. Here's Where To Start.* https://www.forbes.com/sites/peterhorst/2018/01/16/blackrock-ceo-tells-companies-to-contribute-to-society-heres-where-to-start/?sh=390aafb7971d. Accessed: 26. June 2024.

Foss, N. J., Klein, P. G., Lien, L. B., Zellweger, T., & Zenger, T. (2021). Ownership competence. *Strategic Management Journal, 42*(2), 302–328. https://doi.org/10.1002/smj.3222

Freeman, R. E. (1984). *Strategic management: A stakeholder approach.* Cambridge University Press. https://doi.org/10.1017/CBO9781139192675

French Embassy India. (2022). *Speech of the President of the Republic on the occasion of the COP 27: Speech by Mr. Emmanuel Macron, President of the Republic (Sharm el-Sheikh, Egypt - November 7, 2022).* https://in.ambafrance.org/Speech-of-the-President-of-the-Republic-on-the-occasion-of-the-COP-27. Accessed: 26. June 2024.

Friedman, M. (13. September 1970). The social reponsibility of business is to increase its profits. *New York Times Magazine*, pp. 122–126. https://www.nytimes.com/1970/09/13/archives/a-friedman-doctrine-the-social-responsibility-of-business-is-to.html. Accessed: 26. June 2024.

Fujii, H., Iwata, K., Kaneko, S., & Managi, S. (2013). Corporate environmental and economic performance of Japanese manufacturing firms: Empirical study for sustainable development. *Business Strategy and the Environment, 22*(3), 187–201. https://doi.org/10.1002/bse.1747

Fung, A. (2007). Full disclosure: The perils and promise of transparency. *Cambridge University Press.* https://doi.org/10.1017/CBO9780511510533

Gaba, V., & Greve, H. R. (2019). Safe or profitable? The pursuit of conflicting goals. *Organization Science, 30*(4), 647–667. https://doi.org/10.1287/orsc.2018.1280

Galama, J. T., & Scholtens, B. (2021). A meta-analysis of the relationship between companies' greenhouse gas emissions and financial performance. *Environmental Research Letters, 16*(4), 43006. https://doi.org/10.1088/1748-9326/abdf08

Gallego-Álvarez, I., Segura, L., & Martínez-Ferrero, J. (2015). Carbon emission reduction: The impact on the financial and operational performance of international companies. *Journal of Cleaner Production, 103*, 149–159. https://doi.org/10.1016/j.jclepro.2014.08.047

Gamerschlag, R., Möller, K., & Verbeeten, F. (2011). Determinants of voluntary CSR disclosure: Empirical evidence from Germany. *Review of Managerial Science, 5*(2–3), 233–262. https://doi.org/10.1007/s11846-010-0052-3

Garcés-Ayerbe, C., Rivera-Torres, P., Murillo-Luna, J. L., & Suárez-Gálvez, C. (2022). Does it pay more to be green in family firms than in non-family firms? *Review of Managerial Science, 16*(5), 1365–1386. https://doi.org/10.1007/s11846-021-00475-8

Garcés-Ayerbe, C., Rivera-Torres, P., & Murillo-Luna, J. L. (2012). Stakeholder pressure and environmental proactivity. *Management Decision, 50*(2), 189–206. https://doi.org/10.1108/00251741211203524

García-Sánchez, I.-M., Martín-Moreno, J., Khan, S. A., & Hussain, N. (2021). Socio-emotional wealth and corporate responses to environmental hostility: Are family firms more stakeholder oriented? *Business Strategy and the Environment, 30*(2), 1003–1018. https://doi.org/10.1002/bse.2666

Garcia-Torea, N., Larrinaga, C., & Luque-Vílchez, M. (2023). Bridging the understanding of sustainability accounting and organizational change. *Organization & Environment, 36*(1), 17–38. https://doi.org/10.1177/10860266221083339

Gavana, G., Gottardo, P., & Moisello, A. (2017). Sustainability reporting in family firms: A panel data analysis. *Sustainability, 9*(1), 38. https://doi.org/10.3390/su9010038

German Environmental Agency. (2021). *Trends der Treibhausgas-Emissionen in Deutschland*. https://www.umweltbundesamt.de/themen/klima-energie/klimaschutz-energiepolitik-in-deutschland/treibhausgas-emissionen/trends-der-treibhausgas-emissionen-in-deutschland. Accessed: 26. June 2024.

German Environmental Agency. (2023). *Anteil der Treibhausgase an den Emissionen*. https://www.umweltbundesamt.de/daten/umweltindikatoren/indikator-emission-von-treibhausgasen#die-wichtigsten-fakten. Accessed: 26. June 2024.

German Federal Office of Justice. (2022). *Offenlegungspflichten - Rechtliche Grundlagen*. Bundesjustizamt. https://www.bundesjustizamt.de/DE/Themen/OrdnungsgeldVollstreckung/Jahresabschluesse/Offenlegung/Pflichten/Pflichten_node.html#AnkerDokument41086. Accessed: 26. June 2024.

German Federal Statistical Office. (2019). *Statistisches Jahrbuch: Deutschland und Internationales*. Statistisches Bundesamt. https://www.destatis.de/DE/Themen/Querschnitt/Jahrbuch/statistisches-jahrbuch-2019-dl.pdf?__blob=publicationFile. Accessed: 26. June 2024.

Gioia, D. A., Corley, K. G., & Hamilton, A. L. (2013). Seeking qualitative rigor in inductive research: Notes on the Gioia methodology. *Organizational Research Methods, 16*(1), 15–31. https://doi.org/10.1177/1094428112452151

Glaser, B. G., & Strauss, A. L. (1967). *The discovery of grounded theory: Strategies for qualitative research*. Aldine Pub. Co. https://doi.org/10.4324/9780203793206

Godfrey, P. C., Merrill, C. B., & Hansen, J. M. (2009). The relationship between corporate social responsibility and shareholder value: An empirical test of the risk management hypothesis. *Strategic Management Journal, 30*(4), 425–445. https://doi.org/10.1002/smj.750

Gómez-Mejia, L. R., Cruz, C., Berrone, P., & de Castro, J. (2011). The bind that ties: Socioemotional wealth preservation in family firms. *The Academy of Management Annals, 5*(1), 653–707. https://doi.org/10.1080/19416520.2011.593320

Gómez-Mejia, L. R., Welbourne, T. M., & Wiseman, R. M. (2000). The Role of Risk Sharing and Risk Taking Under Gainsharing. *The Academy of Management Review, 25*(3), 492–507. https://doi.org/10.5465/amr.2000.3363318

Gómez-Mejía, L. R., Haynes, K. T., Núñez-Nickel, M., Jacobson, K. J. L., & Moyano-Fuentes, J. (2007). Socioemotional wealth and business risks in family-controlled firms: Evidence from Spanish olive oil mills. *Administrative Science Quarterly, 52*(1), 106–137. https://doi.org/10.2189/asqu.52.1.106

Gottschalk, S. & Lubczyk, M. (2019). *Die volkswirtschaftliche Bedeutung der Familienunternehmen.* ZEW—Leibniz-Zentrum für Europäische Wirtschaftsforschung GmbH Mannheim. https://madoc.bib.uni-mannheim.de/53213/1/Die-volkswirtschaftliche-Bedeutung-der-Familienunternehmen-2019_Stiftung_Familienunternehmen.pdf. Accessed: 26. June 2024.

Gray, R., & Bebbington, J. (2000). Environmental accounting, managerialism and sustainability: Is the planet safe in the hands of business and accounting? *Advances in Environmental Accounting & Management, 1*, 1–44. https://doi.org/10.1016/S1479-3598(00)01004-9

Gray, R., Kouhy, R., & Lavers, S. (1995). Corporate social and environmental reporting. *Accounting, Auditing & Accountability Journal, 8*(2), 47–77. https://doi.org/10.1108/09513579510146996

Grewatsch, S., & Kleindienst, I. (2017). When does it pay to be good? Moderators and mediators in the corporate sustainability-corporate financial performance relationship: A critical review. *Journal of Business Ethics, 145*(2), 383–416. https://doi.org/10.1007/s10551-015-2852-5

Gründinger, W. (2012). *Lobbyismus im Klimaschutz: Die nationale Ausgestaltung des europäischen Emmissionshandelssystems. College.* Springer VS. https://doi.org/10.1007/978-3-531-94070-0

Gulenko, M. (2018). Mandatory CSR reporting—literature review and future developments in Germany. *NachhaltigkeitsManagementForum | Sustainability Management Forum, 26*(1–4), 3–17. https://doi.org/10.1007/s00550-018-0476-9

Gunningham, N., Kagan, R. A. & Thornton, D. (2003). *Shades of green: Business, regulation, and environment.* Stanford Law and Politics.

Günther, E. & Günther, T. W. (2017, Juli). Internationale Studie zur Unternehmenssteuerung und zum Umweltmanagement. *Dresdner Beiträge zur Betriebswirtschaftslehre*(178). https://tu-dresden.de/bu/wirtschaft/bwl/bu/ressourcen/dateien/forschung/veroeffentlichung/internationale-studie-zum-Umweltmanagement.pdf?lang=de. Accessed: 26. June 2024.

Günther, E., Günther, T., Endrikat, J., & [Jan],. (2018). Mehr Umwelt ins Controlling! *Controlling & Management Review, 62*(5), 34–41. https://doi.org/10.1007/s12176-018-0031-0

Günther, E. M., & Hoppe, H. (2014). Merging limited perspectives. *Journal of Industrial Ecology, 18*(5), 689–707. https://doi.org/10.1111/jiec.12125

Habbershon, T. G., Williams, M., & MacMillan, I. C. (2003). A unified systems perspective of family firm performance. *Journal of Business Venturing, 18*(4), 451–465. https://doi.org/10.1016/S0883-9026(03)00053-3

Habibur Rahman, M., Sanguino Galván, R. & Barroso Martínez, A. (2017). Impact of family business on economic development: A study of Spain's family-owned supermarkets. *Journal of Business and Management Sciences, 5*(4), 129–138. https://doi.org/10.12691/jbms-5-4-4

Hahn, R., Reimsbach, D., & Schiemann, F. (2015). Organizations, climate change, and transparency. *Organization & Environment, 28*(1), 80–102. https://doi.org/10.1177/1086026615575542

Hahn, T., Figge, F., Pinkse, J., & Preuss, L. (2010). Trade-offs in corporate sustainability: You can't have your cake and eat it. *Business Strategy and the Environment, 19*(4), 217–229. https://doi.org/10.1002/bse.674

Hamann, P. M., Schiemann, F., Bellora, L., & Guenther, T. W. (2013). Exploring the dimensions of organizational performance. *Organizational Research Methods, 16*(1), 67–87. https://doi.org/10.1177/1094428112470007

Handelsblatt (29. April 2019). Deutsche Familienunternehmen wachsen stärker als Dax-Konzerne: Familienunternehmen sind einer Studie zufolge die Jobmotoren der deutschen Wirtschaft. Das verleiht der Diskussion über Peter Altmaiers Industriestrategie neue Brisanz., 2019. *Handelsblatt.* https://www.handelsblatt.com/unternehmen/mittelstand/familienunternehmer/studie-deutsche-familienunternehmen-wachsen-staerker-als-dax-konzerne/24266932.html. Accessed: 26. June 2024.

Handelsblatt (2022, November). Einigung auf strengere Emissionsvorgaben für EU-Staaten. *Handelsblatt.* https://www.handelsblatt.com/politik/international/fit-for-55-einigung-auf-strengere-emissionsvorgaben-fuer-eu-staaten/28796794.html. Accessed: 26. June 2024.

Hang, M., Geyer-Klingeberg, J., Rathgeber, A., & Stöckl, S. (2018). Economic development matters: A meta-regression analysis on the relation between environmental management and financial performance. *Journal of Industrial Ecology, 22*(4), 720–744. https://doi.org/10.1111/jiec.12573

Haque, F. (2017). The effects of board characteristics and sustainable compensation policy on carbon performance of UK firms. *The British Accounting Review, 49*(3), 347–364. https://doi.org/10.1016/j.bar.2017.01.001

Harms, H. (2014). Review of family business definitions: Cluster approach and implications of heterogeneous application for family business research. *International Journal of Financial Studies, 2*(3), 280–314. https://doi.org/10.3390/ijfs2030280

Hart, S. L. (1995). A natural-resource-based view of the firm. *The Academy of Management Review, 20*(4), 986. https://doi.org/10.2307/258963

Hart, S. L., & Dowell, G. (2011). Invited editorial: A natural-resource-based view of the firm. *Journal of Management, 37*(5), 1464–1479. https://doi.org/10.1177/0149206310390219

Hartmann, J., & Moeller, S. (2014). Chain liability in multitier supply chains? Responsibility attributions for unsustainable supplier behavior. *Journal of Operations Management, 32*(5), 281–294. https://doi.org/10.1016/j.jom.2014.01.005

Hasso, T., & Duncan, K. (2013). Valuation of family firms: The limitations of accounting information. *Australian Accounting Review, 23*(2), 135–150. https://doi.org/10.1111/j.1835-2561.2013.00202.x

Hauswald, H., Hack, A., Kellermanns, F. W., & Patzelt, H. (2016). Attracting new talent to family firms: Who is attracted and under what conditions? *Entrepreneurship Theory and Practice, 40*(5), 963–989. https://doi.org/10.1111/etap.12153

He, R., Le., Luo, Shamsuddin, A., & Tang, Q. (2022). Corporate carbon accounting: A literature review of carbon accounting research from the Kyoto Protocol to the Paris Agreement. *Accounting & Finance, 62*(1), 261–298. https://doi.org/10.1111/acfi.12789

Healy, P. M., & Palepu, K. G. (2001). Information asymmetry, corporate disclosure, and the capital markets: A review of the empirical disclosure literature. *Journal of Accounting and Economics, 31*(1–3), 405–440. https://doi.org/10.1016/S0165-4101(01)00018-0

Heider, A. K., Clauss, T., Hülsbeck, M., Gerken, M., & Rüsen, T. A. (2022). Blood is thicker than water: The role of family willingness and family ability in achieving holistic digitalisation in family businesses. *International Journal of Innovation Management, 26*(3), 1–29. https://doi.org/10.1142/S1363919622400096

Henriques, I., & Sadorsky, P. (1999). The relationship between environmental commitment and managerial perceptions of stakeholder importance. *Academy of Management Journal, 42*(1), 87–99. https://doi.org/10.5465/256876

Hoffmann, E., Dietsche, C. & Hobelsberger, C. (2018). Between mandatory and voluntary: Non-financial reporting by German companies. *NachhaltigkeitsManagementForum | Sustainability Management Forum, 26*(1–4), 47–63. https://doi.org/10.1007/s00550-018-0479-6

Hoy, F., & Sharma, P. (2010). *Entrepreneurial Family Firms.* Prentice-Hall. https://doi.org/10.1177/0894486509357874

Hsueh, J.W.-J., de Massis, A., & Gomez-Mejia, L. (2023). Examining heterogeneous configurations of socioemotional wealth in family firms through the formalization of corporate social responsibility strategy. *Family Business Review, 089448652211463*,. https://doi.org/10.1177/08944865221146350

Huang, Y.-C., Wong, Y.-J., & Yang, M.-L. (2014). Proactive environmental management and performance by a controlling family. *Management Research Review, 37*(3), 210–240. https://doi.org/10.1108/MRR-09-2012-0196

Hummel, K., & Jobst, D. (2021). *The current state and future of corporate sustainability reporting regulations in the European Union.* Vorab-Onlinepublikation. https://doi.org/10.2139/ssrn.3978478

Hummel, K., & Rötzel, P. (2019). Mandating the sustainability disclosure in annual reports—evidence from the United Kingdom. *Schmalenbach Business Review, 71*(2), 205–247. https://doi.org/10.1007/s41464-019-00069-8

Hunt, C. B. & Auster, E. R. (1990). Proactive environmental management: Avoiding the toxic trap. *Sloan Management Review, 31*(2), 7–18. https://sloanreview.mit.edu/article/proactive-environmental-management-avoiding-the-toxic-trap/. Accessed: 26. June 2024.

Hüseyin, D., Marcus, W., & Jörn, B. (2017). Sustainability and environmental behaviour in family firms: A longitudinal analysis of environment-related activities, innovation and performance. *Business Strategy and the Environment, 27*(1), 152–172. https://doi.org/10.1002/bse.1998

International Accounting Standards Board. (2018). *Conceptual Framework for Financial Reporting.* https://www.ifrs.org/content/dam/ifrs/publications/pdf-standards/english/2021/issued/part-a/conceptual-framework-for-financial-reporting.pdf. Accessed: 16. June 2022.

International Monetary Fund. (2021). *Report for Selected Countries and Subjects: October 2021.* https://t.ly/16am. Accessed: 18. October 2022.

Ioannou, I. & Serafeim, G. (2017). *The Consequences of Mandatory Corporate Sustainability Reporting.* (Working Paper No. 11–100). Harvard Business School Research. https://doi.org/10.2139/ssrn.1799589

Ioannou, I. & Serafeim, G. (2019). The Consequences of Mandatory Corporate Sustainability Reporting. In A. McWilliams, D. E. Rupp, D. S. Siegel, G. K. Stahl, D. A. Waldman, I. Ioannou, & G. Serafeim (Eds.), *The Oxford Handbook of Corporate Social Responsibility* (pp. 451–489). Oxford University Press. https://doi.org/10.1093/oxfordhb/9780198802280.013.20

IPCC (2021). Summary for Policymakers. Climate change 2021: The physical science basis. *Contribution of Working Group I to the Sixth Assessment Report of the Intergovernmental*

Panel on Climate Change, 3–32. https://www.ipcc.ch/report/ar6/wg1/. Accessed: 26. June 2024.

ISO. (2023). *ISO - About us*. https://www.iso.org/about-us.html. Accessed: 26. June 2024.

Ivory, S. B., & Brooks, S. B. (2018). Managing corporate sustainability with a paradoxical lens: Lessons from strategic agility. *Journal of Business Ethics, 148*(2), 347–361. https://doi.org/10.1007/s10551-017-3583-6

Iwata, H., & Okada, K. (2011). How does environmental performance affect financial performance? Evidence from Japanese manufacturing firms. *Ecological Economics, 70*(9), 1691–1700. https://doi.org/10.1016/j.ecolecon.2011.05.010

Jensen, M. C. (2000). *Value maximization, stakeholder theory, and the corporate objective function*. Vorab-Onlinepublikation. https://doi.org/10.2139/ssrn.220671

Jensen, M. C., & Meckling, W. H. (1976). Theory of the firm: Managerial behavior, agency costs and ownership structure. *Corporate Governance, 77–132*. https://doi.org/10.1002/9780470752135.ch17

Jiang, Y., Kang, Y., Liang, H., & Yang, Y. G. (2023). *The Externalities of Mandatory ESG Disclosure*. Vorab-Onlinepublikation. https://doi.org/10.2139/ssrn.4355326

Jira, C., & Toffel, M. W. (2013). Engaging supply chains in climate change. *Manufacturing & Service Operations Management, 15*(4), 1–19. https://doi.org/10.1287/msom.1120.0420

Johnson, M., Redlbacher, F., & Schaltegger, S. (2018). Stakeholder engagement for corporate sustainability: A comparative analysis of b2c and b2b companies. *Corporate Social Responsibility and Environmental Management, 25*(4), 659–673. https://doi.org/10.1002/csr.1484

Jones, T. M. (1995). Instrumental stakeholder theory: A synthesis of ethics and economics. *The Academy of Management Review, 20*(2), 404. https://doi.org/10.2307/258852

Kammerlander, N., Dessì, C., Bird, M., Floris, M., & Murru, A. (2015). The impact of shared stories on family firm innovation. *Family Business Review, 28*(4), 332–354. https://doi.org/10.1177/0894486515607777

Kammerlander, N., & Ganter, M. (2015). An attention-based view of family firm adaptation to discontinuous technological change: Exploring the role of family CEOs' noneconomic goals. *Journal of Product Innovation Management, 32*(3), 361–383. https://doi.org/10.1111/jpim.12205

Kammerlander, N., Patzelt, H., Behrens, J., & Röhm, C. (2020). Organizational ambidexterity in family-managed firms: The role of family involvement in top management. *Family Business Review, 33*(4), 393–423. https://doi.org/10.1177/0894486520961645

Kammerlander, N., & Prügl, R. (2016). Innovation in Familienunternehmen. *Springer Fachmedien Wiesbaden*. https://doi.org/10.1007/978-3-658-12315-4

Kaplan, R. S. & Anderson, S. R. (2007). *Time-driven activity-based costing*. Harvard Business School; McGraw-Hill [distributor]. https://www.hbs.edu/ris/Publication%20Files/04-045_d62528d4-7931-4ea1-a205-d9683c639d6e.pdf. Accessed: 26. June 2024.

Kerstin, S. (2022, November). UN-Generalsekretär Guterres: „Sind auf dem Highway zur Klimahölle". *Handelsblatt*. https://www.handelsblatt.com/politik/international/cop27-un-generalsekretaer-guterres-sind-auf-dem-highway-zur-klimahoelle/28792836.html. Accessed: 26. June 2024.

Kim, P., & Bae, H. (2022). Do firms respond differently to the carbon pricing by industrial sector? How and why? A comparison between manufacturing and electricity generation sectors using firm-level panel data in Korea. *Energy Policy, 162*, 112773. https://doi.org/10.1016/j.enpol.2021.112773

King, A., & Lenox, M. (2002). Exploring the locus of profitable pollution reduction. *Management Science, 48*(2), 289–299. https://doi.org/10.1287/mnsc.48.2.289.258

Kirchdörfer, R. (2011). Lexikon Familienunternehmen. *Zeitschrift für Familienunternehmen und Stiftungen*, 32. https://beckassets.blob.core.windows.net/product/readingsample/8745326/fus_01-2011.pdf. Accessed: 26. June 2024.

Klassen, R. D., & Whybark, D. C. (1999). The impact of environmental technologies on manufacturing performance. *Academy of Management Journal, 42*(6), 599–615. https://doi.org/10.2307/256982

Knitterscheidt, K. (2021). Für Mittelständler wird die Dekarbonisierung zum Kraftakt. *Handelsblatt*. https://www.handelsblatt.com/unternehmen/mittelstand/familienunternehmer/schlagmann-poroton-fuer-mittelstaendler-wird-die-dekarbonisierung-zum-kraftakt/27044456.html. Accessed: 26. June 2024.

König, A., Kammerlander, N., & Enders, A. (2013). The family innovator's dilemma: How family influence affects the adoption of discontinuous technologies by incumbent firms. *Academy of Management Review, 38*(3), 418–441. https://doi.org/10.5465/amr.2011.0162

Kotlar, J., & de Massis, A. (2013). Goal setting in family firms: Goal diversity, social interactions, and collective commitment to family-centered goals. *Entrepreneurship Theory and Practice, 37*(6), 1263–1288. https://doi.org/10.1111/etap.12065

Kotter, J. P. (1996). *Leading change* [Nachdr.]. Harvard Business School Press.

Kuyper, J., Schroeder, H., & Linnér, B.-O. (2018). The Evolution of the UNFCCC. *Annual Review of Environment and Resources, 43*(1), 343–368. https://doi.org/10.1146/annurev-environ-102017-030119

La Porta, R., Lopez-De-Silanes, F., & Shleifer, A. (1999). Corporate ownership around the world. *The Journal of Finance, 54*(2), 471–517. https://doi.org/10.1111/0022-1082.00115

La Torre, M., Sabelfeld, S., Blomkvist, M., Tarquinio, L., & Dumay, J. (2018). Harmonising non-financial reporting regulation in Europe. *Meditari Accountancy Research, 26*(4), 598–621. https://doi.org/10.1108/MEDAR-02-2018-0290

Labelle, R., Hafsi, T., Francoeur, C., & Ben Amar, W. (2018). Family firms' corporate social performance: A calculated quest for socioemotional wealth. *Journal of Business Ethics, 148*(3), 511–525. https://doi.org/10.1007/s10551-015-2982-9

Lai, A., & Stacchezzini, R. (2021). Organisational and professional challenges amid the evolution of sustainability reporting: A theoretical framework and an agenda for future research. *Meditari Accountancy Research, 29*(3), 405–429. https://doi.org/10.1108/MEDAR-02-2021-1199

Langenscheidt, F. (2020). *Lexikon der Deutschen Familienunternehmen* (3rd ed.). Springer Fachmedien. https://ebookcentral.proquest.com/lib/kxp/detail.action?docID=6407611. Accessed: 26. June 2024.

Lange-Snijders, R. (2023, 31. Mai). Why private businesses should see ESG reporting as an opportunity. *PricewaterhouseCoopers (PwC)*. https://www.pwc.com/gx/en/services/entrepreneurial-private-business/publications/esg-reporting-opportunity-for-private-businesses.html. Accessed: 26. June 2024.

Lansberg, I. (1988). The succession conspiracy. *Family Business Review, 1*(2), 119–143. https://doi.org/10.1111/j.1741-6248.1988.00119.x

Le Breton-Miller, I., & Miller, D. (2006). Family governance and firm performance: Agency, stewardship, and capabilities. *Family Business Review, 19*, 73–87. https://doi.org/10.1111/j.1741-6248.2006.00063.x

Lee, K., Ko, J., & Jung, S. (2024). Quantifying uncertainty in carbon emission estimation: Metrics and methodologies. *Journal of Cleaner Production, 452*, 142141. https://doi.org/10.1016/j.jclepro.2024.142141

Lee, M.-D.P. (2011). Configuration of external influences: The combined effects of institutions and stakeholders on corporate social responsibility strategies. *Journal of Business Ethics, 102*(2), 281–298. https://doi.org/10.1007/s10551-011-0814-0

Leggett, J. A. (2020). *The United Nations Framework Convention on Climate Change, the Kyoto Protocol, and the Paris Agreement: A Summary*. https://sgp.fas.org/crs/misc/R46204.pdf. Accessed: 26. June 2024.

Leonidou, C. N., Katsikeas, C. S., & Morgan, N. A. (2013). "Greening" the marketing mix: Do firms do it and does it pay off? *Journal of the Academy of Marketing Science, 41*(2), 151–170. https://doi.org/10.1007/s11747-012-0317-2

Levitt, T. (1958). The dangers of social responsibility. *Harvard Business Review, 36*, 41–50.

Lewandowski, S. (2017). Corporate carbon and financial performance: The role of emission reductions. *Business Strategy and the Environment, 26*(8), 1196–1211. https://doi.org/10.1002/bse.1978

Li, M., Wiedmann, T., & Hadjikakou, M. (2020). Enabling full supply chain corporate responsibility: Scope 3 emissions targets for ambitious climate change mitigation. *Environmental Science & Technology, 54*(1), 400–411. https://doi.org/10.1021/acs.est.9b05245

Li, Y., & [Y.], Richardson, G. D. & THORNTON, D. B. (1997). Corporate disclosure of environmental liability information: Theory and evidence. *Contemporary Accounting Research, 14*(3), 435–474. https://doi.org/10.1111/j.1911-3846.1997.tb00535.x

Lipper, L., McCarthy, N., Zilberman, D., Asfaw, S., & Branca, G. (Eds.). (2018). *SpringerLink Bücher: volume 52. Climate smart agriculture: Building resilience to climate change*. Springer. https://doi.org/10.1007/978-3-319-61194-5

López-Pérez, M., Melero-Polo, I., Vázquez-Carrasco, R., & Cambra-Fierro, J. (2018). Sustainability and business outcomes in the context of SMEs: Comparing family firms vs. *Sustainability, 10*(11), 4080. https://doi.org/10.3390/su10114080

Lozano, R. (2015). A holistic perspective on corporate sustainability drivers. *Corporate Social Responsibility and Environmental Management, 22*(1), 32–44. https://doi.org/10.1002/csr.1325

Lumpkin, G. T., Steier, L., & Wright, M. (2011). Strategic entrepreneurship in family business. *Strategic Entrepreneurship Journal, 5*(4), 285–306. https://doi.org/10.1002/sej.122

Lykkesfeldt, P. & Kjaergaard, L. L. (2022). *Investor relations and ESG reporting in a regulatory perspective: A practical guide for financial market participants*. Palgrave Macmillan.

Lyon, T. P., & Maxwell, J. W. (2008). Corporate social responsibility and the environment: A theoretical perspective. *Review of Environmental Economics and Policy, 2*(2), 240–260. https://doi.org/10.2139/ssrn.1011793

Mani, M., & Wheeler, D. (1998). In search of pollution havens? Dirty industry in the world economy, 1960 to 1995. *The Journal of Environment & Development, 7*(3), 215–247. https://doi.org/10.1177/107049659800700302

Margolis, J. D., & Walsh, J. P. (2003). *Misery loves companies: Rethinking social initiatives by business*. Vorab-Onlinepublikation. https://doi.org/10.2307/3556659

Martin, P. R., & Moser, D. V. (2012). A broader perspective on corporate social responsibility research in accounting. *The Accounting Review, 87*(3), 797–806. https://doi.org/10.2308/accr-10257

May, P. (2012). *Erfolgsmodell Familienunternehmen: Das Strategie-Buch*. Murmann.

McWilliams, A., & Siegel, D. (2001). Corporate social responsibility: A theory of the firm perspective. *The Academy of Management Review, 26*(1), 117. https://doi.org/10.2307/259398

Menguc, B., & Ozanne, L. K. (2005). Challenges of the "green imperative": A natural resource-based approach to the environmental orientation–business performance relationship. *Journal of Business Research, 58*(4), 430–438. https://doi.org/10.1016/j.jbusres.2003.09.002

Merriam, S. B. & Tisdell, E. J. (2015). *Qualitative research: A guide to design and implementation,* (4th ed.). John Wiley.

Methven O'Brien, C., & Dhanarajan, S. (2016). The corporate responsibility to respect human rights: A status review. *Accounting, Auditing & Accountability Journal, 29*(4), 542–567. https://doi.org/10.1108/AAAJ-09-2015-2230

Meyer, J. W., & Rowan, B. (1977). Institutionalized organizations: Formal structure as myth and ceremony. *American Journal of Sociology, 83*(2), 340–363. https://doi.org/10.1086/226550

Meyer, M. W., & Gupta, V. (1994). The performance paradox. *Research in Organization Behavior, 16*, 309–369. https://doi.org/10.2307/3381236

de Micco, P., Rinaldi, L., Vitale, G., Cupertino, S., & Maraghini, M. P. (2021). The challenges of sustainability reporting and their management: The case of Estra. *Meditari Accountancy Research, 29*(3), 430–448. https://doi.org/10.1108/MEDAR-09-2019-0555

Micelotta, E. R., & Raynard, M. (2011). Concealing or revealing the family? *Family Business Review, 24*(3), 197–216. https://doi.org/10.1177/0894486511407321

Michelon, G., & Parbonetti, A. (2012). The effect of corporate governance on sustainability disclosure. *Journal of Management and Governance, 16*(3), 477–509. https://doi.org/10.1007/s10997-010-9160-3

Miles, M. B., Huberman, A. M. & Saldaña, J. (2014). *Qualitative data analysis: A methods sourcebook* (3rd ed.). SAGE.

Miles, M. B., Huberman, A. M. & Saldaña, J. (2018). *Qualitative Data Analysis: A Methods Sourcebook*. SAGE.

Miller, D., & Le Breton-Miller, I. (2004). Managing for the long run: Lessons in competitive advantage from great family businesses. *Harvard Business School Press*. https://doi.org/10.1111/j.1741-6248.2005.00046_1.x

Miller, D. & Le Breton-Miller, I. (2005). *Managing for the long run: Lessons in competitive advantage from great family businesses*. Harvard Business School Press. http://www.loc.gov/catdir/enhancements/fy1318/2004019789-b.html. Accessed: 26. June 2024.

Miller, D., & Le Breton-Miller, I. (2006). Priorities, practices and strategies in successful and failing family businesses: An elaboration and test of the configuration perspective. *Strategic Organization, 4*(4), 379–407. https://doi.org/10.1177/1476127006069575

Miller, D., & Le Breton-Miller, I. (2021). Brief reflections on family firm research and some suggested paths forward. *Journal of Family Business Strategy, 12*(1), 100410. https://doi.org/10.1016/j.jfbs.2020.100410

Miller, D., & Le Breton-Miller, I. (2021). Family firms: A breed of extremes? *Entrepreneurship Theory and Practice, 45*(4), 663–681. https://doi.org/10.1177/1042258720964186

Miller, D., Lee, J., Chang, S., & Le Breton-Miller, I. (2009). Filling the institutional void: The social behavior and performance of family vs non-family technology firms in emerging markets. *Journal of International Business Studies, 40*(5), 802–817. https://doi.org/10.1057/jibs.2009.11

Mintzberg, H., Raisinghani, D., & Theoret, A. (1976). The structure of "unstructured" decision processes. *Administrative Science Quarterly, 21*(2), 246. https://doi.org/10.2307/2392045

Misani, N., & Pogutz, S. (2015). Unraveling the effects of environmental outcomes and processes on financial performance: A non-linear approach. *Ecological Economics, 109*, 150–160. https://doi.org/10.1016/j.ecolecon.2014.11.010

Mitchell, R. K., Agle, B. R., & Wood, D. J. (1997). Toward a theory of stakeholder identification and salience: Defining the principle of who and what really counts. *Academy of Management Journal, 22*(4), 853–886. https://doi.org/10.2307/259247

Mittelbach-Hörmanseder, S., Hummel, K., & Rammerstorfer, M. (2021). The information content of corporate social responsibility disclosure in Europe: An institutional perspective. *European Accounting Review, 30*(2), 309–348. https://doi.org/10.1080/09638180.2020.1763818

Mohr, A. T., & Puck, J. (2013). Revisiting the trust-performance link in strategic alliances. *Management International Review, 53*(2), 269–289. https://doi.org/10.1007/s11575-012-0145-0

Moores, K. (2009). Paradigms and theory building in the domain of business families. *Family Business Review, 22*(2), 167–180. https://doi.org/10.1177/0894486509333372

Nederhof, A. J. (1985). Methods of coping with social desirability bias: A review. *European Journal of Social Psychology, 15*(3), 263–280. https://doi.org/10.1002/ejsp.2420150303

Neubaum, D. O., Dibrell, C., & Craig, J. B. (2012). Balancing natural environmental concerns of internal and external stakeholders in family and non-family businesses. *Journal of Family Business Strategy, 3*(1), 28–37. https://doi.org/10.1016/j.jfbs.2012.01.003

Neuman, W. L. (2013). *Social research methods: Pearson new international edition* (7th ed., new international edition). Pearson Education Limited.

Nieto, M. J., Santamaria, L., & Fernandez, Z. (2015). Understanding the innovation behavior of family firms. *Journal of Small Business Management, 53*(2), 382–399. https://doi.org/10.1111/jsbm.12075

Nigri, G., & Del Baldo, M. (2018). Sustainability reporting and performance measurement systems: How do small- and medium-sized benefit corporations manage integration? *Sustainability, 10*(12), 4499. https://doi.org/10.3390/su10124499

North, D. C. (1990). *Institutions, institutional change, and economic performance*. Cambridge University Press. https://doi.org/10.1017/CBO9780511808678

Obloj, T., & Sengul, M. (2020). What do multiple objectives really mean for performance? Empirical evidence from the French manufacturing sector. *Strategic Management Journal, 41*(13), 2518–2547. https://doi.org/10.1002/smj.3198

O'Boyle, E. H., Pollack, J. M., & Rutherford, M. W. (2012). Exploring the relation between family involvement and firms' financial performance: A meta-analysis of main and moderator effects. *Journal of Business Venturing, 27*(1), 1–18. https://doi.org/10.1016/j.jbusvent.2011.09.002

Ocasio, W. (1997). Towards an Attention-Based View of the Firm. *Strategic Management Journal, 18*(Special Issue), 187–206. https://doi.org/10.1002/(SICI)1097-0266(199707)18:1+%3C187::AID-SMJ936%3E3.0.CO;2-K

Olsen, K. H., Bakhtiari, F., Duggal, V. K., & Fenhann, J. V. (2019). Sustainability labelling as a tool for reporting the sustainable development impacts of climate actions relevant to Article 6 of the Paris Agreement. *International Environmental Agreements: Politics, Law and Economics, 19*(2), 225–251. https://doi.org/10.1007/s10784-018-09428-1

Olson, E. G. (2010). Challenges and opportunities from greenhouse gas emissions reporting and independent auditing. *Managerial Auditing Journal, 25*(9), 934–942. https://doi.org/10.1108/02686901011080071

O'Riordan, L., & Hampden-Turner, C. (2021). Corporate social responsibility in Germany. In Samuel O. Idowu & René Schmidpeter (Eds.). *CSR, Sustainability, Ethics & Governance: Current Global Practices of Corporate Social Responsibility*. Springer Nature, 149–192.

Orlitzky, M., Schmidt, F. L., & Rynes, S. L. (2003). Corporate social and financial performance: A meta-analysis. *Organization Studies, 24*(3), 403–441. https://doi.org/10.1177/0170840603024003910

Ottenstein, P., Erben, S., Jost, S., Weuster, C. W., & Zülch, H. (2022). From voluntarism to regulation: Effects of Directive 2014/95/EU on sustainability reporting in the EU. *Journal of Applied Accounting Research, 23*(1), 55–98. https://doi.org/10.1108/JAAR-03-2021-0075

Parker, C. M., Redmond, J., & Simpson, M. (2009). A review of interventions to encourage SMEs to make environmental improvements. *Environment and Planning C: Government and Policy, 27*(2), 279–301. https://doi.org/10.1068/c0859b

Pedersen, E. R. G., Neergaard, P., Pedersen, J. T., & Gwozdz, W. (2013). Conformance and deviance: Company responses to institutional pressures for corporate social responsibility reporting. *Business Strategy and the Environment, 22*(6), 357–373. https://doi.org/10.1002/bse.1743

Pérez, L., Hunt, D. V., Samandari, H., Nuttall, R. & Biniek, K. (10. August 2022). Does ESG really matter—and why? *McKinsey & Company*. https://www.mckinsey.com/capabilities/sustainability/our-insights/does-esg-really-matter-and-why. Accessed: 26. June 2024.

Perino, G., Jarke-Neuert, J., Schenuit, F., Wickel, M. & Zengerling, C. (2022). Closing the implementation gap: Obstacles in reaching net-zero pledges in the EU and Germany. *Politics and Governance, 10*(3). https://doi.org/10.17645/pag.v10i3.5326

Pieper, T. M. (2010). Non solus: Toward a psychology of family business. *Journal of Family Business Strategy, 1*(1), 26–39. https://doi.org/10.1016/j.jfbs.2010.02.003

Plumlee, M., Brown, D., Hayes, R. M., & Marshall, R. S. (2015). Voluntary Environmental Disclosure Quality and Firm Value: Further Evidence. *Journal of Accounting and Public Policy, 34*(4), 336–361. https://doi.org/10.1016/j.jaccpubpol.2015.04.004

Podsakoff, P. M., MacKenzie, S. B., Lee, J.-Y., & Podsakoff, N. P. (2003). Common method biases in behavioral research: A critical review of the literature and recommended remedies. *The Journal of Applied Psychology, 88*(5), 879–903. https://doi.org/10.1037/0021-9010.88.5.879

Porter, M. E., & van der Linde, C. (1995). Toward a New Conception of the Environment-Competitiveness Relationship. *Journal of Economic Perspectives, 9*(4), 97–118. https://doi.org/10.1257/jep.9.4.97

Posch, A., & Speckbacher, G. (2012). Führung in Familienunternehmen: Besonderheiten der Entscheidungsfindung und Verhaltenssteuerung und deren Auswirkung auf den Unternehmenserfolg. *Journal of Business Economics, 82*(S3), 5–23. https://doi.org/10.1007/s11573-012-0566-z

Poza, E. J., & Messer, T. (2001). Spousal Leadership and Continuity in the Family Firm. *Family Business Review, 14*(1), 25–36. https://doi.org/10.1111/j.1741-6248.2001.00025.x

Prencipe, A., Bar-Yosef, S., & Dekker, H. C. (2014). Accounting Research in Family Firms: Theoretical and Empirical Challenges. *European Accounting Review, 23*(3), 361–385. https://doi.org/10.1080/09638180.2014.895621

Preston, L. E., & O'Bannon, D. P. (1997). The Corporate Social-Financial Performance Relationship. *Business & Society, 36*(4), 419–429. https://doi.org/10.1177/000765039703600406

Pringle, H. L., Irwin, D. E., Kramer, A. F., & Atchley, P. (2001). The role of attentional breadth in perceptual change detection. *Psychonomic Bulletin & Review, 8*(1), 89–95. https://doi.org/10.3758/bf03196143

Pugh, Z. H., Choo, S., Leshin, J. C., Lindquist, K. A., & Nam, C. S. (2022). Emotion depends on context, culture and their interaction: Evidence from effective connectivity. *Social Cognitive and Affective Neuroscience, 17*(2), 206–217. https://doi.org/10.1093/scan/nsab092

PwC. (2022). Tackling the scope 3 challenge: Measuring and tracking Scope 3 emissions may be tricky, but companies don't need to do everything at once to make meaningful progress. *PricewaterhouseCoopers (PwC).* https://www.pwc.com/gx/en/services/sustainability/climate/scope-three-challenge.html. Accessed: 26. June 2024.

Ritchie, H., Rosado, P., & Roser, M. (2023). CO_2 and Greenhouse Gas Emissions. *Our World in Data.* https://ourworldindata.org/co2-and-greenhouse-gas-emissions. Accessed: 18. July 2023.

Roberts, R. W. (1992). Determinants of corporate social responsibility disclosure: An application of stakeholder theory. *Accounting, Organizations and Society, 17*(6), 595–612. https://doi.org/10.1016/0361-3682(92)90015-K

Roome, N. (1992). Developing environmental management strategies. *Business Strategy and the Environment, 1*(1), 11–24. https://doi.org/10.1002/bse.3280010104

Rowley, T. J. (1997). Moving beyond dyadic ties: A network theory of stakeholder influences. *The Academy of Management Review, 22*(4), 887–910. https://doi.org/10.5465/amr.1997.9711022107

Russo, M. V., & Fouts, P. A. (1997). A resource-based perspective on corporate environmental performance and profitability. *Academy of Management Journal, 40*(3), 534–559. https://doi.org/10.2307/257052

Ryou, J. W., Tsang, A., & Wang, K. T. (2022). Product market competition and voluntary corporate social responsibility disclosures†. *Contemporary Accounting Research, 39*(2), 1215–1259. https://doi.org/10.1111/1911-3846.12748

Rypdal, K., & Winiwarter, W. (2001). Uncertainties in greenhouse gas emission inventories — evaluation, comparability and implications. *Environmental Science & Policy, 4*(2–3), 107–116. https://doi.org/10.1016/S1462-9011(00)00113-1

Salvato, C., & Moores, K. (2010). Research on accounting in family firms: Past accomplishments and future challenges. *Family Business Review, 23*(3), 193–215. https://doi.org/10.1177/0894486510375069

Sangle, S. (2010). Adoption of cleaner technology for climate proactivity: A technology-firm-stakeholder framework. *Business Strategy and the Environment, n/a-n/a.* https://doi.org/10.1002/bse.692

Sarkis, J., & Cordeiro, J. J. (2001). An empirical evaluation of environmental efficiencies and firm performance: Pollution prevention versus end-of-pipe practice. *European Journal of Operational Research, 135*(1), 102–113. https://doi.org/10.1016/S0377-2217(00)00306-4

Schaltegger, S., & Csutora, M. (2012). Carbon accounting for sustainability and management. Status quo and challenges. *Journal of Cleaner Production, 36*, 1–16. https://doi.org/10.1016/j.jclepro.2012.06.024

Schaltegger, S., Etxeberria, I. Á., & Ortas, E. (2017). Innovating corporate accounting and reporting for sustainability—attributes and challenges. *Sustainable Development, 25*(2), 113–122. https://doi.org/10.1002/sd.1666

Schlacke, S., Wentzien, H., Thierjung, E.-M. & Köster, M. (2022). Implementing the EU Climate Law via the 'Fit for 55' package. *Oxford Open Energy, 1*, Artikel oiab002. https://doi.org/10.1093/ooenergy/oiab002

Schulze, W., Lubatkin, M. H., Dino, R. N., & Buchholtz, A. K. (2001). Agency relationships in family firms: Theory and evidence. *Organization Science, 12*(2), 99–116. https://doi.org/10.1287/orsc.12.2.99.10114

Schulze, W., & Zellweger, T. (2021). Property rights, owner-management, and value creation. *Academy of Management Review, 46*(3), 489–511. https://doi.org/10.5465/amr.2018.0377

Schwager, B. (Ed.). (2022). *Management-Reihe Corporate Social Responsibility. CSR und Nachhaltigkeitsstandards: Normung und Standards im Nachhaltigkeitskontext.* Springer. https://ebookcentral.proquest.com/lib/kxp/detail.action?docID=7077628. Accessed: 26. June 2024.

Science Based Targets. (2022). Science-based Net Zero: Scaling Urgent Corporate Climate Action Worldwide. *Science Based Targets Initiative Annual Progress Report.* https://sciencebasedtargets.org/resources/files/SBTiProgressReport2021.pdf. Accessed: 01. October 2023.

Sharma, P. (2001). Stakeholder management concepts in family firms. *Proceedings of the International Association for Business and Society, 12*, 483–493. https://doi.org/10.5840/IABSPROC20011247

Sharma, P. (2004). An overview of the field of family business studies: Current status and directions for the future. *Family Business Review, 17*(1), 1–36. https://doi.org/10.1111/j.1741-6248.2004.00001.x

Sharma, P., Chrisman, J. J., & Chua, J. H. (1997). Strategic management of the family business: Past research and future challenges. *Family Business Review, 10*(1), 1–35. https://doi.org/10.1111/j.1741-6248.1997.00001.x

Sharma, P., & Sharma, S. (2011). Drivers of proactive environmental strategy in family firms. *Business Ethics Quarterly, 21*(2), 309–334. https://doi.org/10.5840/beq201121218

Sharma, S., & Vredenburg, H. (1998). Proactive corporate environmental strategy and the development of competitively valuable organizational capabilities. *Strategic Management Journal, 19*(8), 729–753. https://doi.org/10.1002/(SICI)1097-0266(199808)19:8<729::AID-SMJ967>3.0.CO;2-4

Shields, J. F., Welsh, D. H., & Shelleman, J. M. (2018). Sustainability reporting and its implications for family firms. *Journal of Small Business Strategy, 28*(1), 66–71.

Sirmon, D. G., & Hitt, M. A. (2003). Managing resources: Linking unique resources, management, and wealth creation in family firms. *Entrepreneurship Theory and Practice, 27*(4), 339–358. https://doi.org/10.1111/1540-8520.t01-1-00013

Smith, W. K., & Lewis, M. W. (2011). Toward a theory of paradox: A dynamic equilibrium model of organizing. *Academy of Management Review, 36*(2), 381–403. https://doi.org/10.5465/AMR.2011.59330958

Song, H., Zhao, C., & Zeng, J. (2017). Can environmental management improve financial performance: An empirical study of A-shares listed companies in China. *Journal of Cleaner Production, 141*, 1051–1056. https://doi.org/10.1016/j.jclepro.2016.09.105

Stechemesser, K., Guenther, E., & [Edeltraud],. (2012). Carbon accounting: A systematic literature review. *Journal of Cleaner Production, 36*, 17–38. https://doi.org/10.1016/j.jclepro.2012.02.021

Stiftung Familienunternehmen. (2019a). *Daten, Fakten, Zahlen zur volkswirtschaftlichen Bedeutung von Familienunternehmen.* https://www.familienunternehmen.de/de/daten-fakten-zahlen. Accessed: 26. June 2024.

Stiftung Familienunternehmen. (2019b). *Die volkswirtschaftliche Bedeutung der Familienunternehmen(5).*

Stiftung Familienunternehmen. (2022). *Definition of the Family Business.* https://www.familienunternehmen.de/en/news/definition-of-a-family-business. Accessed: 21. February 2022.

Stiftung Familienunternehmen. (2023a). *Dates, numbers, facts.* Available at https://www.familienunternehmen.de/en/data-numbers-facts. Accessed: 26. June 2024.

Stiftung Familienunternehmen. (2023b). *Die volkswirtschaftliche Bedeutung der Familienunternehmen: 6. Aufl. und Schwerpunkt „Ausbildungsengagement"*. https://www.familienunternehmen.de/media/pages/publikationen/die-volkswirtschaftliche-bedeutung-der-familienunternehmen-2023/791474aa24-1700133949/die-volkswirtschaftliche-bedeutung-der-familienunternehmen_2023.pdf. Accessed: 25. March 2024.

Strike, V. M., & Rerup, C. (2016). Mediated sensemaking. *Academy of Management Journal, 59*(3), 880–905. https://doi.org/10.5465/amj.2012.0665

Suchman, M. C. (1995). Managing legitimacy: Strategic and institutional approaches. *The Academy of Management Review, 20*(3), 571. https://doi.org/10.2307/258788

Terlaak, A., Kim, S., & Roh, T. (2018). Not good, not bad: The effect of family control on environmental performance disclosure by business group firms. *Journal of Business Ethics, 153*(4), 977–996. https://doi.org/10.1007/s10551-018-3911-5

The Economist. (2023, 29. Januar). *Global inequality is rising again.* https://www.economist.com/finance-and-economics/2022/08/02/global-inequality-is-rising-again. Accessed: 26. June 2024.

Theißen, S., Spinler, S., & Huchzermeier, A. (2014). Reducing the carbon footprint within fast-moving consumer goods supply chains through collaboration: The manufacturers' perspective. *Journal of Supply Chain Management, 50*(4), 44–61. https://doi.org/10.1111/jscm.12048

Tripsas, M., & Gavetti, G. (2000). Capabilities, cognition, and inertia: Evidence from digital imaging. *Strategic Management Journal, 21*(10–11), 1147–1161. https://doi.org/10.1002/1097-0266(200010/11)21:10/11<1147::AID-SMJ128>3.0.CO;2-R

Trumpp, C., & Endrikat[J.], Zopf, C. & Guenther, E [E.], J. (2015). Definition, conceptualization, and measurement of corporate environmental performance: A critical examination of a multidimensional construct. *Journal of Business Ethics, 126*(2), 185–204. https://doi.org/10.1007/s10551-013-1931-8

Trumpp, C., & Günther, T. (2017). Too Little or too much? Exploring U-shaped relationships between corporate environmental performance and corporate financial performance. *Business Strategy and the Environment, 26*(1), 49–68. https://doi.org/10.1002/bse.1900

UK Government. (2022). *PM statement at COP27: 7 November 2022: Prime Minister Rishi Sunak's statement at the COP27 summit in Egypt.* https://www.gov.uk/government/speeches/pm-statement-at-cop27-7-november-2022. Accessed: 26. June 2024.

Umweltbundesamt. (2023a, 19. Oktober). *Treibhausgas-Emissionen in der Europäischen Union.* https://www.umweltbundesamt.de/daten/klima/treibhausgas-emissionen-in-der-europaeischen-union#hauptverursacher. Accessed: 26. June 2024.

Umweltbundesamt. (2023b, 28. Oktober). *Internationale Marktmechanismen im Klimaschutz.* https://www.umweltbundesamt.de/daten/klima/internationale-marktmechanismen#flexible-mechanismen-des-kyoto-protokolls-2008-2020. Accessed: 26. June 2024.

Umweltbundestamt & Deutsche Emissionshandelsstelle. (2023). *Ausgestaltung des EU-ETS.* https://www.dehst.de/DE/Europaeischer-Emissionshandel/EU-Emissionshandel-verstehen/Ausgestaltung-des-EU-ETS/ausgestaltung-des-eu-ets_node.html. Accessed: 26. June 2024.

UN Convention (1992). United nations framework convention on climate change. https://unfccc.int/resource/docs/convkp/conveng.pdf

UNCTAD. (2021). *Empowering family businesses to fast-track sustainable development.* https://unctad.org/news/empowering-family-businesses-fast-track-sustainable-development. Accessed: 26. June 2024.

UNFCCC. (2008). *Kyoto Protocol Reference Manual: On Accounting Of Emissions And Assigned Amount.* https://unfccc.int/resource/docs/publications/08_unfccc_kp_ref_manual.pdf. Accessed: 04. March 2022.

UNFCCC. (2015). *Paris Agreement: What is the Paris Agreement?* https://unfccc.int/process-and-meetings/the-paris-agreement. Accessed: 16. June 2022.

United Nations (2007). *Wie Europäische Union und Vereinte Nationen zusammenarbeiten.* https://unric.org/de/wp-content/uploads/sites/4/2017/02/Leporello_EU-VN_d.pdf. Accessed: 26. June 2024.

United Nations. (2021). *Climate Change 'Biggest Threat Modern Humans Have Ever Faced', World-Renowned Naturalist Tells Security Council, Calls for Greater Global Cooperation.* https://press.un.org/en/2021/sc14445.doc.htm. Accessed: 20. June 2023.

United Nations. (2022a). *Conference of the Parties (COP) | UNFCCC.* https://unfccc.int/process/bodies/supreme-bodies/conference-of-the-parties-cop. Accessed: 26. June 2024.

United Nations. (2022b). *Global Issues | United Nations.* https://www.un.org/en/global-issues. Accessed: 26. June 2024.

United Nations. (2022c). *Secretary-General's remarks to High-Level opening of COP27*. https://www.un.org/sg/en/content/sg/speeches/2022-11-07/secretary-generals-remarks-high-level-opening-of-cop27. Accessed: 26. June 2024.

Unsworth, K., Yeo, G., & Beck, J. (2014). Multiple goals: A review and derivation of general principles. *Journal of Organizational Behavior, 35*(8), 1064–1078. https://doi.org/10.1002/job.1963

Uwer, D. & Schramm, M. (2018). *The Transposition of the CSR Directive into German Commercial Law*. Vorab-Onlinepublikation. https://doi.org/10.14276/2610-9050.1514 (197–221 Paginazione / P.A. Persona e Amministrazione, N. 1 (2018).

van der Byl, C. A., & Slawinski, N. (2015). Embracing tensions in corporate sustainability. *Organization & Environment, 28*(1), 54–79. https://doi.org/10.1177/1086026615575047

van der Gaast, W. (2016). *International Climate Negotiation Factors: Design*. Springer International Publishing. https://doi.org/10.1007/978-3-319-46798-6

van Emous, R., Krušinskas, R., & Westerman, W. (2021). Carbon emissions reduction and corporate financial performance: The influence of country-level characteristics. *Energies, 14*(6029), 1–19. https://doi.org/10.3390/en14196029

Vardaman, J. M., & Gondo, M. B. (2014). Socioemotional wealth conflict in family firms. *Entrepreneurship Theory and Practice, 38*(6), 1317–1322. https://doi.org/10.1111/etap.12126

Velte, P. (2017). Does ESG performance have an impact on financial performance? Evidence from Germany. *Journal of Global Responsibility, 8*(2), 169–178. https://doi.org/10.1108/JGR-11-2016-0029

Venohr, B. & Langenscheidt, F. (2015). *Lexikon der deutschen Marktführer: Das Erfolgsmodell der deutschen Weltmarktführer*. GABAL; (1st ed.) (15 Jan. 2015).

Venturelli, A., Principale, S., Ligorio, L. & Cosma, S. (2021). Walking the talk in family firms. An empirical investigation of CSR communication and practices. *Corporate Social Responsibility and Environmental Management, 28*(1), 497–510. https://doi.org/10.1002/csr.2064

von Stietencron, P. (2013). *Zielorientierung deutscher Familienunternehmen: Der Zusammenhang zwischen Familieneinfluss, Zielorientierung und Unternehmenserfolg*. Springer Fachmedien. https://doi.org/10.1007/978-3-658-00826-0

Wacker Chemie AG. (2020). *Sustainability Report 2019/2020*. https://reports.wacker.com/2020/sustainability-report/production-safety/emissions/air.html. Accessed: 16. June 2022.

Waddock, S. A., & Graves, S. B. (1997). The corporate social performance financial performance link. *Strategic Management Journal, 18*(4), 303–319. https://doi.org/10.1002/(SICI)1097-0266(199704)18:4%3c303::AID-SMJ869%3e3.0.CO;2-G

Walker, D. H. (1997). Choosing an appropriate research methodology. *Construction Management and Economics, 15*(2), 149–159. https://doi.org/10.1080/014461997000000003

Ward, B. (2022). *COP27 Could Be One of the Most Difficult Climate Change Summits in History*. https://www.lse.ac.uk/granthaminstitute/news/cop27-could-be-one-of-the-most-difficult-climate-change-summits-in-history/. Accessed: 12. June 2023.

Wartick, S. L. & Cochran, P. L. (1985). The Evolution of the Corporate Social Performance Model. *Academy of Management Review, 10*(4), 758–769. https://hdl.handle.net/1805/26099. Accessed: 26. June 2024.

WBCSD, & WRI. (2013). *Technical Guidance for Calculating Scope 3 Emissions: Supplement to the Corporate Value Chain (Scope 3) Accounting & Reporting Standard*. https://ghgprotocol.org/sites/default/files/2023-03/Scope3_Calculation_Guidance_0%5B1%5D.pdf. Accessed: 13. March .2023.

WBCSD & WRI (2015). *The Greenhouse Gas Protocol: A Corporate Accounting and Reporting Standard—Revised Edition.* https://ghgprotocol.org/sites/default/files/standards/ghg-protocol-revised.pdf. Accessed: 26. June 2024.

WBCSD, & WRI. (2023). *Greenhouse Gas Protocol: Companies and Organizations.* https://ghgprotocol.org/companies-and-organizations. Accessed: 12. April 2023.

Webb, J. W., Pryor, C. G., & Kellermanns, F. W. (2015). Household enterprise in base-of-the-pyramid markets: The influence of institutions and family embeddedness. *Africa Journal of Management, 1*(2), 115–136. https://doi.org/10.1080/23322373.2015.1024089

Weiss, M., Lammers, D., Ernest-Jones, H., Kadragic, I., Babikian, L., Fettes, N., Wolfrum, M., Freundt, M., Snodin, J., Bailey, R., Davis, J., Liu, L., Sönmez, B. A., & Schmitz, J. (2022). *Now For Nature: The Decade of Delivery: CDP Europe Report 2021.* https://cdn.cdp.net/cdp-production/cms/reports/documents/000/006/132/original/CDP_Europe_Report_-_Now_For_Nature.pdf?1646826774. Accessed: 23. September 2023.

Wilson, D. (2015). Strategic decision making. In C. L. Cooper (Ed.), *Wiley Encyclopedia of Management* (pp. 1–4). Wiley. https://doi.org/10.1002/9781118785317.weom120115

Wintergreen, J., & Delaney, T. (2007). *ISO 14064, International Standard for GHG Emissions Inventories and Verification.* https://www3.epa.gov/ttnchie1/conference/ei16/session13/wintergreen.pdf. Accessed: 22. February 2023.

Wiseman, R. M., & Gomez-Mejia, L. R. (1998). A behavioral agency model of managerial risk taking. *The Academy of Management Review, 23*(1), 133–153. https://doi.org/10.5465/amr.1998.192967

World Economic Forum. (2022). *COP27: The top quotes from climate and world leaders at the UN summit.* https://www.weforum.org/agenda/2022/11/cop27-quotes-climate-leaders/. Accessed: 26. June 2024.

World Economic Forum. (2023, 29. Januar). *Analysis: Global CO2 emissions from fossil fuels hits record high in 2022.* https://www.weforum.org/agenda/2022/11/global-co2-emissions-fossil-fuels-hit-record-2022/. Accessed: 26. June 2024.

Wright, M., Chrisman, J. J., Chua, J. H., & Steier, L. P. (2014). Family enterprise and context. *Entrepreneurship Theory and Practice, 38*(6), 1247–1260. https://doi.org/10.1111/etap.12122

Yin, R. K. (2009). *Case study research: Design and methods* (4th ed.). *Applied Social Research Methods: Vol. 5.* SAGE. https://doi.org/10.33524/cjar.v14i1.73

Yin, R. K. (2018). *Case study research and applications: Design and methods* (6th ed.). SAGE.

Young, S. D. & O'Byrne, S. F. (2001). *EVA and value-based management: A practical guide to implementation.* McGraw Hill.

Zellweger, T. M., Eddleston, K. A., & Kellermanns, F. W. (2010). Exploring the concept of familiness: Introducing family firm identity. *Journal of Family Business Strategy, 1*(1), 54–63. https://doi.org/10.1016/j.jfbs.2009.12.003

Zellweger, T. M., Kellermanns, F. W., Chrisman, J. J., & Chua, J. H. (2012). Family control and family firm valuation by family CEOs: The importance of intentions for transgenerational control. *Organization Science, 23*(3), 851–868. https://doi.org/10.1287/orsc.1110.0665

Zellweger, T. M., & Nason, R. S. (2008). A stakeholder perspective on family firm performance. *Family Business Review, 21*(3), 203–216. https://doi.org/10.1177/08944865080210030103

Zellweger, T. M., Nason, R. S., Nordqvist, M., & Brush, C. G. (2013). Why do family firms strive for nonfinancial goals? An organizational identity perspective. *Entrepreneurship Theory and Practice, 37*(2), 229–248. https://doi.org/10.1111/j.1540-6520.2011.00466.x

The manufacturer's authorised representative in the EU is Springer Nature Customer Service Centre GmbH, Europaplatz 3, 69115 Heidelberg, Germany. If you have any concerns regarding our products, please contact ProductSafety@springernature.com

Printed and bound by CPI Group (UK) Ltd, Croydon, CR0 4YY
30/09/2026
02225434-0005